GENEALOGICAL NOTES

— OF —

BARNSTABLE FAMILIES,

BEING A REPRINT OF THE

AMOS OTIS PAPERS,

ORIGINALLY PUBLISHED IN

THE BARNSTABLE PATRIOT.

Revised and Completed by

C. F. SWIFT,

Largely from Notes Made by the Author.

VOLUME II.

CLEARFIELD

Reprinted by Genealogical Publishing Company
with an Index by
Charles A. Holbrook, Jr.

Index copyright © 1979 by
Charles A. Holbrook, Jr.
Yarmouth, Massachusetts
All Rights Reserved

Volume II
Originally published by
F. B. & F. P. Goss, Publishers and Printers [The "Patriot" Press]
Barnstable Massachusetts
1890

Reprinted, two volumes in one, by
Genealogical Publishing Company
Baltimore, Maryland
1979, 1991

Library of Congress Catalogue Card Number 79-52085

Reprinted, two volumes in one,
for Clearfield Company by
Genealogical Publishing Company
Baltimore, Maryland
2007

Reprinted, in its original two-volume format,
for Clearfield Company by
Genealogical Publishing Company
Baltimore, Maryland
2010

ISBN, Volume II: 978-0-8063-5473-6
Set ISBN: 978-0-8063-0844-9

Made in the United States of America

INDEX TO FAMILIES.

VOL. II.

HERSEY.

This is a Hingham name. William, the common ancestor, wrote his name Hersie. He was of Hingham in 1635, a freeman of the Massachusetts Colony March, 1638, of the Artillery Company in 1652, and died 24th March, 1658, leaving wife Elizabeth. In his will dated March 9, 1658, he names his sons William, John and James, and daughters Frances, Elizabeth and Judith. Frances married Richard Croad 29th May, 1656. Judith married Dec. 1663, Humphrey Wilson. Mr. Savage remarks "that it has been from early days a very prevalent name in Hingham, and it may well be a cause of regret that we have no fuller genealogical account of the family."

Three of this name settled in Barnstable. Dr. James Hersey, Dr. Abner Hersey, and Rev. Henry Hersey, the latter now living, and kindly remembered by all his old parishioners for his urbane feelings and gentlemanly bearing.

Dr. James Hersey, son of James and Mary Hersey, was born in Hingham Dec. 21, 1716. He settled as a physician in Barnstable, purchased a part of the Dimmock estate, which included the ancient stone house built by Elder Thos. Dimmock. A tradition exists that he resided in a house that stood east of the stone house; but it is more probable that he resided in the stone house. He owned it, and it was at that time in good repair. The three sons of James and Mary Hersey, of Hingham, were all physicians. Ezekiel, the elder, graduated at Harvard College in 1728, settled in Hingham, and died Dec. 9, 1770, aged sixty-two years, leaving no children. Dr. James Thacher speaks of him as a man eminent in his profession.

James, the second son, did not receive a public education; he was, however, well educated, and Dr. Thacher speaks of him as a skilful physician, who had at the time of his death, July 22, 1741, acquired an extensive practice in the County. Tradition gives him a good name. He married July 27, 1737, Lydia, daughter of Col. Shubael Gorham. She died Nov. 9, 1740, leaving one son, James, born Nov. 9, 1738.

For his second wife Dr. James Hersey married April 9, 1741,

Mehitable, daughter of John Davis, Esq., of Barnstable, by whom
she had born in Barnstable,

I. Ezekiel, Jan. 14, 1741-2, five months and twenty-two days
after the death of the father.

The widow Mehitable Hersey's history has already been
given, and it is unnecessary to give only an abstract thereof in
this connection. She married 1st, James Hersey, by whom she
had Ezekiel. 2d, Capt. John Russell, by whom she had Lothrop.
3d, John Sturgis, Esq., by whom she had John and Sarah, and
4th, Hon. Daniel Davis, by whom she had Daniel.

Sept. 9, 1741, Ezekiel Hersey, of Hingham, physician, and
Mehitable Hersey, of Barnstable, were appointed by Hon. Sylva-
nus Bourne, Judge of Probate, Administrators of the estate of
James Hersey, late of Barnstable, in the County of Barnstable,
Physician.

Sept. 2, 1741, "Ezekiel Hersey, Hingham, in the County of
Suffolk, was appointed by Josiah Willard, Judge of Probate, to
be Guardian 'unto ye nephew James Hersey, a minor, aged about
three years'—to take into your custody such part and portion of
estate as accrues to him in right of his father James Hersey, late
of Barnstable, in the County of Barnstable, deceased."

James Hersey, 2d, was a physician and probably studied
medicine with his uncle Ezekiel at Hingham, and removed to Kittery, Maine, where he died in 1758 aged twenty years. Oct. 13,
1758, Solomon Davis, of Boston, merchant, was appointed administrator of his estate.

Feb. 1763, Ezekiel Hersey, the brother of James, 2d, was of
legal age, and his uncle Solomon Davis resigned his trust, and he
was appointed administrator on the estate of his brother James.
On other deeds and papers recorded in the County of Suffolk,
James of Kittery, is called a physician.

I have been thus particular in quoting from the records, because a question has arisen involving the identity of James, the
father, and James, the son. I think it perfectly certain that both
were physicians. James, the younger, was only twenty when he
died, unmarried. His heirs were, his brother Ezekiel, who was
about sixteen years of age, and his mother, who was then the
wife of John Sturgis, Esq. Neither were legally eligible, and
therefore his uncle Solomon Davis, Esq., was appointed administrator, till Ezekiel, the brother, was of legal age, and then he resigned and Ezekiel was appointed.

That a young man, who had not completed his twentieth
year, should have been a practicing physician at Kittery seems
improbable, but there is no doubt of its accuracy. His uncle
Abner had an extensive practice in Barnstable when only 19.

Ezekiel Hersey, son of James, born Jan. 14, 1741-2, was a
clerk in the store of his uncle Solomon Davis, merchant, of Bos-

ton. He died early, tradition says, at 22, leaving no issue.

Dr. Abner Hersey, son of James and Mary Hersey, born in Hingham in 1721, was employed till 18 in husbandry with his father. He had few opportunities for acquiring an education, and is represented as a rude and illiterate young man. He came to Barnstable in 1740 to study medicine with his brother James. The late Dr. James Thacher, of Plymouth, says that Dr. Abner studied medicine with his brother James of Barnstable, a physician of reputation and extensive practice, enjoying entire confidence and popular favor wherever known. He studied one year, and at nineteen succeeded to his brother's practice. He was young and suffering under the disadvantages of a penurious education, when he began his career, and afterwards pursued it with a zeal and fidelity in the highest degree honorable to his character. For many years he commanded without a rival the whole practice of Cape Cod, then containing seven or eight thousand inhabitants. Sound judgment and correct observation supplied defects of education. As a physician he was indefatigable, faithful, punctual and successful. As a surgeon, judicious, and skilful; but he performed no capital operations. He was honest. No one suffered injustice by him. He was a strict observer of the Sabbath, never absenting himself from public services. He was moderate in his charges, and punctual in making his annual demands.

Dr. Hersey was subject to hypochrondiac affections, and in his domestic character he was eccentric in the extreme—a mere compound of caprice and whim. Domestic happiness and social intercourse were strangers to his family.

He never had the small pox, and that disease was a great terror to him. He once visited a patient who had the symptoms of the disease—he was sorely frightened and shut himself for a week in his house, firmly believing that his last day was near at hand.

He was abstemious, eating no animal food, and drinking no ardent spirits or wine. His diet consisted chiefly of milk and vegetables. His garments were cut after a fashion of his own, large, loose and lined with baize. His bed was the same summer and winter. It is said that the Chinese estimate the degrees of cold by *jackets*. Dr. Hersey adopted a similar rule. He had on his bed a dozen all-wool, fulled blankets. In the summer he turned down one or two. When the weather became cool in autumn, he turned down three or four, and during the coldest weather in winter he buried himself under the whole. With him the weather was from one to ten blankets cold.

Such is the character given to him by one who was his pupil five years. Its truthfulness I have no reason to doubt. I have conversed with many who knew him intimately, and they all confirm the statement that he was "a mere compound of caprice and whim." The pathology of disease no one understood better than he, and that was the secret of his success. The great art of the physician is to judge rightly, to read the character of the disease in its symptoms. He that can do this is a good physician, for a very simple man can prescribe safely if he know certainly the character of the disease.

He prepared his own medicines, employing Mr. Edward Childs to do the labor   For days and weeks together Mr. Childs used the pestle and the mortar under his direction.

In politics he was doubtful—he took sides with neither the whigs nor the tories. He avoided conversation on political subjects, and no one could say with certainty to which party he belonged. He suffered much pecuniarily by the depreciation of continental money. One spring during the Revolution he sold a cow for $30, and in the fall paid the whole sum for a goose.

Some years since I collected many curious anecdotes illustrative of his character, but I have mislaid the paper and cannot now recall them to memory. Dr. Thacher relates several : On a hot day after chasing a flock of sheep, he sweat most profusely, and pulling off his wig he said : "This is not strange, for I have more wool on my back than the whole flock of sheep."

Mrs. Davis, widow of his brother, and another lady, proposed making him a visit ; greatly agitated at the proposition, he replied : "Madame, I cannot have you here, I am sick, and my wife is sick—I have no hay or corn for your horses ; and I have no servants in my family, and I had rather be chained to a galley oar than to wait on you myself."

Whenever anything vexed him the latter part of the above quotation varied to suit the circumstance, was a common saying with him. He usually repeated it in this form : "I had rather be chained to a galley oar than to suffer such vexation."

He had a great coat made from seven calf skins, tanned and prepared for the purpose by Mr. Joseph Davis, which he wore in stormy weather. Huge cowhide boots, home made breeches, coat and waistcoat, lined with baize, a shirt of the same cloth, and a red buff cap, was his usual dress. If such an apparition should now appear, he would be called insane. Clothed in this strange and uncouth dress, no physician in Massachuestts ever had a more extensive practice, and no one ever secured so completely as he did the confidence of his patients. That he should have secured the practice of the whole County, as stated by Dr. Thacher, and as his will confirms, seems almost incredible, yet there is no doubt of the fact. At that time obstetrics was not included in the practice of the regular physician. A class of persons, known as midwives, absorbed all that practice, many of whom were eminent in their day.

Dr. Hersey could not have secured the practice of a region of country extending seventy miles in length without being orderly in all his arrangements. Eccentric as he was, he was the most punctual and orderly of men. He established *"his rounds,"* and on a certain day he visited each town. That day was known, and if the roads were not blocked up with snow he was certain to be at an appointed place at a particular hour. He travelled his "rounds" whether he had or had not a patient to visit. The people on his route who needed his services kept a watch for him on the roads he uniformly passed. Everybody knew him, and if they did not, he could be easily described so that the most simple could not mistake him.

Most of his days he spent on horseback or in his carriage, which was as oddly constructed as his dress. He used it only in the winter, or during violent storms. It was built somewhat like a common sulky, closed up on every side, with two small openings in front, one for the reins and the other for him to see to guide his horse.

The money which he acquired in his practice he invested principally in real estate. At one time a tract of woodland was to be sold at auction on the day that he would be at Cape Cod. He called on a neighbor and asked him to bid it off for him. The neighbor inquired how long he should bid. "Till I come back," was the Doctor's laconic reply.

He was very exact in his accounts, keeping debtor and creditor with all with whom he dealt, and making annual settlements. Mr. Jonathan Davis, on receiving his annual bill, found thereon the following credit : "For chasing a calf and not catching it, 4 d."

He employed many workmen on his farms. Every man must do what he was told to do, and nothing else. Mr. Oris Bacon settled a spring curb for him and the Doctor examined the work at noon and was pleased with it. After dinner the Doctor ordered him to take an armed chair and sit in a cool place by the door. Mr. Bacon did so. At four o'clock the Doctor ordered him a mug of flip, and at sunset Mr. Bacon went home, having done nothing during the afternoon. At the annual settlement Mr. Bacon found that the Doctor had credited him for a full day's work.

Mr. Edward Childs, as has been already stated, worked for him for several successive years. One day the Doctor said to him, "I have given you £100 in my will, what do you intend to do with it?" "Dress up and marry off my girls," was the reply. The Doctor was irritated and said, "I will change my will, none of my money shall be spent in buying finery for girls."

The Doctor had a favorite mare. She was as stubborn as she was sleek, and at times neither coaxing or the whip would urge her forward. Edward, after exhausting his patience in trying to urge her along, struck her a violent blow over the head, killing her instantly. He dare not see the Doctor that day, but on the following went to his work as usual. He expected the Doctor would be vexed with him, but on meeting the Doctor was unusually pleasant, and never thereafter named the matter to him.

These anecdotes show that the Doctor was a perfectly honest man, that as eccentric as he was, he would never willingly wound the feelings of a man.

Dr. Abner Hersey married Oct. 3, 1743, Hannah, daughter of Mr. James Allen, of Barnstable. She belonged to one of the most fashionable families in town, and was well educated for the times. It was an ill-assorted match, and as Dr. Thacher informs us, was productive of no domestic felicity. They had one child. Mary, born Jan. 19, 1749, who died young.

Dr. Abner Hersey died Jan. 9, 1787, in the 66th year of his age. His widow died in May, 1794, in the 71st year of her age, according to the church records; but according to the town, in her 73d year.

In his will he divided his estate among the several churches in the County in the proportion which each town had employed him as a physician.

Annually the Deacons of the several churches assembled to set-tle the accounts and receive their several proportions of the income. So long as the woodland lasted the Deacons' fund was looked forward to as anxiously as their annual meetings; when the wood was gone, the income of the lands barely paid expenses; they therefore petitioned the Legislature to allow them to make a compromise with the heirs at law, and sell and divide the proceeds in the proportions named in the will. The Leg-islature granted the prayer of the petitioners, the property was sold and deeded. At the end of a century the Doctor said he would re-turn, and examine the accounts of the Deacons. That century has now nearly elapsed, and if he returns may all of us stand ready to welcome his second advent to this wicked world. Let the Deacons tremble.

Dr. Abner Hersey owned the ancient Dimmock house bought of the heirs of his brother James. There is no tradition that he re-sided therein, but he probably did till his marriage in 1743, and per-haps a few years later. He bought of the Lothrops the estate which was Tritram Hull's, situate opposite the County Jail on the north side of the County road. His residence was a high single house, pleasantly situated, with convenient outbuildings, surrounded by a large orchard of choice fruit trees which bore abundant crops.

His farm contained about seventy-five acres of planting land, not in one tract, but in several, all lying in the East Parish. He also owned salt meadows, and large lots of woodland which, at the time of his death, was covered with a heavy growth of wood and timber.

In the selection of his lands he exercised a sound judgment. Poor land with a sandy soil he uniformly rejected, because the crops would not pay for fencing as he fenced, and cultivating as he cultivated. Prior to his time, a more skilful and scientific farmer had not resided in the County of Barnstable. As regardless as he was of his own personal appearance, he was yet the most orderly of men in all his business arrangements, and as neat as he was orderly. His wooden fences were five railed, and every post was set two and one-half feet into the ground. His stone walls, of not fully four feet high, were hemmed with two rails, or heavy poles. No loose stones or rails were allowed to lie beside them, and no briars or rank weeds to grow near to mature seed to be scattered over his fields.

In the cultivation of his lands, it was his invariable rule to return more to the soil than the crop drew from it. This is the secret art of good husbandry. From year to year his lands increased in fertility. The stranger passing through the town might select every field which he owned, by observing his neat and substantial fences, his luxuriant crops of grain, vegetables or grass. Towards the close of his life, his lands became the standard to which his neighbors referred when speaking of the fertility of land. "It is naturally as rich as Dr. Hersey's," was a common remark of those who had lands to sell.

He exhibited the same good sense and sound judgment in the selection and management of his stock. He selected the best breeds, never keeping a poor animal, and in the care and management thereof very few were more careful or skilful than he.

Dr. Hersey did good service for the farming interest of the County. The exhaustive system of cultivation, universally practiced by our fathers, he repudiated. He introduced a better system of cultivation and management which many of his neighbors adopted.

In his time agricultural products were comparatively higher than at the present time. The price of labor was regulated by the price of grain, consequently, with judicious management, there was a profit in farming even when the labor was hired. Dr. Hersey's object in cultivating was not mainly for profit. His great object was improvement, and incidently to give employment to the industrious and collect debts due him which he would have lost, if he had insisted on cash payments.

At his death his farm was under high cultivation. After the death of his widow in 1794, its sole management devolved on the deacons of the several churches. However pious they may have been, they certainly were not good farmers. They re-inaugurated the old system of croping without manure. Every spring the land was leased at public auction, either for pasturing or planting.

During the twenty-nine years that the deacons managed the fertility of the soil had diminished, and the expense, repairs and taxes, nearly absorbed all that was obtained from rents, and the sale of wood.

In 1815 the deacons became convinced that in a few years more the expenses would equal the income. A compromise was made with the heirs at law, legal authority from the Legislature was obtained, and in 1816 the whole property was sold. Dea. Nathaniel Lewis, of Barnstable, and Dr. Calvin Tilden, of Yarmouth, were the active and efficient men in effecting the sale.

In summing up the character of Dr. Abner Hersey, I am decidedly of the opinion that a higher rank should be awarded to him, than that given by his pupil Dr. James Thacher. I know he had better individual opportunities to judge than I have had, and if the decision depended on us, my opinion should be rejected and his received. But the question is not between us. I could name twenty individuals who had as good opportunities for forming a correct judgment as Dr. Thacher, and they unanimously said in reply to my inquiries that, forgetting his eccentricities, he was a most skilful physician, a man whose moral character was unimpeached, of good sense, of sound judgment, a good neighbor and citizen and an exemplary and pious member of the church.

He had one ——— fault, call it so if you please, he was a hypochrondiac, an affection which, the doctors say, "is attended by uneasiness about the region of the stomach and liver, or the hypochrondiac region." It is a disease which causes melancholy feelings, low spirits, spleen, and a disordered imagination. The person who is thus afflicted is no more to blame than the blind man because he cannot see, or the deaf for not hearing. Uniformly persons having that disease have power to restrain their feelings when in the presence of strangers, but at home, in the presence of their own families, they cannot. This is universally true of the hypochrondiac.

We may smile when the stories of his eccentricities are repeated, but can we condemn Dr. Hersey ; ought we to forget his many good qualities because he had an incurable disease. With equal propriety we might censure the rheumatic or the consumptive.

Dr. Hersey has been called rude and illiterate. It is true he was not a gay or a fashionable man, neither did he have a public education. He could not have been rude in the common acceptation of that term. If he was rude he was not a hypochrondiac, for all thus affected are remarkable for the suavity of their manners when abroad. Tradition represents him as gentlemanly in his address, and as one who studiously avoided giving cause for offence. The Doctor, his family and relatives, had much reason to lament his misfortune, the public had no right to complain, and Dr. Thacher, for giving publicity to private matters, was injudicious, and trod on ground he had no moral right to enter upon.

I have quoted substantially what he has published, and I have so done that the bane and the antidote might appear side by side. If Dr. Hersey had been a bad man, it would have been unjust to have veiled his faults; but no man is to be condemned because God, in his allwise Providence, has afflicted him with an incurable disease. He is a subject for our piety and our commiseration.

Dr. Hersey has left a good record.—Very few a cleaner or a better one. When he signed his will he thought he had immortalized his name—that it would be venerated by the wise and the good in all coming time. He was mistaken. As a physician he had then erected a monument to his own memory more enduring than marble or brass. Of what other physician can it be said that for forty-five successive years he commanded all the practice of a County extending seventy miles in length. There were other physicians at the time in the County; but no one would employ another in a difficult case, if by any means his services could be secured. All had the utmost confidence in his skill—nothing could impair their confidence in him as a man or a physician. His memory and his reputation will brighten as time advances, and the future writer of the biographies of the eminent physicians of our land will never pass over in silence the name of Abner Hersey.

His body has now rested nearly a century in the grave, yet he is not forgotten—his memory is embalmed in the popular mind and centuries will not eradicate it. He was a good man—he left his mark on the age in which he lived.

The will of Dr. Abner Hersey is dated Oct. 21, 1786, and the codicil thereto 23d Dec. next following, and proved in 1787.

Its several provisions are very clearly stated, his meaning and intention cannot be misunderstood. It was probably drawn up by himself, and is too long to copy verbatim. After the usual preliminary articles he says:

"I give to my wife Hannah the use and improvement of all my real estate, with this special restriction that she shall not suffer more than two crops in the term of twelve years to be taken off said real estate, and that she cut no more wood off said real estate than what is sufficient for her own firing and fencing said estate, provided she cannot procure fencing stuff otherwise."

After paying off his debts and legacies she was to have the improvement of his whole estate, real, personal and mixed.

The following bequest shows clearly that however "penurious" his own education may have been, he did not despise learning and science. His brother Ezekiel had been a benefactor of Harvard College, and the founder of a professorship.

"I give and bequeath the sum of five hundred pounds lawful

money ($1,666.67) for the sole use and benefit, and for the encouragement and support of a professor of Physic and Surgery at the University in Cambridge, in the County of Middlesex, and Commonwealth of Massachusetts, aforesaid; or any other town or county in said Commonwealth where such professor shall be appointed to reside, the one moity or half part thereof to be paid by my executors hereafter named in four years after my decease, and the remaining moity or half part thereof to be paid by my executors hereafter named after the decease of my wife."

In the codicil the whole is made payable after the decease of his wife.

He also bequeathed to the University at Cambridge, to be deposited in its library,

10 Books of Bishop Butler's Analogy of Natural and Revealed Religion.

6 Books by Rev. Henry Grove on the Lord's Supper, and

3 sets of Dr. Evans' Sermons on the Christian Temper.

After the decease of his wife and the payment of the legacy 'to Harvard College, he devised the use and improvement of the remainder of his estate, forever, to the thirteen Congregational Churches in the County of Barnstable. In making this division, he proportioned the amount given according to the amount of practice he had obtained in each of the several parishes. This fact is not stated in the will, but I have it on good authority. I have reduced his fractions to their least common denominator, 56, instead of using 8th, 14th, 28th and 56th, as he does.

To the Congregational Church in the East Precinct in Barnstable, (of which he was a member,)		7	56ths.
To the West Church, Barnstable,		5	"
" Church in Sandwich,		4	"
" " in Falmouth.		4	"
" West or First in Yarmouth,		6	"
" East or Second,		4	"
" North or First, Harwich,		4	"
" South or Second,		3	"
" Church in Chatham,		4	"
" " South Eastham,		5	"
" " North "		3	"
" " Wellfleet,		3	"
" " Truro,		4	"

56 56ths.

The east parish in Yarmouth is now the town of Dennis; the north in Harwich, Brewster, and the south in Eastham, Orleans; Provincetown was included in Truro.

Respecting the management of his real estate after the decease of his wife, he directed as follows :

"And it is my will and I hereby order that the deacons of the churches for the time being, or such persons as they shall appoint, do from time to time, let out or rent such real estate for as much as it will fetch, (under this special restriction, that there shall not be taken off from said real estate more than two crops in twelve years.) And I do hereby order that the buildings and fences be kept in repair, and the same be paid for, with all other reasonable charges and costs, out of said rents, being the net profits of said divised premises, together with the said personal or mixed estate, be paid by the said deacons of said thirteen churches to the ministers of their respective churches for the time being, who are, or shall be regularly settled and ordained, and for whose support their respective towns, districts, precincts or parishes, are by law liable to be taxed."

The rents so received by said ministers to be applied,

1-3 thereof in the purchase of Dr. Dodridge's Rise and Progress of Religion.

1-3 Dr. Evans' sermons on the Christian Temper, and the remaining 1-3 as follows :

12 63ds in the purchase of the Rev. Henry Grove's discourse on the Lord's Supper.

18 63ds in Dr. Dodridge's discourses on Regeneration, and two sermons on Salvation by Faith.

9 63ds in Dr. Dodridge's discourse to young people.

12 63ds in Dr. Dodridge's discourses on the education of children.

12 63ds in Dr. Dodridge's discourses on the power and grace of Christ, and the evidences of the Christian Religion.

"And that each of said ministers do distribute said books in his church as he shall think most conducive to and for the interests of religion and virtue."

The net income of his estate he ordered to be so applied for one hundred years. After the expiration of a century, the ministers of the several churches were authorized to purchase, three years out of every period of four years, such other books as they shall judge best calculated for the promotion of piety and religion.

He named as the executors of his will his wife Hannah Hersey, Dea. Nathaniel Lewis, and Dr. John Davis, and in the codicil thereto added the name of Mr. Joseph Davis. Witnesses to the will, Timothy Phinney, Joseph Annable, Edward Childs. To the codicil, Richard Bourne, Ebenezer Hinckley, Prentiss Mellen and Edward Childs.

His estate was apprised, in lawful money, as follows :

His homestead and 34 acres of land,	£705
Calves Pasture, 10 acres,	180
The Dimmock farm and land adjoining, 68 acres,	906
230 acres of Woodland,	450,15
Salt Meadows,	188

Personal Estate,   332,17,4
Notes due him,   1035,17,6
                                                   _____
                                                   £3798,09,10
equal to $12,611.64.

The deacons held an annual meeting at Lydia Sturgis' tavern, and in those days neither ministers nor deacons refused to partake of good liquors, could smoke their pipes and be as merry as the merriest. Lydia Sturgis' tavern at that time was the head-quarters of a company of men who met to play cards, drink and gamble in a small way, often stopping till the small hours of the morning. Common rumor at the time, said that some of the deacons preferred the jovial company of card players in "Hagar's Bed Room," to the staid and religious conversation of the ministers and the gray haired deacons.

Dr. Hersey placed no restriction in his will on the sale of his wood, and as long as that lasted a small sum was annually distributed among the thirteen churches, and the books ordered were purchased. When the wood was gone the rents barely paid taxes and repairs. The expenses of the annual meetings of the deacons were large. The testator presumed that the ministers and deacons would manage his estate gratuitously; but it was not so. Some of them had to travel forty miles to attend the annual meetings, and were absent from home nearly a week, and they had to be compensated, at least for the amount of their traveling expenses.

In their petition to the Legislature they state that the management of said real estate in common is attended with great inconvenience and expense and that the same has heretofore been managed in an unproductive manner. On the 12th of February, 1816, the General Court authorized the churches to make a compromise with the heirs-at-law, namely, of the children of Dr. Hersey's sister Molly, who married David Lincoln, and of his sister Rachell, who married Ephraim Otis, and to sell the estate, and after paying to the heirs such proportion as should be agreed upon, to divide the remainder to and among the thirteen churches, in the proportions ordered by the testator. Dr. Calvin Tilden of Yarmouth, was appointed the agent of the churches, and Barney Smith, Esq., of Milton, the attorney of the heirs-at-law. They sold the estate at auction in October, 1816.

A goodly sum was realized from the sale. Like prodigal children, the churches have wasted their heritage. Not content with the golden egg, (the income) they have killed the goose that laid it. They have devoted the money to other purposes than those for which it was given. Little, very little now remains of the Hersey fund. The churches have forgotten their benefactor, and the deacons no longer remember him in their prayers.

DR. JAMES HERSEY.

Dr. James Hersey died intestate. The account of his estate and the settlement thereof on the probate records, is entered very minutely. The inventory taken September 28, 1741, by Joseph Lothrop, Ebenezer Lewis and Robert Davis, is very particular. The furniture in each room is apprised by itself. It is evident from this document and the division of the estate, that he owned and resided in the old Dimmock fortification house. At the time he occupied it, there was a leanto on the rear or north side.

The following are taken from the inventory:

Bed with the furniture belonging thereto, in the Great Room, or parlor, at the southeast corner, on the lower floor,	£29,10,0
Bed and its furniture in the Great or Front Chamber,	39,00,0
Bed in the Leanto Chamber,	15,00,0
Bed in the Leanto,	20,00,0
Bed, small and trundle,	1,10,0
	£105,00,0

He had a looking-glass in the great and in his bed-room, both valued at £8,00,0, and one in his great chamber valued at £2,10. He had 23 oz. of silver plate valued at £34, showing that the price of silver was then 3,75, a much higher price than it has reached during the present war. His house was well furnished, and it appears that he lived in good style for those times. He had four horses and a colt valued at from 10 to £15 each; a pair of oxen £23; 3 cows and a steer. If these figures are called dollars instead of pounds, it would represent the value in gold or silver money. Indian corn is apprised at 10 shillings a bushel, equal to 45 or 50 cents in coin; rye at 12 shillings, peas at 20 shillings, and potatoes at six shillings currency. I do not recollect of seeing potatoes named in the records at an earlier date. They were not cultivated by the first settlers, but the precise period of their introduction I am unable to give.

He had £177,47 due him on notes, and a large amount on book account of uncertain value. His medicines on hand were apprised at £46,17.

His real estate in Hingham in the County of Suffolk, was apprised at £476,09,0
In the County of Barnstable, 1540,00,0

£2,015,00,0
From his personal estate there was realized, £1345,6,3
Debts and expenses of settling, 1,487,19,8
leaving the net value of his estate less than £2,000, estimated in a depreciated currency, in reality only 2000 dollars in silver money.

His real estate consisted of that part of the ancient Dim-

mock Farm, extending on the road from the dwelling-house of
Asa Young, Esq., to the run of water on the west of the dwelling-house of Mr. Job Handy. It contained twenty-eight acres of
upland, more than half of which was on the north of the stream
of water running into the mill pond. He also owned the meadows adjoining his land, and on the south side of the creek to the
western boundary of the old Dimmock Farm. He also owned
about forty acres of woodland. His estate was divided Dec. 6,
1757. To the widow, then the wife of John Sturgis, Esq.,
twelve acres of the north part of the homestead. Of the remainder James was assigned five eighths and Ezekiel three. James
had the southwesterly part of the farm, containing nine acres.
His boundary on the east was the present range of fence on the
west of Alvan Howes' residence, and included all the land on the
south of the creek to the run of water above named on the west,
with all the meadows adjoining, and to the west, on the south of
mill creek. Ezekiel had the eastern part of the farm, containing
seven acres, bounded easterly by the land of Samuel Sturgis, now
Asa Young's, southerly by the highway, and westerly by James
and his mother's land. These heirs and the widow afterwards
sold out to Dr. Abner Hersey.

    [Hinckley is the article next in order, but I have decided to
publish an account of the Hull family first, because it chronologi-
cally comes first. The byographies of Rev. Joseph Hull and Gov.
Thomas Hinckley, will cover the most interesting portion of the
history of the town of Barnstable, that is from its first settlement
till 1705. If Gov. Hinckley had written an account of the first
settlement, given us the personal history of the first settlers, all
of whom he knew, he would have conferred an obligation on the
present and future generations for which they would have ever
been thankful. He omitted to do it, and now the history of these
men has to be gleaned from the few records and the perishing
memorials which the remorseless hand of time has left.]

HULL.

Of the early history of this gentleman little is known. In Mather's Magnalia the name of Mr. Hull is placed in his "first classis," that is, "such as were in the *actual exercise* of their ministry when they left England, and were the instruments of bringing the *gospel* into this wilderness, and of settling churches here according to the order of the *gospel.*" May 5, 1635, twenty-one families from England, with Mr. Hull as their minister, settled at Wessaguscus, now Weymouth. On the 8th of July following, the lands on which they settled were granted to them by the Massachusetts Colony. In September, 1635, he became a freeman of that Colony, and he was a deputy to the General Court in September, 1638, and at the March term in 1639.

Sept. 6, 1638, Mr. Joseph Hull, Edmond Hobart, Sen., and Mr. Richard Browne were elected magistrates for the town of Hingham, to hear and determine actions where less than 20 shillings was claimed.

In the spring of 1639, Mr. Hull and several families from Weymouth and Hingham decided to remove to Barnstable, with the company to be organized by Mr. Collicut of Dorchester. On the 5th of May, 1639, it is stated in Hobart's journal that he preached his farewell discourse to his people in Weymouth.

Mr. Bliss in his history, quoting from a dedication sermon delivered by Rev. Josiah Bent, Jr., Nov. 28, 1832, remarks that "Mr. Hull did not preach in Weymouth much over a year if any." He draws this inference from the fact that Mr. Thomas Jenner was settled in the ministry at Weymouth in 1636, and Mr. Robert Lenthal, previous to 1638. The fact that Mr. Hull did not preach his farewell discourse till May, 1639, is fatal to the supposition of Mr. Bent that he was the minister only one year. If he was dismissed in 1636, he would not have delayed preaching that sermon three years, until he was on the eve of removing to Barnstable.

In early times the churches that were able, maintained a pastor and a teacher, and both were called ministers.   Mr. Hull was probably pastor, and perhaps Jenner and Lenthal were successively teachers of the same church.

Weymouth was early settled, and its population was scattered over a wide extent of territory, and there may have been two churches.   In early times there were men in that town of almost every shade of religious opinion, and it is probable that there were two churches or religious societies therein before 1639 when Mr. Samuel Newman, one of the ablest and learned of the divines who came to New England, was settled as the successor of Mr. Hull, and under his ministry all the people were united.

Mr. Hull came to Barnstable in May, 1639, Elder Thomas Dimmock was there in the preceding March.   To them the Plymouth Colony Court granted the lands in the town, on the customary conditions and making the usual reservations.   They were the founders of the town, and Mr. Hull, being the minister, on him devolved the greater responsibility.

At that time the woodman's axe had seldom resounded through the forest.   The country, excepting a few fields which had been cleared by the Indians, was a vast wilderness.   The old common-field, which still retains its name, had only a few scattering trees thereon, and the new common-field, which extended from the old to the bounds of Yarmouth, contained little forest. There were planting lands near Goodspeed's, now Meeting House Hill, at the Calves Pasture, and on some of the sandy soils at West Barnstable.   Near the Indian ponds there were large tracts of lands, called by our fathers *plain lands*, by which I understand cleared or planting lands.   At Chequaquet and at Hyannis there were also Indian fields.

In 1639 the Indian population probably exceeded five hundred.   They were a quiet inoffensive race, with whom our ancestors ever lived in peace.   Though all were Pokonokets and acknowledged the supremacy of Massasoit as their great sachem or chief ruler, they were divided into numerous tribes, each of which was ruled by its own sagamore.

Iyannough, the sachem of the Mattakeset Indians, had been dead fifteen years, and his territory was divided among many claimants.   He had no children of sufficient age to succeed him. Nepoyitan was the sachem of the northeasterly part of the town. He had given half his lands to Twaconniecus, and there were other claimants.   The sachem of the Indians at Hyannis, was called by the English John Hianna, for what reason I cannot decide.   The Indians of Chequaquet and in the southwest part of the town, belonged to the Massapee or Marshpee tribe, and their sachem, Paupmunnucks, resided on the neck of land at the Indian

Ponds. At West Barnstable the Indians belonged to the Scorton tribe and their sachem, Secuncke,* resided in Sandwich.

Sandwich had been settled two years, and Yarmouth less than one, when Mr. Hull came to Barnstable. There were in the plantation about fifteen families, settled in two villages, one near Goodspeed's, now Meeting House Hill, and the other near Coggins' Pond. The settlement at Old Town, in the northeasterly part of the town, commenced by Mr. Bachiller and his company in the cold winter of 1637-8, had been abandoned. Mr. Hull and Dimmock laid out the lands between the two villages into lots, and those who came with Mr. Hull settled thereon. Mr. Dimmock had then selected a farm for himself and built a house thereon, probably the fortification house that has so often been named in these papers.

Mr. Hull built for himself a farm house where Capt. Thomas Harris now resides. The first Meeting House was on the opposite side of the road, where the ancient burying-ground now is. I infer from the fact the first settlers often held their meetings at his house, that it was as large and convenient as any in the settlement.

Tradition informs us that Mr. Hull held his first meeting, and preached his first sermon, beside the great rock lying in the road near the house of Mr. Edward Scudder. Formerly it stood on the bluff on the south side of the way, but it was gradually undermined by the rains, and finally rolled down to its present position. When the present jail was built a portion of it was split off and used in the construction of the foundation of that building.

At the December term of the Plymouth Colony Court Mr. Hull and Mr. Dimmock were deputies from Barnstable, and at the same court he was admitted to be a freeman of the Plymouth Colony.

His name does not occur on the Church records, as the pastor or teacher. Dec. 11, 1639, a day of thanksgiving was held at his house "for God's exceeding mercy in bringing us hither, safely keeping us healthy and well in our weak beginnings, and in our church estate. The day being very cold our praises to God in publique being ended, we divided into three companies to feast together, some at Mr. Huil's, some at Mr. Mayo's, some at Brother Lombard's, Senior."

April 15, 1640, Mr. Hull assisted at the ordination of Rev. John Mayo as teaching elder of the Barnstable church.

"May 1, 1641, Mr. Hull was excommunicated for his willful breakeing of communication with us, and joyneing himselfe a member with a companie at Yarmouth to be their pastour ; contrary to the advise and counsell of our church."

---

*Secuncke's (or Black Goose's) father was perhaps sachem in 1639. Secuncke was, however, an aged man in 1682.

There is no record of the excommunication of his wife, but the following record makes it certain that she was, and for the same offence.

"Our syster Hull renewed her covenant with, renouncing her joyneing with the [not legible] at Yarmouth confessing her evil in soe doeing with sorrow March 11, 1642."

"Mr. Hull in the acknowledgeing of his sin, and renewing his covenant was received againe into fellowship with us Aug. 10, 1643."

March 7, 1642-3, the Plymouth Colony Court "ordered that a warrant shall be directed to the constable of Yarmouth, to apprehend Mr. Joseph Hull, (if he do either exercise the ministry amongst them or administer the seals,) to bring him before the next magistrate, to fynd suffieient sureties for his appearance, the next General Court, to answere his doings, (being an excommunicant.)"

Mr. Hull desisted from his attempt to preach in Yarmouth, and that spring removed to Dover. Gov. Winthrop under the date of May 10, 1643, when the articles of confederation of the United Colonies were adopted, says: "Those of Sir Ferdinando Gorge his province beyond Pascataquack, were not received nor called into the confederation, because they ran a different from us both in their ministry and civil administration; for they had lately made Acomenticus (Dover) a poor village a corporation, and had made a taylor their mayor, and had entertained one Hull, an excommunicated person and very contentious, their minister."

Mr. Hull after his settlement returned to Barnstable, where as above stated he was again received into fellowship, and no proceedings were had against him on the warrant which had been issued for his arrest.

His daughter Joanna had in 1639 married Mr. John Bursley who traded with the Eastern Indians at Dover and in that vicinity. On his return Mr. Hull removed his family, and thereafter did not reside in the Plymouth Colony.

Precisely how long he remained at Dover I am unable to state. Governor Winthrop speaks of him as the minister at Dover in the beginning of the year 1646, and names circumstances not creditable to a son of Mr. Hull. Cotton Mather, in his Magnalia Book VII, describing the perils of the Widow Elizabeth Heard at the famous assault of the Indians on Cocheco, in 1689, calls her "a daughter of Mr. Hull, a reverend minister."

Bishop, in his New England Judged, part 1, page 386, in his relation of the persecutions of the Quakers at Dover and that vicinity previous to 1660, speaks of Mr. Hull as being then the minister at Dover or Oyster River. He does not clearly state at which place he was settled, but that the two places were not distant. He says Mary Tompkins and Alice Ambrose on the Sabbath attended Mr. Hull's place of worship, and both standing up "before the old man he began to be troubled; and having spoken something against women's preaching, he was confounded, and knew not well what to say, whereupon Mary standing up declared the truth to the people." She was put down and carried out of the house, and Bishop says that in the melee, "the Priest pinched her arms." In the afternoon the Quakers held a separate meeting, to which nearly all of Mr. Hull's parishioners resorted.

A little time after he removed to the Isles of Shoals, or Smith's Isles, and preached in a Meeting House on Hog Island, built in 1641. It would seem by a notice of Mr. Hull in Neals History of New England, that he went to those desolate islands earlier than 1659. In the publications of the Massachusetts Historical Society it is also stated that the Rev. John Brook was the minister from about the year 1650 to 1662.

Rev. Joseph Hull died Nov. 19, 1665. He was called aged, though the number of years that he lived is unknown. His wife Agnes administered on his estate. Inventory, £52,5,5. It appears that the Island then owed him £20 for his ministry.

In tracing the history of "poor Mr. Hull" I have quoted from the records and the writings of his contemporaries. I have done so because I cannot endorse the opinions of Gov. Winthrop, or those of Mr. Savage, in his edition of the Governor's history or in his Genealogical Dictionary. In his criticisms of Dr. Cotton Mather, Mr. Savage is severe, and I am satisfied that on re-examination of the subject he will conclude that he has confounded the histories of two men, Benjamin and Joseph Hull. I have also carefully collected what others have said of him because I believe that no better men, as a class, than the first settlers of Barnstable, came into New England. The treatment which Mr. Hull received during his short residence, from Mr. Lothrop and his church, I cannot approve. I feel that full justice has not been done to his memory.

There is another consideration that should have an influence. All the records and all the early notices we have of Mr. Hull were written by men who for some reason or other appear to have been his personal enemies, and some allowance should be made for their prejudices. In the following review of his character I state my own opinions, and I think the judicious reader will concur with me therein.

The Rev. Joseph Hull came from England in 1635, and settled with twenty families beside his own at Weymouth, as their minister. He remained there four years, when he was dismissed from the church, preaching his farewell discourse to his people May 6, 1639.

That he was a man of good standing, clearly appears by the records. Soon after his arrival he was made a freeman of the Massachusetts Colony, and in 1638 was a deputy to the General Court, and was appointed a magistrate to try small cases. These offices he continued to hold until his removal to Barnstable. The people of Weymouth were not at that time unanimous in their religious opinions. There were Episcopalians; men who had danced with Morton around the May-pole, set up at Merry Mount; puritans; and men who belonged to no sect. Settled among a people whose opinions were so variant, it is not surprising that there were some who called him "a contentious man."

The salary paid to Mr. Hull was inadequate for the support of his large family. He was engaged in agriculture, particularly in the raising of cattle and horses for market, which then sold at high prices. It appears by a deed of Richard Standuwick, of Broadway, Somersett, England, recorded in vol. 1, page 160, of the Plymouth Colony records, that he took the care of cattle which had been sent out from England for a portion of the increase. This was a common practice at that time, and as cattle sold for high prices, the adventurers obtained a profit.

The great inducements held out to people to remove to Barnstable, or Mattakeset, as it was then called, were the extensive salt meadows and the great facilities for raising stock which the place afforded. These considerations induced the first settlers of Barnstable to leave the older settlements, where they complained that "they were straightened for lands." To raise cattle in a new country covered with forest requires a large extent of land for pasturage, and if there are no natural meadows on which hay can be cut, it will be many years before large stocks can be kept. In 1639 the raising of stock was a very profitable business, and Mr. Hull and those who came with him expected to realize fortunes in the business; but in a few years emigration having almost ceased, the demand was greatly diminished, and prices fell, and with them their visions of lordly wealth.

Mr. Lothrop and his church came Oct. 21, 1639, N. S. The town had been incorporated, many houses had been built, and a civilized community were dwelling among the Indians. Mr. Hull and the other settlers welcomed them to their homes, assigned them lands, and assisted them in putting up their first rude cabins. Mr. Lothrop's church constituted a majority of the people, they preferred their own pastor with whom they had suffered persecution in England. Mr. Dimmock and others of the first comers preferred to sit under the preaching of Mr. Lothrop rather than that of Mr. Hull. In consequence Mr. Hull was left in a small minority. Rev. John Mayo had been ordained teacher of the church, and Mr. Hull held no office therein.

In municipal affairs Mr. Lothrop and his church assumed the whole control. Mr. Hull was not re-elected deputy to the Court in June, 1640, and he does not appear to have held any office whatever. Lands that he had sold Samuel Hinckley the town took possession of, and Mr. Hinckley sued Mr. Hull for damages. The matter was referred to the Governor, and assistants, and their decision was in accordance with the offer Mr. Hull had made, that he should refund to Samuel Hinckley 20 shillings, and that the town should return one-half of the land taken. As the decision was in exact accordance with the tender made by Mr. Hull; and as this was the only lawsuit, or controversy, as it is called, in which his name appears, it does not prove that he was "a contentious man."

Human nature is ever the same. All men are ambitious,— some seek distinction in one form, some in another. Whether a community be large or small, to be the leading man therein is a mark of honor, and to be rudely thrust from that position is a dishonor to which very few men can calmly and quietly submit. In October, 1639, Mr. Hull was the leading man in the town—he had procured the grant of the lands—the act incorporating the town—as chairman of the town committee, had the general management of its municipal affairs—was deputy to the Colony Court—and pastor of the church and congregation. He was the founder of a civil community and however small or however weak it may have been, and though no Homer or Virgil has sung his praises, nor any Demosthenese or Cicero has trumpeted his fame, yet he may honestly and truly have said, I was the instrument in the hands of God to build up this little community ; and to convert the savage Indians from enmity to friendship.

In one short year thereafter he fell from his high position, he was excluded from office ; he had lost his influence ; he was unpopular, many of his early friends had deserted him, and others reaped the fields he had sown. He felt chagrined ; and the ungenerous treatment he thought he had received, induced him to remove. A few friends still adhered to him—they deeply sympathized with him, and they desired that he should continue to be their leader in temporal, and minister unto them in spiritual things.

In Yarmouth the Rev. Marmaduke Matthews, a Welchman, was the settled minister. He was witty and learned ; but not distinguished for depth of thought or sound judgment. Many were dissatisfied with him as a minister, among whom were Dr. Thomas Starr, Mr. William Nickerson, Hugh Tilley, and Joshua Barnes.* These men probably invited Mr. Hull to come to Yarmouth, and in the spring of 1641 he removed, and was the pastor of a small congregation, composed partly of his Barnstable friends and partly of the opponents of Mr. Matthews. For thus presuming to worship God in the manner and in the place they desired, the church in Barnstable hurled letters of excommunication against him and those who had dared to follow him. Those letters had no effect. The power of the civil magistrate was invoked, and in March, 1642-3, a

---

*These men were presented as "scoffers and jeerers of religion" and as disturbers of the proceedings of a town meeting. The plain English of this is, they opposed Mr. Matthews, the regularly settled minister, and favored Mr. Hull, the pastor of the second or irregularly established church.

warrant was issued for the arrest of Mr. Hull for the crime of "preaching at Yarmouth, he being an excommunicated person." However strenuously he might deny the authority of the church, and however ardently he might oppose the policy of the law, yet as a good citizen he felt bound not to resist the power of the civil magistrate—he submitted, and soon after removed to Dover.

His settlement at that place gave great offence to Gov. Winthrop and the other delegates of the United Colonies of New England, who held their first meeting at Boston in May, 1643. Because the little town of Dover elected a mechanic to be its mayor, and called Mr. Hull to be its minister, the colony of Sir Fernando Gorges, embracing the territory now included in the states of New Hampshire and Maine, and then called Georgiana, was denied the right, and was excluded from membership, as one of the United Colonies.

Surprising and incredible as this may appear, the fact is clearly and distinctly stated in the passage which I have quoted from Winthrop's History. If the delegates of Sir Fernando had been admitted, perhaps different counsels might have prevailed, perhaps some of the long, bloody and cruel wars, between the English on the one side, and the French and the Indians on the other, might have been avoided.

When on the first day of May, 1641, the church in Barnstable excommunicated Mr. Hull, for neglecting to commune with them, the members could hardly have imagined that they were committing an act which would be remembered in all coming time. They had a perfect right to dismiss Mr. Hull, and that was probably all they intended by the vote, for when Mr. Hull on the 10th of August, 1643, acknowledged he had done wrong in breaking off communion with the church, they received him again into fellowship. If he had been an immoral man, or even "a contentious man," they would not have welcomed him again into their fellowship. This act of the church in Barnstable is a complete vindication of the moral character of Mr. Hull.

The vote of the church passed in May 1641, had been communicated to the Plymouth Colony Court, and they had thereupon ordered a warrant to be issued for the apprehension of Mr. Hull if he continued to preach in Yarmouth. Gov. Winthrop of Massachusetts had been informed of these proceedings; but that the church had recinded its vote of excommunication, and that the constable had never had an occasion to serve the warrant, are facts that probably never came to his knowledge. If they had, it is not probable that he would have allowed his record to have remained uncorrected, and the stigma of being a "contentious man" to have rested on Mr. Hull's character. Fortunately thro' the efforts of Rev. Hiram Carleton, of West Barnstable, the records of Mr. Lothrop have been rescued from the oblivion in which they have slept nearly two centuries, and furnish the means of vindicating the character of Mr. Hull.

Dr. Cotton Mather, however bigoted he may have been, however credulous, however fond of the mavellous, and however strong may have been his faith in the super-natural, on all occasions speaks kindly and well of Mr. Hull.

Misfortunes followed in his footsteps in all his wanderings. Every recorded act of his life exhibits him as a man of peace, of a quiet and yielding disposition, as a good man and a sincere christian. In his controversy with Samuel Hinckley, he yielded all that he was asked to yield. His dealings with the church in Barnstable is a continual series of concessions on his part—he conceeded till he had nothing left to concede. At Yarmouth, when he found that the gathering of a second church gave offence to his former friends and to the Court, he withdrew and in a spirit of meekness, bordering on pusilanimity, "acknowledged that he had sinned," in preaching the gospel to that people.

At Dover, when the quakeress preachers invaded, on the Sabbath, his house of worship, and disturbed the order of exercises, by assuming a high place therein, and attempting to address the congregation, Bishop says that John Hill was belligerent, and thrust them down, and "that old Mr. Hull in leading Mary out pinched her arm." Bishop is usually truthful, and I presume the pinching must be admitted; that is, as aged as he was, he did not mean that she should escape from his grasp. In the afternoon Mr. Hull allowed the quakeresses to do as their spirits moved—he did not disturb their meeting, and to avoid all contest with their adherents he removed to the Isles of Shoals. In these desolate isles, where the rocks and sterility contend for the mastery, and where a single spring furnishes the water, and where the people breakfast, dine and sup on fish, there being nothing to tempt intrusion, poor Mr. Hull spent the remainder of his days, and there died in peace.

I have extended this review to a greater length than I intended. Circumstances seemed to require it. Mr. Hull was the founder of the town of Barnstable ; his character as a man and a minister was shrouded in doubt, and uncertainty. I felt it to be a duty to attempt to remove that shroud, and present his character in its true light. To succeed in this, it was necessary that the examination should not only be full, but exhaustive. How well I have succeeded in performing that duty, the reader will judge. If he decides that Mr. Hull was "a contentious man" and a heterodox teacher of religion, I fear that he will have to travel many a weary mile to find a peaceful man and a sincere christian.

Of Mr. Hull's family little is certainly known. His wife and several children came over with him. Judging by the disparity between the ages of his children he probably married twice. It is also difficult in some cases to discriminate between his and Mr. Benjamin Hull's children.

His daughter Naomi was baptized in Barnstable, 22 March, 1640, and Ruth 9th of May 1641. Beside these he had other children. His daughter Joanna, born in England, married 28 Nov. 1639, Mr. John Bursley, and afterwards Dolar Davis. Elizabeth, who married John Heard, of whom Mather gives so full an account of her escape from the Indians in 1689, I am confident was his, not Benjamin Hull's daughter, as stated by Mr. Savage. She was the mother of eleven children, among which the names of Joseph and Tristram occur. He had a son to whom reference has already been made. Josias, of Windsor, Conn., tradition says, was his son. Reuben, of Portsmouth, was probably another son. He had a large family, and it is of no profit to guess at their names. Tristram, of Yarmouth and Barnstable, I feel confident was the son of Rev. Joseph, though there is no record by which to establish the fact.

Tristram Hull, probably a son of Rev. Joseph Hull, went to Yarmouth with his father in 1641, but does not appear to have returned to Barnstable till 1644, all his children are recorded as born in Barnstable.

His houselot containing ten acres was bounded northerly by the meadow, easterly partly by the land of Barnabas Lothrop and partly by William Casely, southerly by the highway, and westerly by the land of Mr. Thomas Allyn, formerly Mr. Mayo's. This land is now owned by Mr. Isaiah Hinckley, and was a part of Dr. Hersey's farm. He also owned three acres of meadow on the north of his homelot, and four acres at Sandy Neck, at a creek yet known as Hull's creek.

Tristram Hull was a prominent man in Barnstable. He was of the board of Selectmen, and held other offices of trust. His wife was named Blanch, and is frequently named on the records as a woman whose reputation was not creditable to herself, her family or her friends. In 1655 she married for her second husband Capt. William Hedge of Yarmouth, but the change in her residence did not improve her manners. Capt. Hedge cut her off with a shilling in his will, full eleven pence more than she deserved.*

Children of Tristram Hull born in Barnstable :

I.   Mary, Sept., 1645.
II.   Sarah, March, ———.
III. Joseph, June, 1652.
IV.   John, March, 1654.
V.   Hannah, Feb., 1656.

---

*A question may arise whether it is right to publish such passages as this. Some squeamish persons object. I think it not only clearly right; but unjust to suppress them. Is it right that the reputations of such persons as Martha Foxwell, Capt. John Gorham, and Capt. William Hedge, should suffer because they unavoidably came in contact with a bad woman? I think not. History is of no value when the exact truth is suppressed. No line of distinction can be drawn between not telling the whole truth and the wilful misstatement of facts.

In his will dated Dec. 20, 1666, he names his five children and wife Blanch.

Joseph, a cooper by trade, inherited the paternal estate. He married Oct. 1676, Experience Harper, and had Tristram, born 8 Oct., 1677. Feb. 7, 1678, he sold his estate for £85 to Capt. John Lothrop, his mother Blanch and his wife Experience releasing their rights of dower. From Barnstable he removed to Falmouth, and purchased of Jacob Perkins for £105 an estate which he bought 31 Oct., 1677, of William Weeks, Sen'r.

Capt. John Hull, son of Tristram, removed to Rhode Island, where he has descendants. He sailed a ship between Newport and London. Charles Magee, afterwards the celebrated and well-known Sir Charles Magee, was an apprentice to Capt. Hull.

Hannah Hull married Sept. 15, 1674, Joseph Blush, of West Barnstable, and was the mother of twelve children. She died Nov. 15, 1732, aged 75.

HINCKLEY.

To write a full genealogy and history of the Hinckley family, a volume would afford insufficient space. I shall condense the materials I have collected into the smallest compass that I can, without rendering the narrative obscure. Omitting Gov. Thomas Hinckley, the same traits of character, with very few exceptions, have been transmitted from the first to the ninth generation.

SAMUEL HINCKLEY.

Samuel Hinckley, the common ancestor of all of the name in this country, is the type of the race. 'He was a dissenter, though on the 14th of March, 1734-5, in order to escape out of his native country, he was obliged to swear that he "conformed to the order and discipline of the church" of England.* He was honest, industrious and prudent, qualities which have been transmitted from father to son down to the present time. The Hinckley's are zealous in the advocacy of whatever opinions they adopt, and I never knew one who was dishonest, lazy or imprudent. He was not a distinguished man or prominent in political life. To be a juryman or surveyor of highways, filled the measure of his political aspirations. He appears to have been a man of good estate for the times, and all his children were as well educated as his means would permit. Very few of his descendants have amassed wealth, and a smaller number have been pinched by poverty.

In 1628 it appears by the colony records that Elder Nathaniel Tilden, of Tenterden, purchased lands in Scituate. He is spoken of

---

*This oath, whether taken with or without mental reservation, was perjury, according to the laws of England. Many of our ancestors were compelled to take it, or remain in England. They did outwardly "conform," in order to save themselves from imprisonment or persecution. Many of the first settlers of Barnstable would not outwardly conform, and in consequence suffered two years imprisonment in the vile dungeons of the city of London. Mr. Hinckley thought it politic to outwardly conform, and most persons, under the same circumstances, would have done the same. The sin consisted in compelling such men to take the oath, rather than in the taking thereof. The Union men of the South are in precisely the same circumstances at the present time, and no man condemns them for outwardly conforming to the requirements of the rebels.

as being at that time in this country. He was a man of wealth, and before removing his family probably came over, as many did, to examine the country and fix on a place for his future residence. In the spring of 1635 Mr. Tilden, Samuel Hinckley, John Lewis, and James Austin, of Tenterden, in the County of Kent, in England, and several other families from that County, making a company of 102, counting men, women, children and servants, resolved to emigrate to New England. In the latter part of March they sailed from Sandwich in the ship Hercules, 200 tons, Capt. John Witherly. Circumstances make it probable that they intended to join the Rev. John Lothrop, who, with several members of his church, had taken passage in the Griffin for Boston the preceding summer. More than half of the passengers who came over in the Hercules were afterwards inhabitants of Scituate.*

Samuel Hinckley brought with him his wife Sarah and four children, and immediately after his arrival in Boston went to Scituate and built a house which Mr. Lothrop calls No. 19. Three of his fellow passengers also built houses in that town in the summer of 1635, namely, William Hatch, No. 17, John Lewis, No. 18, and Nathaniel Tilden No. 20. The street on which they built was called Kent street. Samuel Hinckley continued to reside in Scituate till July, 1640, when he sold his house, farm and meadows, and removed to Barnstable.

Samuel Hinckley bought his lands of the Rev. Joseph Hull, and respecting the title he afterwards had some trouble with the town. There is no record of his lands ; but their location is well known. His houselot was bounded south by his son Thomas', and west by Rowley's pond, near which, according to tradition, he built his house, a small one-story building, with a thached roof. Precisely how long he resided in that house, I am not informed. He was one of the very first who removed to West Barnstable, where he owned one of the best farms in the town, now owned by Levi L. Goodspeed, Esq. His son-in-law, John Smith, owned the adjoining lands, since known as the Otis farm

In 1637 Mr. Samuel Hinckley, as he was called in the latter part of his life, took the freeman's oath, though his name appears on the list of the preceding year. As before remarked, he was not a prominent man, though his name frequently occurs on the records

---

*Moore, in his "Lives of the Governors of New Plymouth and Massachusetts," pages 201 and 2, states that Samuel Hinckley, in 1623, removed with Rev. John Lothrop from Egerton, in the County of Kent, to London, that he came over in 1634 in the ship Griffin with Mr. Lothrop, arrived in Boston Sept. 18, 1634, and on the 27th of the same month removed to Scituate, and that he removed to Barnstable in 1639. His son Thomas, he says, was born in 1621, and that he "came to New England soon after his father had made a settlement in Barnstable." Mr. Moore makes these statements as matters of fact. To say that he was mistaken in his suppositions, does not excuse him. He inferred or guessed that Mr. Hinckley came over with Mr. Lothrop, and recorded his guess as a truth of history. Mr. H. came from Tenterden in the ship Hercules in March 1635, bringing his wife and four children, as the Custom House records at the port of Sandwich show.

as a juror, a surveyor of highways, and as one of the granters of the
lands at Suckinesset.

As a church member he does not appear to have been intolerant.
The fact that he was twice indicted for "entertaining strangers,"*
indicates that he belonged to the liberal party, of which his friends
Cudworth, Hatherly and Robinson, and his son-in-law, Rev. John
Smith, were prominent members.

He married his first wife in England, and she and his four children came over with him. The names of his children are on the
Custom House record; but their names are omitted in the history of
the town of Sandwich, England, from which Mr. Savage copied.

Children of Samuel Hinckley.

2   I.   Thomas, born in England, 1618. (See below.)
3   II.   Susannah, born in England, married in 1643, Mr. John
        Smith, of Barnstable, and had a large family. (See Smith.)
4   III.   Sarah, born in England, married by Mr. Prince Dec. 12,
        1649, to Elder Henry Cobb, and was his second wife. (See
        Cobb.)
5   IV.   Mary, born in England. It appears by her father's will
        that she married and had a family, and was living in 1662.
6   V.   Elizabeth, born in Scituate, baptized Sept. 6, 1635, mar-
        ried July 15, 1657, Elisha Parker. (See Parker.)
7   VI.   Samuel, born in Scituate, bap. Feb. 4, 1637-8, buried in
        Barnstable March 22, 1640-1, aged three years.
8   VII.   A daughter, born in Scituate, and buried in Barnstable
        July 8, 1640.
9   VIII.   Twins born in ⎫   buried Feb. 6, 1640-1.
10   IX.   Barnstable, ⎭   buried May 19, 1640-1.
11   X.   Samuel, born in Barnstable 24 July, 1642, and baptized
        same day. (See below.)
12   XI.   John, born in Barnstable 24 May, 1644, and baptized
        26th of same month. (See account below.)

Mrs. Sarah Hinckley died Aug. 18, 1656, and Samuel Hinckley
married Dec. 15, 1657, for his second wife, Bridget Bodfish, widow
of Robert of Sandwich.

Samuel Hinckley died Oct. 31, 1662. In his will dated Oct. 8,
1662, he gives to his wife Bridget the use of his house, a garden and
some land; his two cows, Prosper and Thrivewell, and "all the
household stuff she brought with her." His daughters Susannah,
Mary, Sarah and Elizabeth, are named, and he gives to each of
them and to each of their children, one shilling each. As Mr.
Hinckley had a large property, the presumption is that he had given
a dower to each of his daughters at the time of their marriage. He

---

*"Entertaining strangers." We are commanded to "entertain strangers," and are told
that some have thereby "entertained angels unawares." By "strangers" our ancestors
"Quakers," and thence the criminality of the act.

gives legacies to his grandchildren Samuel, Thomas, Mary, Bath-shea, children of his son Thomas, and to his grandsons Samuel and Jonathan Cobb. His personal estate was apprised at £162,16, and he had a large real estate which he gave to his three sons, Thomas, Samuel and John.

Gov. Thomas Hinckley, son of Samuel, married for his first wife, Dec. 4, 1641, Mary Richards,* daughter of Thomas of Weymouth. She died June 24, 1659, and he married March 16, 1660, for his second, Mary Glover,† widow of Nathaniel Glover. Her grandson, Rev. Thomas Prince, says "she was the only child of Mr. Quartermaster Smith by his first wife, formerly of Lancashire, in England, and afterwards of Dorchester, in New England," and "was born in Lancashire in 1630. Her parents living under the ministry of the Rev. Mr. Richard Mather at Toxteth in that shire, they came up and brought her with them to Bristol in order for N. E. in April, 1635. Her father and others settling at Dorchester, and a new church gathered there Aug. 23, 1636, the said Mr. Richard Mather became the Teacher ; under whose ministry she lived, unless when sent to school at Boston. She married to Mr. Nathaniel Glover, a son of the Hon. John Glover, of said Dorchester, by whom she had Nathaniel and Ann. And then this husband dying she remained a widow till when she married the Hon. Thomas Hinckley, Esq., of Barnstable." Her daughter married July 11, 1673, William Rawson, and her son Hannah Hinckley.

Mrs. Mary Hinckley is represented to have been beautiful in person, and the most accomplished and intelligent woman in the Colony. Her daughters bore a striking resemblance to the mother, and in her grandsons seems to have been concentrated the intellectual vigor of the grandfather, and the accomplishments of the grandmother. This is remarkable, but perhaps not more so than the other facts named, that the distinguished traits in the character of the ancestor of this family have been transmitted from father to son to the present generation.

Mrs. Hinckley died July 29, 1703, in the 73d year of her age. To her may truly be applied the words frequently occurring in ancient eulogies, "She lived greatly beloved and died greatly lamented." Gov. Hinckley, then 85 years of age, wrote some verses to her memory which have been printed. She was buried in the ancient burying-ground in Barnstable, and a monument was

---

*Her sister Alice married Deputy Gov. William Bradford, making him brother-in-law to Gov. Hinckley.

---

†Mrs. Glover's friends were opposed to the marriage. She had two children and Mr. Hinckley eight, and they urged this as a reason against the marriage. About the time of his marriage Mr. H. carried with him some apple tree grafts from his own orchard. These he set in a tree which is said to be yet in bearing in Quincy, and known as the Hinckley apple tree.

erected to her memory, which has now crumbled to pieces. The inscription has however been preserved.

HERE LYETH Ye
BODY OF Ye TRULY
VIRTUOUS AND PRAISE-
WORTHY MRS. MARY
HINCHLEY, WIFE TO
Mr. THOMAS HINCKLEY,
DIED JULY Ye 29, 1703,
IN Ye 73d YEAR OF
HER AGE.

Gov. Thomas Hinckley died April 25, 1705, aged 87, not 85, as stated on the monument recently erected to his memory.

Mr. Moore, in his Lives of the Governors of Plymouth and Massachusetts, has furnished the most extended notice of Gov. Thomas Hinckley that has been published. He obtains his facts mainly from the colonial records, consequently it is little more than a synopsis of his official acts. In relation to his individual history, he furnishes little information and of that little, much is wanting in accuracy.

I confess that I do not feel competent to write, as it should be written, the biography of Gov. Thomas Hinckley. I may however attempt it in an article separate from this genealogy. I can collect the facts, and lay a foundation on which another can build. During half a century he held offices of trust and power in the Old Colony, and had a controling influence over the popular mind. He was the architect of his own fortune in life; the builder of his own reputation. He was a man of good common sense, and of sound judgment; honest and honorable in all his dealings; industrious, persevering and self-reliant; and, if it be any praise, it may be added, he was the best read lawyer in the Colony. He had some enemies—it would have been a miracle if so prominent and so independent a man had had none. Barren trees are not pelted. The Quaker influence was arrayed in hostility to him. He examined every question presented to him in its legal aspects, and viewing his acts from that stand-point, he was very rarely in the wrong. He was a rigid independent in religion, and his tolerant opinions, though in advance of his times, did not come up to the standard of the present. Some of his acts I shall leave for others to defend; but that he was the intolerant and cruel man that some of the infatuated bigots of his time represented him to be, the facts will not sustain. He was a living man, never allowed his faculties to rust by inaction, and to the last could draft an instrument with as much clearness and precision as in his early manhood.

Children of Gov. Thomas Hinckley born in Barnstable:

13. I. Mary, 3d Aug. 1644, baptized Aug. 4, 1644. She mar-

ried a man named Weyborne, perhaps John, a son of Thomas Weyborne who came from Tenterden to the "Castle" in Boston harbor in 1638, and probably acquaintances before they came over. She was living in 1688.

14. II.   Sarah, 4th Nov. 1646, baptized Dec. 6, 1646, married March 27, 1673, the second Nathaniel Bacon. She died Feb. 16, 1686-7, aged 40, leaving four children. (See Bacon.)

15. III.   Meletiah, 25th Nov. 1648, bap. next day. She married 23d Oct. 1668, Josiah Crocker of West Barnstable, and was the mother of a most respectable family of ten children. Benjamin, the youngest, graduated at Harvard College in 1713, and was many years teacher of the Ipswich Grammar School. She survived her husband 26 years, and died 2d Feb. 1714-15, aged 66 years. In her will dated 21st Jan. 1713-14, she names her five sons and three daughters then living. (See Crocker.)

16. IV.   Hannah, 15th April, 1651, bap. April 27, 1851, married Capt. Nathaniel Glover, son of her mother-in-law by a former husband. She died in Dorchester Aug. 20, 1730, aged 79 years, 4 months, 5 days. She had a daughter Hannah born Dec. 3, 1681, and died 6th Jan. 1724.

17. V.   Samuel, 14th Feb. 1652-3, bap. Feb. 20, 1652-3. (See account below.)

18. VI.   Thomas, 5th Dec. 1654. He died in 1688, aged 34, leaving no issue. In 1686, when the County road was laid out, his house is named as standing on the south side of the road between the houses of George Lewis and Samuel Cobb, probably the same house that he gives in his will to his nephews, and that was afterwards owned by his nephew Samuel. As he was a householder in 1686, it is probable that he did marry and that his wife died early, according to a tradition preserved in the Crowell family.

In his will dated 27th July, 1688, and proved on the 13th of Sept. following, he bequeaths to his honored father Thomas Hinckley, all the lands which his father had given him excepting the portion he had sold Samuel Cobb, and his horse. To his brother Ebenezer he gave one-half of all his uplands within the Common Field gate, and all the rest of the lands he had bought with the housing thereupon, equally to his sister Crocker's eldest son, and to his brother Samuel's eldest son. All his meadows in Barnstable and in Yarmouth, he gave in equal proportions to his brother Ebenezer and to his said sister Crocker's and brother Samuel's eldest sons. He also bequeathed to his honored mother £10 in money ; to his well beloved friend, Faith Winslow, daughter

of Nathaniel, £5 in money; to Mr. Jonathan Russell £3 out
of his estate; to his sisters Mary, Thankful, Abigail and
Reliance, each a cow; to his brother John his two four year
old steers; to each of his sisters, Hannah, Bathshua, Mehitabel, Mary and Experience, 10 shillings. His lands were at
the east end of the town, and were bought of the Lumbards,
and his house was probably that afterwards owned by Dea.
Gershom Davis.

19. VII.   Bathshua, 15th May, 1657, married June 6, 1681,
Samuel Hall, of Dorchester, had Bathshua Nov. 14, 1683.
She was living in 1688.

20. VIII.   Mehetable, 24th March, 1659. She married Samuel
Worden of Yarmouth, who was afterwards of Boston. She
had Samuel, baptized at Barnstable Feb. 24, 1683-4. Her
husband died early, and she married 25th Aug. 1698, William Avery of Dedham, his third wife.

21. IX.   Admire, 28th Jan. 1660, died 16th of Feb. following.

22. X.   Ebenezer, 22d Feb. 1661, died, 2 weeks after.

23. XI.   Mary, 31st July, 1662.   She was the second wife of
Samuel Prince, Esq., of Sandwich, Middleboro', and Rochester. She was the mother of the Rev. Thomas Prince,
born May 1687, graduate Harvard College 1707, a most as-
siduous annualist, whose services in perpetuating evidence
relative to our early history, exceeds, says Mr. Savage, that
of any other man since the first generation. When young he
resided at Barnstable with his grandfather Hinckley, whose
papers he filed and preserved; but it is to be regretted that
many of them have since been scattered and lost. She also
had Nathan a graduate of Harvard College, 1718, a man of
superior talent to his brother, but of less value to society.

24. XII.   Experience, Feb. 28, 1664. She married James
Whipple, of Barnstable.   She is named in her brother
Thomas' will dated 27th July, 1688, but it seems that she
died soon after that date, leaving no issue. He married for
his second wife 25th Feb. 1692, Widow Abigail Green of
Boston, a daughter of Lawrence Hammon, born 27th April,
1667, and by her had nine children. He removed to Boston
in 1708. He owned the estate afterwards owned by Hon.
Sylvanus Bourne, and his son Dr. Richard.

25. XIII.   John, 9th June, 1667.   (See account below.)

26. XIV.   Abigail, 8th April, 1669.   She married 2d Jan.
1697-8, Rev. Joseph Lord, graduate Harvard College, 1691
of Dorchester, Mass., founder of Dorchester, South Caro-
lina, and afterwards minister of Chatham.   He was a school
master, physician, and clergyman.   I have a volume of his
manuscript sermons and a portion of his diary, beautifully
executed. She had nine children, and died on the night of

Dec. 14, 1725, aged 56.   He married Nov. 16, 1743, for his second wife Bethia Smith.   He died in 1748, aged 76.

27.   XV.   Thankful, 20th Aug. 1671, married 12th Nov. 1675, Rev. Experience Mayhew, of Martha's Vineyard, teacher of the Indians there, and the author of several books in relation to them.   She was the mother of a most remarkable family of children ; namely : Joseph, Harvard College 1730 ; Nathan, Harvard College 1731 ; Lecariah, a missionary to the Indians who died 6th March, 1806, aged 88 ; and Jonathan, Harvard College 1744, one of the most distinguished divines of the country.

28.   XVI.   Ebenezer, 23d Sept. 1673.   (See act. below.)

29.   XVII.   Reliance, 15th Dec. 1675, baptized Dec. 19, 1675, being on that Sunday of the great Narraganset Swamp fight.   The father was an officer in Capt. Gorham's company, and Rev. Mr. Russell, the minister, gave the name. She married 15th Dec. 1698, Rev. Nathaniel Stone of Harwich, and was the mother of twelve children.

Samuel Hinckley, son of Samuel, resided on his father's estate at West Barnstable.   He was a farmer.   He married 14th Dec. 1664, for his first wife, Mary, daughter of Roger Goodspeed. She died Dec. 20, 1666, aged 22, and he married Jan. 15, 1668-9, Mary, daughter of Edward Fitzrandolphe.   He died intestate Jan. 2, 1726-7, aged 84, and his estate was divided on the 31st of the same month, by a mutual agreement between his four sons, Benjamin, Joseph, Isaac, Ebenezer and Thomas, who appear to have been all the surviving heirs.   His widow signs her name as "Elizabeth Bursley," wife of John B.

Children born in Barnstable.

30.   I.   Benjamin, 6th Dec. 1666.   (See below.)

31.   II.   Samuel, 6th Feb. 1669, died 3d Jan. 1676.

32.   III.   Joseph, 15th May, 1672.   (See below.)

33.   IV.   Isaac, 20th Aug. 1674.   (See below.)

34.   V.   Mary, May 1677, died 15th June, 1677.

35.   VI.   Mercy, 9th April, 1679.

36.   VII.   Ebenezer, 2d Aug. 1685.   (See below.)

37.   VIII.   Thomas, 1st Jan. 1688-9.   (See below.)

John Hinckley, son of Samuel, resided at West Barnstable. He was a man of some note, often employed in town affairs, and ensign of the militia company, an office of honor in his day.   He married for his first wife July 1668, Bethia Lothrop.   She was a member of the church, but does not appear to have been an exemplary sister.   She died 10th July, 1697, and he married Nov. 24th, 1697, for his second wife, Mary Goodspeed.

Children of Ensign John Hinckley born in Barnstable.

38.   1.   Sarah, end of May, 1669, married John Crocker 22d June, 1721.

39. II. Samuel, 2d Feb. 1670-1. He removed to Stonington, Conn., and was living in 1710.
40. III. Bethia, latter end of March, 1673. She died 12th April, 1715, aged 32, according to her gravestones in West Barnstable churchyard.
41. IV. Hannah, middle of May, 1675, married June 2, 1708, Benjamin Lewis. (See Lewis.)
42. V. Jonathan, 15th Feb. 1677.
43. VI. Ichabod, 28th Aug. 1680.
44. VII. Gershom, 2d April, 1682.

The above are all the children named on the town record; but in the settlement of his estate, and in the will of Bethia in 1715, and of Mercy in 1707, the following are also named, probably children of the second wife:

45. VIII. Mary.
46. IX. Abigail.
47. X. Mercy. She died single in 1718, leaving £100 estate mostly in money. She names her sisters Sarah, Hannah Lewis, Mary and Abigail. Her brother Job, Thomas Crocker, Jr., Walley Crocker, Rev. Mr. Lord, and her *loving cousin Joseph Lothrop*, whom she appoints executor.

Ensign John Hinckley died 7th Dec. 1709. Inventory by Joseph Smith and Daniel Parker Dec. 13, 1709. Real estate £431,10; personal, £200,15,4, and was sworn to by his widow Mary. His sons Ichabod and Gershom administered. His estate was divided to his wife Mary, eldest son Samuel of Stonington, Ichabod, Bethia, Hannah Lewis, Jonathan, Gershom, Job, Abigail, Mercy and Sarah.

(17.) Samuel Hinckley, son of Gov. Thomas, called junior, to distinguish him from his uncle of the same name, resided at West Barnstable. His father in his will says he gave to him the greatest part of his great lot where his son built his house. The boundaries of his great lot are not on the record. It was probably a part of the tract at West Barnstable, known as the "Timber Lands." Samuel Hinckley, Jr., was not a prominent man. He married Nov. 13, 1676, Sarah, daughter of John Pope of Sandwich. His death is recorded with commendable particularity, "Sam'l Hinckley, son of Mr. Thos. Hinckley, deceas'd, ye 19 March, 1697," new style I presume, aged 46 years, and his widow married Aug. 17, 1698, Thos. Huckins, 2d. This family residing remote from the principal settlements, and had few advantages for obtaining an education. The mother and her son Thomas signed with their marks Dec. 17, 1700. This family removed to Harwich and some of the members afterwards to Maine.

Samuel Hinckley in his will dated March 12, 1696-7, gives

half of his land and "housing" to his wife Sarah, and the other half to his son Thomas, provided he confirms the conveyance of the lands of his son which he sold unto Samuel Cobb and Henry Cobb which were given to his son by his brother Thomas Hinckley, also all the money due him from Richard Child, Eleazer and Jonathan Crocker, being a part of the money the land sold for. He appoints his wife executrix, and his brothers, Capt. Seth Pope and Josiah Crocker, overseers. Inventory April 2, 1698, by Job Crocker, Josiah Crocker and Daniel Parker. Personal estate £137,1.

Children born in Barnstable.

48. I.   Mercy, 22d July, 1678, married Samuel Bangs Jan. 13, 1706, of Harwich.

49. II. Mehitabel, 28th Dec. 1679, died in Harwich April 30, 1718.

50. III. Thomas, 19th March, 1680-1, married Mercy ———— and had born in Harwich Joshua, March 29, 1707, Thomas, March 11, 1708-9. He died in Harwich and administration on his estate was granted to his widow Oct. 11, 1710. She married 2d William Crosby April 26, 1711. Joshua married Lydia Snow March 31, 1726, and had in Harwich, Thomas, March 4, 1726-7 ; Joshua, Aug. 15, 1728 ; Josiah, May 5, 1730 ; Elkanah, July 1, 1732 ; Nathan, June 1, 1734 ; Lydia, April 1, 1736 ; Ruth, Feb. 2, 1738 ; Isaac, Feb. 5, 1740 ; and Benjamin, June 8, 1744. He had other children whose names are not on the town records, for his son Reuben was baptized April 9, 1748. In 1753 Joshua Hinckley and his wife Lydia were dismissed from the Harwich church to the church in Oblong. He was a worthy, respectable man ; but unfortunately very poor. Thomas, son of Thomas, married March 31, 1730, Ruth Myrick of H. March 7, 1765, Lydia Nickerson of Chatham, and July 31, 1766, Hannah Severance of H. He is called a blacksmith and resided near Hinckley's Pond in H. The record of his family is lost. He had Nathaniel baptized July 30, 1738 ; Mary, 1741 ; Ruth, 1743 ; Mercy, 1745 ; Isaac, July 12,. 1747. He died in 1769, leaving a widow Hannah and a minor son Elijah. His widow married perhaps in 1771, John Burgess of Yarmouth. Nathaniel of this family married 1760 Mercy Nickerson of Chatham and Mary, Nathan Crowell Jan. 1, 1761.

51. IV. Seth, 16th April, 1683. April 5, 1711, letters of administration were granted to Samuel Hinckley of Harwich, on the estate of his brother Seth, late of Barnstable, deceased. His heirs were his brothers Job, Shubael, Josiah, Elnathan, sisters Mary Bangs, Mehitabel Hinckley and Mer-

cy Crosby, and to the two children of Thomas Hinckley, another of the brothers deceased.

52. V. Samuel, 24th Sept. 1684, married Mary, daughter of Edmond, and grand daughter of Major John Freeman. His children born in Harwich were Seth, Dec. 25, 1707; Shubael, March 15, 1708-9; Samuel, Feb. 12, 1710-11; Mary, Feb. 12, 1710-11, twin, died March, 1710-11; Edmond, Nov. 20, 1712; Reliance, Nov. 21, 1714 (this date is doubtful). She is recorded as the eldest child, date probably 1704. Samuel Hinckley and his wife were dismissed from the Harwich to the church in Truro in April 1719.

53. VI. Elnathan, 8th Sept. 1686, living in 1711.

54. VII. Job, 16th Feb. 1687-8, living in 1711.

55. VIII. Shubael, 1st May, 1699, married first, Lydia, daughter of Capt. Jonathan Bangs, 1712, had Sarah March 2, 1712-13, who probably died early; and Samuel, Jan. 5, 1714-15. His uncle Edward Bangs appointed his guardian 1728. He married for his second wife Oct. 7, 1718, Mary Snow. This is probably the Shubael Hinckley of "Old York," Me., mentioned in the April number, 1854, of the Genealogical Register, who moved to the neighborhood of the Kennebec, had four wives, twenty children, and died at Hallowell aged 92. His son James married Mary McKenney of Georgetown, Me., and had born in Topsham, James, 14th Aug. 1769; Thomas, April 3, 1772; Mercy, Dec. 17, 1775; Nicholas, April 2, 1778; Ebenezer, Oct. 20, 1780; Clark, May 10, 1783; Levi, May 29, 1785; Olive O., Aug. 24, 1787; Mehitabel, May 18, 1790; and Mary, March 18, 1793. He has descendants in Maine.

56. IX. Mercy, 11th Jan. 1692, married by Joseph Doane, Esq., to William Crosby April 24, 1711, and had seven children.

57. X. Josiah, 24th Jan. 1694-5. He was a blacksmith and lived in Truro. Married Lydia Paine.

58. XI. Elnathan, 29th Dec. 1697, (?1695.)

I am indebted to Josiah Paine, Esq., of Harwich, for much information respecting the family of Sam'l Hinckley (son of Gov. Thomas.) That a woman having eleven children, the oldest only twenty years of age, should have deserted her family and married a man having eight children, is what mothers do not often do.*

(25.) John Hinckley, son of Gov. Thomas, born 9th June, 1667, was a farmer, and as the stock and tools of a shoe maker are apprised as a part of his assets, I infer that he had learned

---

*Her son Jabez Huckins was born 20th July, 1698, and her marriage to Thomas Huckins was solemnized on the 17th of Aug. next following. If the reader will turn to the Huckins genealogy, the reason why the children left their unnatural mother will be apparent. Tho' some of this family removed to Truro, those of the name now resident in that town are not descendants of Samuel; but of his brother John.

that trade. In those times, many who did not work regularly at the trade, made and mended the shoes for their own families. This was probably the fact in regard to John Hinckley. He was a witness to the will of the Rev. Samuel Newman of Rehobeth, Nov. 18, 1681, and Mr. Savage thence infers that he was then a pupil of Mr. Newman. He occupied for a time a part of his father's house. He was honest, industrious, and prudent, a member of the church, but did not possess much talent or business capacity. He married May 1, 1691, Thankful, daughter of Thomas Trott of Dorchester. He died in 1706, and his widow married Mr. Jonathan Crocker of West Barnstable, Feb. 1710-11. He died in 1746, leaving her again a widow. His father gave him the westerly half of his dwelling house, and of his farm and land at the Calves Pasture. He outlived his father less than a year, and was only thirty-eight at his death. Letters of administration on his estate were granted to his widow Thankful Hinckley March 22, 1705-6. His real estate was apprised at £100, and his personal at £93,10. Among the articles apprised were his leather and shoemaker's tools £1, and a servant boy and a girl £12. Slaves or servants in those days do not appear to have been valued very highly. The final settlement of his estate was made May 27, 1722, by "Thankful Crocker, formerly Thankful Hinckley." She appears to have been a good manager, for beside the support of her family the personal estate had increased in value £60. John Hinckley bought out his sisters Abiah and Thankful, and four-fifths were divided to him and one-fifth to his brother James. John had all the lands on the north side of the road and at the Calves Pasture, excepting the dwelling house which had been sold to Samuel Allyn, and the lot by the hill on the south of the pond where he afterwards built his house, now owned by the heirs of Robinson T. Hinckley, deceased.

Children of "Mr. John Hinckley, Jr.," born in Barnstable.

59. I.   John, 29th March, 1692, died Aug. 24, 1694.
60. II. Mary, 24th Feb. 1694, died in 1722.
61. III. Abiah, 24th March, 1696, baptized Abigail, married Dec. 8, 1715, Dea. Samuel Chipman. (See Chipman.)
62. IV. Thankful, 14th July, 1699, married Oct. 11, 1724, James Smith. (See Smith.)
63. V.   John, 19th Feb. 1701. He was a carpenter, and was extensively engaged in building in Barnstable and the adjacent towns. He built the Meeting House at Marshpee in 1757, and in 1762 added the high steeple to the Meeting House in the East Parish in Barnstable. He was a man of sound judgment, good business habits, and exercised a wide and controlling influence. He was a deacon of the east church, of which he was one of the most respected and exemplary members. In 1743 he was Lieutenant of the troop

of horse in the County of Barnstable, and in 1757 Captain. The following order has an historical interest, and I therefore copy it from the original, preserved among Dea. Hinckley's papers.*

"First Regiment in the Co. of Barnstable, the 15th of August, 1757.
To Capt'n John Hinckley, Captain of the Troop in the County of Barnstable,   GREETING:
[L. S.] Having received intelligence this day from his EXCELLENCY THE GOVERNOUR that a very large body of the French and Indian enemy have made themselves masters of fort William Henry, near Lake George, and have likewise invested fort Edward; and there being reason to apprehend that the enemy will penetrate farther into the country unless large reinforcements are sent to oppose their progress, and he has ordered me to send off without delay the Troop of horse belonging to this Regiment, being completely furnished with arms and ammunition according to law, and with what provision, &c., they can carry to SIR WILLIAM PEPPEREL, Lieutenant-General of the Province, wheresoever he shall be, and then to put themselves under his command and to receive his further orders.

These are therefore in his Majesty's name, to require you forthwith to muster the Troop of horse under your command compleat in arms, and with ammunition and provision as abovesaid to meet to-morrow at twelve of the clock at the house of the widow Mary Chipman in Barnstable, to be ready forthwith to march from thence to Sir William Pepperel as afores'd wherever he be, and then to put yourselves under his command and to receive his further orders. Hereof you may not fail. Given under my hand and seal the day and year aboves'd.

JAMES OTIS,
Coll'n of sd Regiment.

Dea. Hinckley received a common school education. His accounts are remarkable for their compactness and clearness. All the accounts of the materials and labor of building a house, he would condense into a space not larger than the hand. The following are his entries respecting the building of the steeple of the east Meeting House:

"Feb. 21, 1762, then began to cut timber for the steeple. July the 6, then raised the steeple." The accounts for labor are

---

*Among his papers there is an order from Gov. Thomas Pownal, dated Aug. 4, 1758, by which he is "authorized and empowered to take upon you the charge of seventy men and to conduct them to the regiments to which they belong," &c. Also a letter from Hon. Thomas Hubbard, dated Boston, Oct. 4, 1757, in which he advises Dea. H. that he has bought ten thousand feet of seasoned boards, and 16 m of good shingles for the Meeting House at Marshpee, to be landed at Barnstable.

Dea. Hinckley's mode of keeping the accounts of the men that he employed occupied but little space, and was as exact as any other mode. A full weeks work he entered thus,
$\frac{111111}{111111}$ four days, thus, $\frac{110111}{100110}$ the cyphers representing absence.

set down weekly, noting the days that each worked. The whole amount of labor in constructing the steeple was as follows:

Dea. Hinckley,	40	days.
"Adino," his son,	4 1-2	"
"Nic," probably Nicholas Cobb,	49	"
"Jab," his son Jabez Hinckley,	68 1-2	"
"Ben,"	61	"
	223	

Paid for Iron,	£16,3
Hinges	1,10
11 1-2 m Shingles,	74,15

He married Sept. 17, 1726, Bethia, daughter of Joseph Robinson, Esq., of Falmouth, a descendant of Rev. John, of Leyden. His residence was a little distance west of his grandfather's.

Children born in Barnstable.

1, Thankful, 7th Oct. 1727, married Aug. 12, 1745, David Cobb of B. ; 2, Bethia, 1st Feb. 1730., married Jan. 31, 1754, Henry Cobb ; 3, Martha, 28th April, 1734, married Jan. 15, 1756, Mr. Barnabas Howes ; 4, Adino, 12th Dec. 1735, married Dec. 16, 1762, Mercy, daughter of Solomon Otis, Esq., and was the father of Solomon, Adino and Robinson T. Hinckley, recently deceased ; 5, Hodiah, 6th Oct. 1738, married March 25, 1762, Simeon Jenkins, father of Dea. Braley and others ; 6, Jabez, 24th Oct. 1741, married 1764, Deborah Wing, and died Feb. 1817. His children were, James, 28th Aug. 1766 ; Josiah, 8th April, 1769 ; Anna, 4th Jan. 1773, died young ; Anna, 18th Dec. 1775 ; Joshua, 2d March, 1779 ; Vicy, 7th Dec. 1785, single woman. 7, Abiah, 13th Oct. 1746, married Cornelius Crocker, (see Crocker) ; and 8, John, 13th Sept. 1748, father of Isaiah, Charles, Capt. Matthias Hinckley and others now living. He died Oct. 1, 1835, aged 87. He recollected many who had conversed with the first settlers. Dea. John Hinckley, the father, died April 11, 1765, aged 64.

64. VI. James, 9th May 1704. He married Dorcas and removed to Falmouth, where he died in 1746 insolvent. The Hinckleys at Truro I think are his descendants.

(28.) Ebenezer Hinckley, son of Gov. Thomas, born in Barnstable 23d Sept. 1673, resided in his native town till 1716, when he removed to Braintree. His father gave him the east part of his house. He is called in deeds a yeoman, and was not distinguished in public life.* He married Nov. 1706 Mary Storn of Sudbury. He died Oct. 17, 1721, leaving a widow and two children. In his will dated July 5, 1720, he devises to his daughter

---

*John and Ebenezer, the two surviving sons of Gov. Hinckley, would have been entitled to more respect if they had erected a monument to the memory of their father, instead of quarreling about the division of his estate.

Rachel £140 to be paid to her when of age, and a copy of Mr.
Flavel's works ; to his son Ebenezer £160 when of age, and the
"three biggest books" mentioned in my father's will, his gun,
sword and *iron back.* The balance of his property, about £300,
he devises to his wife Mary, who married Nov. 5, 1722, John
George. His children were:

65.   I.   Rachel, born in Barnstable Nov. 1, 1707, married May
        27, 1742, Samuel Spear, Jr.

66. II.   Ebenezer, born in Braintree March 14, 1713, married
        July 11, 1732, (aged 19?) Hannah Nightingale, whom he
        survived. He was a shipmaster, and according to tradition
        died in the West Indies. He left seven children. 1, Eben-
        ezer, who married Ann Morton, a sister of the Hon. Perez
        Morton, and had Joseph, who married his cousin Abigail
        Hinckley ; John, who settled in Albany and had eight chil-
        dren ; Lucy, who married Isaac Prescott ; Anna, unmar-
        ried ; Sophia, married John D. Howard, Jr., of Boston ;
        and Herman, unmarried. 2d, Thomas was a shipmaster,
        settled at first in Wellfleet and afterwards removed to Bos-
        ton. He married Susannah Hewes of Wrentham. He died
        aged 34 during the Revolution, leaving a widow and four
        children, some of whom were born in Wellfleet. 3d, John
        was an auctioneer in Boston and a member of the Ancient
        and Honorable Artillery Company in 1772. He married
        Abigail Kneeland of Boston, and had Abigail who married
        her cousin Joseph, and had no children ; Mary married Ed-
        ward Church, merchant of Boston, and died Nov. 1858,
        aged 87 ; John, who died unmarried in 1855 at Andover ;
        Sophia, Harriet and Eliphalet, died young. 4th, Eliphalet,
        a mariner, died unmarried. 5th, Mary, died unmarried ;
        Hannah, died unmarried ; and Nancy, who married Benja-
        min Gorham.

    (30.) Benjamin Hinckley, son of the second Samuel, resi-
ded at West Barnstable on a part of the Hinckley farm. I find
no settlement of his estate on the probate records. He was living in 1745, aged 79. He married 27th Dec. 1686, Sarah, daughter of James Cobb. He had nine children, five the record says
"dyed," and their names and ages are not recorded, neither do
they appear on the church records.

Children born in Barnstable.

67.   I.   Benjamin, 18th July 1694, married Nov. 2, 1716, Abi-
        gail, daughter of Joseph Jenkins. He died in 1745, leaving
        an estate apprised at £920,13,6. His homestead at West
        Barnstable was valued at £380, but the currency was then
        depreciated, a yoke of oxen being valued at £30, about
        double their value fifty years before. He had a family of
        eleven children born in Barnstable, namely : 1, Abigail, born

July 30, 1718, married Nathaniel Fuller April 5, 1739?; 2, Edmond, Jan. 30, 1719-20, married Sarah Howland Dec. 6, 1744, and had Edmond Nov. 10, 1745, Abner, Nov. 25, 1747, Mary, July 11, 1749, Enoch, March 27, 1751, Heman, Jan. 27, 1754, Anna, Dec. 6, 1757, and Benjamin, Dec. 24, 1761 ; 3, Samuel, Oct. 16, 1721 ; 4, Joseph, Oct. 23, 1723, married Mary Davis of Sandwich Feb. 1751 ; 5, Benjamin, April 28, 1727, married Nov. 22, 1750, Lydia Phinney, and had Nymphas Sept. 13, 1753, and probably others; 6, Sylvanus, April 7, 1729, married 31st May, 1753, Sarah Phinney, and had Zacheus 7 19th March 1754, Sylvanus, 25th Aug. 1 56, Prince, 27th Dec. 1758, Lydia, 8th June, 1761, Levi, 17th May, 1764, Elizabeth, 23d Sept. 1766, and Reliance, 26th March, 1769 ; 7, Nathaniel, April 7, 1732,* married Joanna Lewis Oct. 13, 1761 ; 8, Martha, April 24, 1734, married Daniel Fuller Nov. 1, 1753 ; 9, Bathsheba, April 14, 1736, married Nath'l Ryder March 7, 1754 ; 10, Timothy, April 16, 1738, married Mary Goodspeed 1766 ; and 11, Zaccheus,† Oct. 6, 1740. I notice that the mother Abigail was appointed guardian of her son Timothy March 12, 1745, why it does not appear.

(31.) Joseph Hinckley, son of the second Samuel, married 21st Sept. 1699, by Col. Thacher, to Mary Gorham. He resided at West Barnstable on the estate which was his grandfather's. His house yet remains, and is now owned by Levi L. Goodspeed, Esq. He was a man of wealth, and it appears by his will that in addition to his farming business he was engaged in the tanning and currying business. He died in 1753, aged 81 years. In his will dated 11th Sept. 1751, proved Aug. 7, 1753, he names his son John, to whom he gave all his real estate in the East Precinct, &c., &c. ; to Isaac lands at West Barnstable and at Hebron, Conn., a pew in the West Meeting House, bedding he had at College, latin books, tanning and currying tools, &c., &c. He names his son Samuel, deceased. To his daughter Mercy Bourn he devises his negro girl "Sarah," bought of Hopkins, his biggest silver porringer, &c., &c. To his daughter Mary Davis he gave his negro girl "Anne," bought of his brother Isaac, &c. He also names the children of his daughter Thankful, deceased, his granddaughter Mary Bourne, grandson Joseph Davis, and granddaughter Mehitabel Dillingham. His negro servant "Peg" to reside with either child she may desire. His sons John and Isaac executors. He had ten children born in Barnstable, namely : 1, Mercy, 19th Aug. 1700, married Mr. John Bourne March 16, 1722 ; 2,

---

*A Nathaniel Hinckley, called 2d, married Nov. 24, 1758, Elizabeth Chipman. The first Nathaniel was 48 at his first marriage, and I may have confounded them.

---

†I think Zaccheus lived, and that I remember him as a very old man; but I may be mistaken.

Joseph, 6th May, 1702, married 1725, Mary Otis of Scituate, had a son Joseph Oct. 4, 1738, probably died young, the father died Sept. 9, 1738, the mother March 21, 1738-9 ; 3, Mary, 25th Feb. 1703-4, married Dea. Gershom Davis Sept. 23, 1731 ; 4, Samuel, 24th Feb. 1705-6, died early ; 5, Thankful, 9th June, 1708, married James Davis Dec. 2, 1727. She died Aug. 24, 1745, leaving seven children, the father being also deceased, the children were brought up by their grandfather Hinckley ; 6, Abigail, 30th Oct. 1710, married Mr. John Dillingham of Harwich Jan. 3, 1742, she died Sept. 9, 1749, leaving a daughter Mehitabel ; 7, Elizabeth, 4th Jan. 1712-13 ; 8, Hannah, 10th June, 1715 ; 9, John, 16th Nov. 1717, called junior. He resided in the ancient brick house that belonged to Henry Bourne, and was subsequently occupied by Rev. Thomas Walley and the Russels, as a parsonage. He married Jan. 24, 1744-5, Bethia Freeman, and had eight children : 1, Joseph, Nov. 10, 1745, died Nov. 21, 1745 ; 2, Bethia, Aug. 25, 1747, died Feb. 23, 1775 ; 3, Mary, Aug. 9, 1749, died April 2, 1820 ; 4, Elizabeth, April 9, 1752 ; 5, John, Oct. 15, 1754, called "Brick John" to distinguish him from "Farmer John," and because he lived in the ancient brick house, he married Dec. 4, 1778, Hannah Ide of Rehoboth, and was the father of the late Isaac Hinckley and others ; 6, Freeman, June 27, 1757, he was a silver smith, married Sabra Hatch of Falmouth May 17, 1771. He died early leaving no issue, and his widow became the fourth wife of John Thacher ; 7, James, April 2, 1760 ; and Sarah Oct. 28, 1763.   6, Isaac, born 31st Oct. 1719, Harvard College 1740, was a classmate of Samuel Adams and other distinguished men. He resided at West Barnstable in the house which was his father's. During the Revolution he was an active patriot. He was many years town clerk, and one of the selectmen of the town. He died Dec. 1802, aged 83 years. He married Dec. 18, 1748, Hannah Bourne, and had 1, Richard, Oct. 29, 1749 ; 2, Hannah, March 25, 1751 ; 3, Abigail, Feb. 13, 1753 ; 4, Joseph, March 6, 1755 ; 5, Elizabeth, April 30, 1757 ; 6, Isaac, June 18, 1760, an enterprising shipmaster, removed to Hingham and has descendants ; 7, Charles, Nov. 1, 1762 ; and 8, Eunice, July 14, 1765.

(33.) Isaac Hinckley, son of the second Samuel, born 20th Aug. 1674, resided at West Barnstable for a time. He married for his first wife, June 6, 1712, Mrs. Elizabeth Gookin of Sherborn. She was the daughter of the Rev. Mr. Gookin, and was born 20th May, 1690, and was sixteen years younger than her husband. There is no record of his family on the town books or settlement of his estate on the probate records. He was of Barnstable in 1703, and after that his name disappears.

(36.) Ebenezer Hinckley, son of the second Samuel, born Aug. 2, 1685, resided in the East Parish, and owned nearly all the ancient Allen estate. He married for his first wife Mrs.

Sarah Lewis June 17, 1711; she died March 21, 1737-8, aged 46, and he married for his second wife, July, 1739, Mrs. Thankful Miller of Yarmouth. He died April 12, 1751, aged 65, (gravestones.) In his will dated on the day preceding his death he made provisions that were unsatisfactory to his widow and children, but they had the good sense to settle the trouble satisfactorily among themselves. He bequeathed to his wife all the property she brought to him *excepting her clock and negro woman*, and the use of one-third of his estate so long as she remained a widow. To his three sons, Eben, Thomas and Samuel, he gave all his real estate. To Eben his negro boy Boston, and his Indian boy, &c.; to Thomas and Samuel his negro boy "George"; to his daughter Susannah Hinckley his negro girl "Barbara," &c.; and to his daughter Mary Hinckley his negro boy "Jethro." His wife's negro woman he undertook to make the common property of his five children, but that matter and the clock was set right by the sons. His children born in Barnstable were: 1, Ebenezer, 10th Sept. 1712, married in 1743, Mehitable Sturgis of Yarmouth, and had Sarah April 19, 1744, Temperance Jan. 20, 1748, and Ebenezer Sept. 23, 1754, the latter married, had a family, and lived to great age—the mother died Nov. 14, 1773, aged 53; 2, Daniel, 8th July, 1714, died Aug. 8, 1714; 3, a son, 24th Sept. 1715, died Sept. 27, 1715; 4, Thomas, 27th July, 1717, married Nov. 9, 1752, Phebe Holmes of Plymouth, and had Daniel March 20, 1754, Phebe, Aug. 8, 1755, Patience July 16, 1757, Temperance, Thomas and James. He resided in a house that stood opposite the present residence of Mr. Solomon Hinckley in Barnstable. He died April 30, 1775, aged 59; 5, Susannah, April 18, 1722; 6, Samuel, 7th Sept. 1727, a sea captain, had the westerly part of his father's estate, on which he built a splendid mansion, married, and had one daughter who married Samuel Allyn. He died early in life, leaving a large estate. His widow survived him many years, and died in the Alms House; 7, Mary, born 12th April, 1729, married Feb. 20, 1752, Samuel Childs.

(37.) Thomas Hinckley, son of the second Samuel, born 1st Jan. 1688-9, resided at West Barnstable. He was a tanner and died in 1756. aged 68, leaving four children, two of whom, Mercy and Mary, were of feeble minds and incapable of taking care of themselves. His real estate was apprised at £944, and his personal at £863,5,6. Seth Hamblen was appointed guardian to Mercy and Mary, to each of whom was assigned £182, paid by their brother Elijah, to whom four-fifths of the estate was set off, and to his sister Temperance Otis, one-fifth. The children of Mr. Thomas Hinckley, born in Barnstable, were: 1, Seth, Aug. 17, 1720, died Sept. 20, 1720; 2, Mercy, Feb. 11, 1721; 3, Temperance, Jan. 20, 1725, married John Otis, Esq., Dec. 3, 1741; 4,

Elijah, Dec. 1, 1725 ; 5, Mary, Sept. 30, 1727 ; 6, Isaac, April 18, 1731, died 20th Oct. 1731.

(43.) Ichabod Hinckley, son of Ensign John, born Aug. 28, 1680, married for his first wife 7th Jan. 1702, Mary Goodspeed ; she died Oct. 1, 1719, and he married for his second wife Aug. 3, 1721, Mary Basset, of Sandwich. His children born in Barnstable were : Mary, 27th Nov. 1704, died 2d March, 1718 ; John, 4th Jan. 1710-11, died Feb. following ; Benjamin, 19th June, 1707 ; David, 1st March, 1709 ; John, 7th March, 1712 ; Eben, 7th July, 1714 ; Thankful, 1st Aug. 1716 ; Mary, 26th Sept. 1718 ; Thankful, 2d Dec. 1723 ; and Mercy, 22d Nov. 1726.

(44.) Job Hinckley, son of Ensign John, married 15th Nov. 1711, Sarah Lumbert, and had Hannah, who perhaps married Sept. 11, 1742, Samuel Claghorn, and Huldah who married Nov. 29, 1739, Benjamin Casley, Jr., and had a large family. Of the descendants of Ensign John Hinckley I have little information. Samuel removed to Stonington, Conn. Ichabod and Job remained in Barnstable. Jonathan and Gershom probably removed.

HOWLAND.

Several of the name of Howland come over early. Arthur who settled in Marshfield as early as 1643 ; Henry of Duxbury 1633, John who came in the Mayflower, 1620, and Zoar of Newport 1656, the latter may have been a son of Henry. As carefully prepared genealogies of this family have been published, it will be unnecessary for me to repeat that which is accesible to those who take an interest in the families.

The Barnstable family descends from John Howland who came over as a servant or attendant of Gov. Carver. His name is the thirteenth on the Covenant made at Cape Cod Nov. 11, 1620. Till the recent discovery of Gov. Bradford's history, it was a current tradition that he married Elizabeth daughter of Gov. Carver. He married soon after his arrival Elizabeth daughter of John Tiley, an only child, her parents dying in the first sickness. He was after a representative, and an assistant of the Governor in 1633-4 and 5, and was a prominent man in the colony. He died 23d Feb. 1672-3 aged over 80. Excepting Mr. John Alden, he was the last male survivor of the adult passengers in the Mayflower. In 1679 there were twelve living who came over in that ship. Samuel Fuller of Barnstable one of the twelve died Oct. 31, 1683. In 1690 there were three survivors, Resolved White, Mary Cushman daughter of Isaac Allerton, and John Cook son of Francis. Mrs. Cushman the last survivor of those who came in the first ship, died in 1699, "over 90 years old."

John Howland sen'rs will is dated 29th May, 1672, in which he names his ten children whether in the order of their births, is not known, as no family record has been preserved.

Children of John Howland born in Plymouth.
The order of their births is not certainly known.

2. IV.   John, eldest son, born Feb. 24, 1627.
3. I.   Desire, married Capt. John Gorham 1644, died 13th Oct. 1683.   (See Gorham.)
4. VI.   Jabez, of Duxbury, married Bethia, daughter of Antony Thacher of Yarmouth, was a lieutenant in Philip's war,

afterwards removed to Bristol, where he kept a public
house. He had nine children and has many descendants.
5. VII. Joseph, married 7th Dec. 1664, Elizabeth Southworth.
6. V. Hope, born 1629, married John Chipman. (See Chipman.)
7. II. Elizabeth, married Sept. 13, 1649, Ephraim Hicks, and
10th July, 1651, John Dickenson of Barnstable.
8. III. Lydia, married James Brown of Swansey.
9. VIII. Hannah, married Nathaniel Bosworth.
10. IX. Ruth, married Nov. 1664 Thomas Cushman.
11. X. Isaac, youngest son, Middleboro', married Elizabeth
Vaugham, he was a soldier in Philip's war, kept an inn in
1684, and was often representative to the Colony Court, and
died in 1724.

Lieutenant John Howland, second of the name, was born in
Plymouth Feb. 24, 1626-7, as he informed Chief Justice Sewall
when at Barnstable in 1702. He removed from Plymouth to
Marshfield, and thence to Barnstable about the year 1658. His
farm at West Barnstable contained about 90 acres, and in 1672 he
conveyed by deed the easterly half thereof to his brother-in-law
Elder John Chipman. A portion of his estate is yet owned by his
descendants. He held many town offices and was lieutenant of
the military company. He was admitted a freeman of the colony
in 1658. There is some evidence that in early life he favored the
Quakers. He certainly was opposed to the intolerant party of
which George Barlow of Sandwich was the leading man. His
wife joined the church Nov. 22, 1691. He and two other aged
men, Joseph Lothrop and James Lewis, joined the church on the
18th of June, 1699.

He married 26th Oct. 1651, Mary, daughter of Robert Lee.
He probably had two children born in Marshfield, his other eight
children were born in Barnstable.
12. I. Mary.
13. II. Elizabeth, born 17th May, 1655, married John Bursley
1673.
14. III. Isaac, 25th Nov. 1659. (See below.)
15. IV. Hannah, 15th May, 1661, married Jonathan Crocker
20th May, 1686. She died previous to Feb. 1711.
16. V. Mercy, 21st Jan. 1663.
17. VI. Lydia, 9th Jan. 1665.
18. VII. Experience, 28th July, 1668.
19. VIII. Ann, 9th Sept. 1670, married 18th Sept. 1691,
Joseph Crocker.
20. IX. Shubael, 30th Sept. 1672. (See below.)
21. X. John, 31st Dec. 1674. (See below.)
14. Isaac Howland, son of John, born 25th Nov. 1657,

married Anne Taylor Dec. 27, 1686. He resided at West Barnstable, and had

22. I. Ebenezer, 7th Sept. 1687, married June 26, 1712, Elizabeth Justice? and removed to Sandwich, where he was living in 1730, and is named by Mr. Fessenden as the head of a family.

23. II. Isaac, 3d July, 1689, married May 14, 1719, Elizabeth Jennings of Sandwich. He died 8th Nov. 1751, aged 63. His children born in Barnstable were: 1, Anne, Sept. 4, 1721, married Joseph Lumbert Feb. 6, 1746; 2, Sarah, July 23, 1722, married Edmond Hinckley Dec. 6, 1744; 3, Joseph, May 10, 1726, married Elizabeth Lovell March 1763; 4, Benjamin, 22d Nov. 1729, married Anna Crocker March 15, 1763; 5 and 6, Rachel and a child, twins, Dec. 22, 1734; 7, Lemuel, Jan. 30, 1740-1, removed to Sandwich, married Dec. 11, 1765, Abigail Hamblin, died 1805.

24. III. Mary, Oct. 1691.

25. IV. Ann, Dec. 1694.

26. V. John, Feb. 2, 1696, married Alice Hamblen 1728. He died in 1747 and his widow married May 22, 1648, Samuel Hinckley. Children: 1, Desire, June 15, 1732, married Jonathan Bodfish May 3, 1753, died April, 1813, aged 81. She was the mother of a remarkable family, (see Bodfish); 2, Susannah, Dec. 22, 1734, married Ignatius Smith Nov. 21, 1759; 3, David, Aug. 8, 1737, married Mary Coleman Dec. 15, 1763; 4, Jonathan, twin with David, removed to Sandwich where he died in 1812, aged 75; 5, Deborah, Oct. 25, 1739, married Nov. 1763, Richard Sparrow of Eastham.

27. VI. Joseph, July 1702, married 1st Rachel Crocker, Jan. 18, 1739, who died May 9, 1742, and 2d, Maria Fuller, May 16, 1746, and had 1, Hannah, Aug. 8, 1738, married Christopher Taylor Jan. 15, 1761; 2, Mary, Sept. 9, 1740; 3, Rachel, May 2, 1742, married Nathan Jenkins Dec. 9, 1762; 4, Ann, Sept. 19, 1747.

28. VII. Noah, baptized 16th July, 1699, probably died early and therefore omitted on town record.

20. Shubael Howland, son of John, born 30th Sept. 1672, married Mercy Blossom 13th Dec. 1700. He died in 1737, and in his will names his wife Mercy, who died in 1759, his sons Jabez and Zaccheus, and his daughter Mercy Jenkins.

Children born in Barnstable.

29. I. Jabez, 16th Sept. 1701, married Elizabeth Percival Dec. 22, 1727. He died in 1765. His children were: 1, James, born June 30, 1729, married Rebecca Hall, and had Abigail Dec. 31, 1754; Rebecca, March 26, 1757; Elizabeth, Aug. 11, 1759; Joseph and Jabez, twins, Jan. 29, 1762; Mercy,

Aug 5, 1767; and James, Aug. 7, 1771; 2, Jabez, Jan. 27,
1730-1, killed in the French war; 3, Elizabeth, Oct. 26,
1732, married Francis Wood Dec. 17, 1756; 4, Mercy,
Aug. 15, 1734, a woman of feeble health died unmarried;
5, Nathaniel, Oct. 9, 1736, married Martha Thacher of
Wareham, Dec. 15, 1762, and removed to Lee; 6, Ansel,
Dec. 3, 1738, a firm believer in witchcraft, married Elizabeth Bodfish; and 7, Mary, Jan. 31, 1741, married John
Bursley.

30.   II.   Mercy, 21st May, 1710, married Joseph Jenkins July
15, 1736.

31.   III.   Zaccheus.   No other mention is made of him on the
record.   A man of this name married, had a family, and
died very aged, though intemperate.

21.   John Howland, son of Lieut. John, born Dec. 31, 1674,
resided at West Barnstable.   He died March, 1738, aged 64.   In
his will dated Feb. 8, 1737-8, and proved 29th March, 1738, he
gives to his wife Mary the use and improvement of all his *housing*, lands and meadows, during her widowhood, excepting suit
able house-room and firewood for his two daughters Mary and
Joanna, so long as they remain single, and all his personal estate,
"excepting what I hereafter dispose of."   To his son George five
shillings, he having already had his portion by deed; to his son
John half of the upland and meadow that came by his mother,
and one-half my wearing apparel; to his son Job the other half,
and the remainder of his homestead; and "my will is, if my son
John should fail of being brought up to College, then he shall
come in equal partner with my son Job in my real estate.   To his
daughter Hannah he gave five shillings, and to each of his daughters Mary and Joanna, £30.   His estate was apprised at £1088,8,
corn being then worth 8 shillings a bushel.

He probably married three times.   1st, Mary Lothrop, Sept.
8, 1697, (the record says James, but there being no James Howland I think John was intended.)   2d, Yet Mercy Shove, (tho'
record says Josiah) Nov. 29, 1709; 3d, Mary Crocker, June 18,
1709.

Children born in Barnstable.

32.   I.   George, 30th Dec. 1705, married Abigail Crocker Oct.
28, 1731, and had, 1, Hannah, Aug. 4, 1732, died Sept. 5,
1732; 2, Seth, March 17, 1734-5; 3, John, June 2, 1738;
4, Shove, June 18, 1741; 5, George, April 25, 1743.

33.   II.   Hannah, 2d Feb. 1708, died young.

34.   III.   Mary, 11th Aug. 1711.

35.   IV.   Hannah, 8th Jan. 1715, married John Allen of Hingham Dec. 28, 1752.

36.   V.   John, 13th Feb. 1720-21, Harvard College 1741, ordained at Carver Sept. 24, 1746, (in the church records

called the church in the south part of Plympton) died in
1804, aged 84, married —— Lewis, had four sons and
three daughters who survived him.
37.   VI.   Job, June, 1726, married Hannah Jenkins Dec. 6,
1753, and had, 1, Mary July 21, 1755 ; 2, John, March 31,
1757 ; 3, Shove, Dec. 28, 1759 ; 4, Hannah, May 20, 1762 ;
5, Job, July 24, 1764 ; 6, Joanna, July 28, 1766 ; 7, Benjamin, Aug. 7, 1768, died young ; 8, Benjamin, June 18,
1770 ; 9, Mehitable, June 23, 1773 ; 10, Southworth, March
29, 1775 ; 11, Timothy, Sept. 17, 1777.
38.   VII.   Joanna, married Mr. James Lewis April 12, 1750,
his third wife.

I find others of the name of Howland on the records which I
am unable to arrange, not having a copy of the records of the
Sandwich families. A Joshua Howland of Yarmouth died in
1814, leaving descendants ; but I am unable to state to what family he belonged.

HOWES.

___

Samuel Howes, as he generally wrote his name, or House, as it is generally written on the records, and as his descendants spell their name, probably came over in 1634 with the Rev. John Lothrop. He first settled in Scituate, was a freeman Jan. 1, 1634-5, and was one of the founders of the church there Jan. 8, 1634-5. He built the 12th* house in that town, situate between the houses of Richard Foxwell and Mr. Lothrop. This he afterwards sold to Nicholas Simpkins. He was one of the first settlers in Barnstable, and probably came with his brother-in-law Rev. Mr. Lothrop in 1639. In regard to his residence in Barnstable, I can furnish few facts. He did not remain long, for in 1642 he was a resident in Cambridge. In 1646 he had returned to Scituate, and was that year appointed to gather the excise in that town. In 1652 and 3 he was a grand juryman, and tho' appointed to note the short comings of his neighbors, the following record shows that he, like many others, did not note his own. "1659, June, Samuel House is enjoyned by the Court to take some speedy course with a dogg, that is troublesome and dangerous in biting folks as they go by the highwaies."

In a deed dated at Cambridge, Mass., Nov. 13, 1643, in which he conveys to Joseph Tilden fifty acres of upland and nine acres of marsh land situate near the North River in Scituate, he styles himself a shipcarpenter, and also in another deed to Thomas Rawlins, dated Jan. 22, 1646-7.

The fact that he was a shipcarpenter, accounts for his frequent removals. Neither the records nor tradition furnish any evidence that any vessels were built in Barnstable before 1675. John Davis had a large boat, or small vessel, at the time of the settlement, which was used in the transporting of articles from

___

*In the copy of the church records this name is written Watts House, a mistake in transcribing. Other records show that Samuel House dwelling was No. 12.

Scituate and other places to Barnstable. The "bark Desire," Capt. Samuel Mayo, appears to have been the first vessel of any considerable size that hailed from Barnstable. She is named in 1650. None appear to have been built at that early period, though there was an abundance of material, and many of the first settlers were mechanics.

Samuel House died in Scituate in 1661, leaving four children. Samuel and Elizabeth were appointed Oct. 1, administrators on their father's estate. His estate in Scituate was apprised at £241,14, and in Barnstable, by John Chipman and Tristram Hull at £249,17, a large estate in those times. William Paine, of Boston, a man of great wealth, who died in 1660, bequeathed "to my kinswoman Elizabeth, daughter of Samuel House, £10." She was his grandniece.

Whether or not Samuel was a relative of Thomas, the ancestor of the Howes family of Dennis, I have been unable to ascertain. His name is also sometimes written House. Samuel married Elizabeth, daughter of William Hammond of Watertown. She was born in England in 1619, and was a member of the Watertown church. Mr. Lothrop has the following entry on his records : "Elizabeth Hammon, *my sister*, having a dismission from the church at Watertown was joined April 14, 1636." The meaning of "my sister" in this record is perhaps doubtful, though in a note in the Dimmock article I have not considered it so. She was not then a sister of his church without she had joined in London as early as 1632. She was at the latter date only thirteen, which renders it very doubtful ; and if she had been he would not have called her "*my* sister," but simply "sister." No instance occurs on his records of his applying to the brethren or sisters of his church the word *my*, without a relationship actually existed. William Hammond came from Lavenham, in the County of Suffolk, England, and it is very improbable that his daughter Elizabeth should have joined Mr. Lothrop's church in London. I infer from this that Ann, the second wife of Mr. Lothrop, was Ann Hammond, baptized 14 July, 1616. In no other manner can the known relationship between the parties be explained.

Children of Samuel House born in Scituate.

2. I.   Elizabeth, baptized Oct. 23, 1636.
3. II.   Samuel, there is no record of his birth or baptism.

Born in Barnstable.

4. III. Sarah, baptized Aug. 1, 1641.

Born in Cambridge.

5. IV.   John, born 6th Dec. 1642, baptized in Barnstable May 18, 1645.

All these children it appears by the will of the grandfather Hammond, dated July 1, 1662, one year after the death of Samuel

House, were then living and the widow Elizabeth. According to
the usages in the Old Colony, the widow Elizabeth was entitled to
letters of administration, but for some reason that does not appear, administration was granted to the two elder children, Elizabeth and Samuel. The final settlement I do not find on record.
It seems that some trouble arose ; for Aug. 4, 1663, the Court
summoned John Sutton and Mr. Tilden, to give an account of the
division and disposed of the estate before the next October term
of the Court, if they "doe not end it in the interem," as no record appears, the presumption is, that it was ended "in the interem."

In what part of Barnstable Samuel Howes settled I am unable to fix certainly. Probably at West Barnstable, for reference
is made to meadows owned by him near Scorton Creek. The
lands purchased of Serunk or *Seconke* (Wild Goose) Sachem of
Scorton, which he confirmed to the town of Barnstable by deed
dated Aug. 26, 1644, were at the northwesterly corner of the
town, and probably included Sandy Neck, then considered of little
value. Mr. Freeman is mistaken in calling this the "first purchase." The Indian title to the lands in the northeasterly part of
the town, (excepting the reservation at the corner) was the first
purchase.

In the deed of Seconke he bounds the lands conveyed, easterly by the lands of "Pexit another Indian." These lands were at
West Barnstable, and do not appear to have been an extensive
tract. To whom Pexit sold, I do not find stated on record. This
is of little importance ; yet it would be satisfactory to show, that
every acre of land in Barnstable was obtained by fair purchase of
the aboriginies. In early times a considerable tract northwesterly
from Dea. William Crocker's farm was called the "Gov.'s" land
and meadows, probably Gov. Bradford, for Hinckley was not then
entitled to that honor. Samuel House's meadows were in the
same vicinity, and probably his lands.

If House's lands were in any other portion of the town, there
are records by which the precise location could be fixed. Barnstable, at the time of House's settlement, was almost an unbroken
wilderness. A few English had settled in the vicinity of Goodspeed's Hill and Coggin's pond. The Indian population was
numerous. They had villages and cleared lands. They however
frequently removed from place to place. Tradition says that they
usually fixed their residences on the north shore in the summer and on the south in the winter, and there are records which
partially confirm the tradition. House had been accustomed to
an active life, in the busy marts of trade of his native land ; his
wife was the daughter of a man of considerable wealth, and in
early life had been accustomed to enjoy all the conveniences, and
many of the luxuries of civilized life. He built himself a shanty

in the forest, probably more than a mile from an English neighbor. Week after week he did not see a white man, and the Indians in his vicinity were his constant and almost only visitors. Under such circumstances it is not surprising that he desired to change his residence. He was of Cambridge in 1642, having probably removed from Barnstable in 1641.

His lands and meadows were unsaleable and he let them remain. At the time of his death in 1661, many families had then removed to West Barnstable and lands had appreciated in value, and for that which he considered almost worthless, his heirs obtained as already stated a handsome sum. Speculating in wild lands was a mania that in early times prevailed to a very considerable extent; but it may be doubted whether many succeeded better than House.

3.   Samuel House, the second of the name, was also a ship carpenter. His ship yard, probably his father's, was near Hobart's Landing in Scituate. He married in 1664 Rebecca Nichols, daughter of Thomas of Scituate. His children were :

6.   I.   Samuel, 1665, married Sarah Pincin.
7.   II.   Joseph, 1667.
8.   III. Rebecca, 1670.
9.   IV.   John, 1672.
10. V.   Sarah, 1678, married in 1710 James Cushing.

Samuel, 3d, died in 1718 and left sons Joseph, David, James, Samuel and John. As this is not a Barnstable family, I shall not pursue the inquiry.

HUCKINS.

Mr. Thomas Huckins, the ancestor of this family, was born in the year 1617. Of his early history little is known. He came over before he was twenty-one years of age, and was a resident of Boston, or its vicinity,* for he was one of the twenty-three original members of the Ancient and Honorable Artillery Company chartered in 1638, and in 1639 bore its standard. To be the ensign of that company, was a mark of honor. At that time aristocratic notions had far more influence than at the present time, and it was very rare indeed that a young man in the twenty-second year of his age was elected to an office of honor or profit, without he belonged to an influential family in the mother country.

His name is written Hutchins, Huckins, Huchens, and Huggins, the latter being the manner in which it was pronounced in early times. A Robert settled in Dover in 1640, who had a son James; George in Cambridge, freeman 1638; John at Newbury, 1640, or earlier; and Joseph of Boston, married 1657. There was also a Richard Hutchins who requested to be admitted a freeman 19th Oct. 1630, and who probably came over in the fleet with Gov. Winthrop. There is no record that he took the oath, and Mr. Savage infers that he died that year or returned home. The names in these early families indicate that they were relatives.

Among the wealthy and influential promoters in England, of the settlement of Massachusetts, was a Mr. Thomas Hutchins.— He was an assistant of the Governor, while the administration of the affairs of the company were conducted in England. His name

---

*There is some evidence that he was of Dorchester. In 1638 there was a stream on the boundaries between that town and Dedham, called "Huggins Creek." This was the manner in which the name was pronounced in early times, and often written. The name of that creek proves that a man of the same name resided in its vicinity, for all the names of creeks and places not having well known Indian or legal names are thus derived. Mr. Richard Collicut, also a charter member of the Artillery Company, to whom the lands in Barnstable were first granted, was a Dorchester man, and his associates were principally from that town. Thomas Huckins' lot was one of those laid under the authority of Mr. Collicut, bore one of the earliest dates of grants, Sept. 14, 1640. This combination of circumstances may have been accidental, but in the absence of better evidence, I think that it may be safely inferred that Thomas Huckins was one of the associates of Mr. Richard Collicut, and one of the earliest settlers in Barnstable.

appears in all the records prior to 1630; but after the removal it ceases to appear. He did not come over; but having a pecuniary interest in the success of the settlement, it is probable that those of the name who did come belonged to, or were connected with his family. The fact that our Thomas Huckins, when a young man, and before he had become in any manner distinguished, should have been elected ensign of the Artillery Company, seems to prove that he was connected with influential families. To be able to trace our ancestry to the renowned in the father land, adds nothing to our own merit. When they left their native shores they began as pilgrims in a foreign land, and resolved to be the architects of their own fortunes in life. No patent of nobility granted to an ancestor, can confer so much honor on a man as to be able to trace his descent from a member of Mr. Robinson or Mr. Lothrop's church. These were honest men, the other may have been a Sir John Fallstaff or a Lord Jeffries, distinguished only for their crimes and debaucheries.

Mr. Thomas Huckins was an exemplary member of Mr. Lothrop's church. The criminal calendar records only one charge affecting his moral character. He is charged with having abused a poor servant. No details are given, and no opinion can be formed of the heniousness of the offence. The Colony Court considered itself the guardian of the poor boys sent over as apprentices, and always lent a willing ear to their complaints. There appears not to have been much foundation, for Mr. Huckins was only required to pay the expenses, as he was obliged to do as the boy's master; no fine nor punishment being imposed on him, and we may therefore safely infer that the offence was not grievous. As a business man he perhaps had no superior in the colony, certainly not in the town. His neighbor, Nicholas Davis, the quaker, did more business but was not so careful or successful a man. Mr. Huckins had a landing place or wharf near his house, where he discharged and received freights. He was one of the "farmers" or partners that hired the Cape Cod fisheries.

In 1670 considerable quantities of tar were manufactured in the colony, and he was appointed one of the purchasers, and instructed to pay eight shillings for small barrels and twelve shillings for large.

Oct. 4, 1675, he was appointed Commissary General of the Colony, and had the sole management in procuring supplies, and forwarding them to the soldiers engaged in the Indian war.* The arduous duties of this office he performed ably, and to the entire satisfaction of the court.

---

*His friend and associate, Mr. Collicut, held the same office by appointment of the Mass. Colony during the Pequat war, and in my notice of that gentleman I have stated that the business connected with that office prevented him from settling in Barnstable as he had intended.

Mr. Huckins held numerous town and colonial offices, and was a man in whom the people placed the utmost confidence for his integrity and ability. He was propounded as one of the freeman of the Colony in 1646, but it does not appear to have taken the oath till 1652. He was constable of Barnstable in 1646, and several years afterwards; he was one of the board of Selectmen in 1668, '70, '71, '72, '74, '75, '77, and '78; deputy to the colony court in 1669, '70, '71, '72, '74, '75, '77 and '78. June 5, 1671, he was elected a member of the council of war for the colony, and in 1676 of the town council. In 1669, 1670 and 1672, he was a member of the committee to audit the colony accounts, and in 1677 on a committee to adjust the claims against the colony for expenses incurred during the Indian war. Beside these offices his name appears as surveyor of highways, as a member of the grand and petit juries, and in 1670 and 1671 he and Mr. Thomas Hinckley were appointed by the court "to look after the minister's rate," which at that time was not so readily paid as in earlier times.

In addition to his other duties, March 1, 1652-3, he was licensed "to sell wines and strong waters until the next June Court." June 1, 1663, he was approved by the court, and "his former liberty renewed to keep an ordinary at Barnstable." From this it appears that he had formerly been licensed to keep a public house, probably the liberty which had been granted to him in 1653 had been continued to that time. He was several years a receiver of the excise imposed on the importation of wines and liquors and on powder and shot. The return for 1663 presents some noteworthy items. It appears that he was captain of the packet that year, and that he brought into the town for himself 35 gallons of wine and 9 of brandy; for Joseph Lothrop 10 gallons of rum; for Nicholas Davis and his man, 4 gallons, and one case of liquors, and 50 pounds of shot; for Trustrum Hall 100 gallons, and six cases of liquors, and one barrel of powder, and 200 pounds of shot; and for Mr. Thomas Clark (of Harwich) 20 gallons of rum. Calling the case three gallons, 179 would be the amount used in Barnstable in 1663, or about three gallons for every adult white male. The Indians however probably drank the largest proportion of the liquors, for the English then used malt liquors as* their common beverage. The same year about the same quantity

*The quantity of malt liquor used in early times was large. It was a substitute at meals for tea and coffee. There were certainly three if not four malt houses, within the present limits of the East Parish. Gov. Hinckley had one that stood in the little yard enclosed by stone wall opposite the house of Mr. Jabez Nye; the Lewis' had one that stood where Edward Phinney afterwards built his house, near the residence of Mrs. F. W. Crocker, and Mr. Samuel Sturgis had one that stood to the eastward of the house of Mr. Wm. W. Sturgis. In addition the Crockers I believe had one that stood near the bounds of the two parishes. They were not used exclusively for the manufacture of malt, they were used as smoke houses for curing fish and meats in the Indian mode. The natives had smoke houses and the places when put up were hence called agamam, also shawme, shawmet, sqam, &c., meaning a place where fish are cured by smoking.

of liquors were brought into the town of Yarmouth.   The other towns do not appear to have made returns.

The enumeration of the important offices which he held proves that he was not only a business man, but a good business man, and a man in whom his townsmen placed implicit confidence as a man of integrity and ability.   Our annals furnish the names of few men who, taken in all the relations of life, show a finer record than Thomas Huckins.   The history of the formation of the Artillery Company shows that he was a man of liberal views, and an opponent of the bigotry and narrow sectarianism which ruled in Massachusetts at that time.   The original members of that company, with few exceptions, were the friends of Wheelwright, consequently were looked upon with suspicion by the government, and it is said that if they had not chosen for their captain Robert Reayne, a man presumed to hold different views, the charter of the company could not have been obtained.   After the death of Mr. Lothrop the Barnstable church ceased to act in harmony. Mr. Huckins adhered to the party that invited Mr. William Sergeant to become its pastor.   This faction belonged to the political party that in 1656 had become dominant in the Colony, and had adopted the narrow sectarian policy that had always ruled in Massachusetts.

That Mr. Huckins adopted the intolerant policy of the party to which he belonged does not appear.   Though constable in 1657, he lived on friendly terms with his neighbor Nicholas Davis, and as the notorious Barlow of Sandwich was employed to search the house of Davis, it may be inferred that Huckins declined to act officially in the case.   In 1662 Mr. Huckins cordially united with the other faction of the church in the settlement of Mr. Walley, a man of peace and an able advocate of the tolerant principles of the Rev. Mr. Lothrop.

Mr. Huckins owned a large real estate.   He did not have the grant of his houselot recorded until Feb. 3, 1661, and then the record was made to correspond with the facts as they then existed. "Six acres of upland granted (as appears per order of town bearing date ye 14th 7 mo. 1640) to his houselot butting on a little creek that comes out of ye great creek by Rendevous Creek and runs up into ye woods,"(thus far seems to be quoted from the old grant) which is now bounded north by Goodman Blush, southerly by Goodman Cob, and easterly partly by Goodman Blush and partly by Goodman Cob.   As the roads were then only rights of way through gates or bars, they are not mentioned.   This land is now owned by Elijah Lewis, 2d, Loring and Nathan Crocker. It was originally bounded on the north by the lot of Dolar Davis. The "little creek" was afterwards called Huckins Creek.   From the earliest to the present time there has been a wharf and landing place near its northern terminus, where it joins the "Great Creek." Nicholas Davis, son of Dolar, appears to have been the earliest who transacted a mercantile business in that vicinity. His wharf or landing place was on the Great or Mill Creek. The name of Huckins' wharf has changed as often as its owners have changed. In modern the Lewis' had a shipyard thereon, and the upper part of the "little creek" where salt water flows has recently been known as shipyard creek. The salt meadows terminated at the south-west corner of Huckins' lot, and from that point the record informs that little creek "runs up into the woods." At the head of the meadows the "little creek" made a sharp turn to the eastward, crossing the present wharf road on the south of Elijah Lewis, 2d's, house and was the outlet of the surplus water of the low lands as far east as the Agricultural Hall. Then this tract was covered either by ponds, swamps or a dense growth of maple, hornbeam, &c., and was of no value for agricultural purposes. Much of it was not included in the adjoining allotments, and remained some time as common lands. At some former time the low lands on this tract were covered by cedar trees of immense size. In some violent commotion these gigantic trees were all prostrated, and remaining for centuries covered with water, peat accumulated over them and a growth of maple, hornbeam, &c., succeeded. When Mr. Huckins settled there, a stream of fresh water run all the year on the south of his house, through a morass impassable by teams. In this isolated spot he kept an ordinary, as taverns were then called, for the accommodation of travellers. It is however to be presumed that the lovers of "strongwaters" knew the paths that lead to his house.

In addition to his houselot he owned nine acres of land in the old common-field, two in the new, adjoining Mattakeese pond; 3-4 of an acre of land by the "horse prison," (near where the dwelling-house of the late Mr. Edward Gorham stood,) 11 acres of meadow at Sandy Neck, and two acres of marsh, more or less, lying by his house, bounded westerly by the creek, easterly by ye upland, northerly to ye creek. These two acres included all the meadows on the west of his, and the Davis or Blush lots to the creeks, consequently he owned the ancient wharf or landing-place, and hence the creek and wharf were called by his name.

He also owned, in partnership with Nathaniel Bacon and John Phinney, ninety-six acres of upland and fresh meadows situate on the east and south of the Bursley farm at West Barnstable. He also bought the farm of Isaac Robinson, when the latter removed to Falmouth.

Mr. Thomas Huckins married for his first wife, in 1642, Mary, daughter of Isaac Wells of Barnstable. She was buried 28th July, 1648. By her he had three daughters, two of whom died

in infancy. He married for his second wife 3d Nov. 1648, the
widow Rose Hyllier of Yarmouth. He was cast away in his vessel in a gale Nov. 9, 1679, and he and his son Joseph perished.—
He was in the 62d year of his age, and his son 24. The widow
Rose Huckins died in the year 1687, aged about 71 years.
I do not find a settlement of his estate on the Probate Records.
His daughter Mary married Dec. 6, 1666, Samuel Storrs, resided
on the Dexter farm at Scorton Hill. She died 24th Sept. 1683,
leaving seven children. The family afterwards removed to Windham, Conn. John resided in Barnstable. He was constable in
1672. He married Aug. 10, 1670, Hope, daughter of Elder John
Chipman. He died Nov. 10, 1678, in the 29th year of his age,
leaving four daughters. His widow married March 1, 1682-3,
Jonathan Cobb, and removed to Middleboro. Hannah married
Feb. 24, 1673-4, James Gorham and had a large family. She
died 13th Feb. 1727-8, aged 74. (See Gorham, 5 IV.)

Thomas Huckins, the second of the name, was a carpenter.
He resided on the Robinson farm in Barnstable, owned a large
real estate, and was a man of good character and influence. By
an entry on the town records June 1, 1688, it appears that he
bought the lands of the Rev. Mr. Thomas Walley. He also owned
the Great Neck at Cooper's Pond, on the west of Joseph Bearse's
land, on which he built a house. This tract is yet owned by his
descendants. He married May 1, 1680, Hannah, daughter of
Elder John Chipman. She died Nov. 4, 1696, aged 37. For his
second wife he married Aug. 17, 1698, Sarah, widow of Samuel
Hinckley. His estate was settled Dec. 11, 1714, and he probably
died that year. His son Thomas administered. To John, the
eldest son, was set off "all the homestead, both upland and
meadow, together with the dwelling house, barn and housing,* and
orchard thereon," (only excepting so much meadow reserved out
of the same as will yield hay enough to winter fifteen head of neat
cattle yearly,) woodland and other property. To Thomas and
Samuel, the other two then surviving sons, was set off the Neck
Farm, with "the dwelling-house, barn and other out housing thereon standing," together with the meadow reserved out of John's
portion, woodland and other property. John being the eldest son,
according to the law at that time, was entitled to a double portion,
consequently had one-half of the estate after the widow's dower
was set off, and the portions of the two surviving daughters, Hope
and Hannah, paid.

His real estate was apprised at £1,085,12. Personal, including carpenter's tools, £66,05.

Joseph, the oldest son of the second Thomas, married 18th

*"Housing." This word is here used as meaning other buildings beside a dwelling-
house. The word seems to have been used in the same sense as the word "out-house" is
now used.

Sept. 1702, Sarah Lothrop. He died in 1705, leaving no issue. His widow administered and one third of his estate was set off to her, and the remainder divided to his brothers and sisters. The widow married John Trap 14th Oct. 1708.

James Huckins, another son of the second Thomas, died unmarried about the time of the death of his father. His brother John was appointed administrator on his estate July 17, 1714. His estate was settled, and the property divided 26th Sept. 1716, to the same persons and in the same proportions as the father's estate was.

Samuel Huckins, son of Thomas, died unmarried in 1718. His will is dated 22d Aug. 1718, and was proved on the 20th Oct. following. He gave to his brother Thomas all his land at the Neck, where he then lived, and all his meadow lying north of his brother John's estate. He names "his mother's dower" which it appears he owned. He gave legacies to his sisters Hannah Huckins, and to the widow Hope Hamblin.

After the decease of Samuel the old Huckins estate was owned by the brothers John and Thomas. I do not find that John ever married, or if he did that he had issue. I have not carefully examined into the matter ; but as his estate was afterwards owned by the descendants of his brother Thomas, I infer that he died childless.

Thomas, the third of the name, had a large family, most of whom lived in celibacy. James, the eighth child, born April 11, 1730, died June 25, 1818, aged 88. From him I believe all of the name now living descend. Capt. James Huckins, of Boston, is his grandson.

Thomas, 3d, married Rachell (Snow?) He owned the large Huckins estate and was a wealthy farmer. His wife died March 22, 1765, aged 70. He died March 3, 1774, aged 86.

Genealogy of the Huckins family :

1. Thomas Huckins married 1st Mary Wells, 1642, who was buried 28th of July, 1648 ; 2d, the widow Rose Hyllier, of Yarmouth, Nov. 3, 1648, who died in 1687, aged about 71 years. (By her first husband, Hugh Hyllier, she had Deborah 30th Oct. 1643, and Samuel 30th July, 1646.) "Mr. Thomas Huckins was cast away ye 9 November, 1679, and died in the 62d year of his age. His son Joseph lost with him at the same time, aged 24 years, 1679."—[Barnstable town records.

Children born in Barnstable.

2. I.   Lydia, 4th July, 1644, buried 28th July, 1644.
3. II.   Mary, 29th March, 1646. (See Stores.)
4. III.   Elizabeth, 27th Feb. 1647-8, buried 8th Dec. 1648.
5. IV.   John, 2d Aug.1649.
6. V.   Thomas, 25th April, 1651. ᴸᵈ
7. VI.   Hannah, 14th Oct. 1653. (See Gorham.)

8. VII.   Joseph, 21st Feb. 1655, drowned Nov. 9, 1679.
5. John Huckins married 10th Aug. 1670, Hope, daughter of Elder John Chipman. "John Huckins died ye 10 Nov. 1678, in ye 29th year of his age." (Barnstable town records.) His widow married March 1, 1682-3, Jonathan Cobb, and removed to Middleboro.'

Children born in Barnstable.

8. I.   Elizabeth, 1st Oct. 1671, married 4th June, 1695, Dea. John Lewis, died July 12, 1741, aged 70.
10. II.   Mary, 3d April, 1673, married 1690 Nathan Bassett of Sandwich.
11. III.   Experience, 4th June, 1675, married Thomas Lewis, son of George, 28th Sept. 1699.
12. IV.   Hope, 10th May, 1677, married Thomas Nelson. She died Dec. 7, 1782, at Middleboro', aged *one hundred and five years, six months and twenty days*, the longest liver of any of English descent born in Barnstable.
6. Thomas Huckins married for his first wife Hannah, daughter of Elder John Chipman, May 1, 1680. She died Nov. 4, 1696, aged 37; and for his second wife married Aug. 17, 1698, Sarah, widow of Samuel Hinckley. Her maiden name was Pope. He died in 1714, widow Sarah surviving.

Children born in Barnstable.

13. I.   Hannah, 6th April 1681, died 29th Oct. 1698.
14. II.   Joseph, 6th Oct. 1782. (See notice above.)
15. III.   Mary, 13th June, 1684, married Samuel Bacon 30th March, 1704, and died before 1708.
16. IV.   John, 1st May, 1686. (See notice above.)
17. V.   Thomas, 15th Jan. 1687-8. (See below.)
18. VI.   Hope, 21st Sept. 1689, married James Hamblen.
19. VII.   James, 20th Aug. 1691, died 1714, unmarried.
20. VIII.   Samuel, 19th Aug. 1693, died 1718, unmarried.
21. IX.   Jabez, 20th July, 1698, baptized Jan. 31, 1697-8. He died June 1699.
22. X.   Hannah, 22d Aug. 1699, baptized Aug. 27, 1689. She is mentioned in the settlement of her father's and brother's estate.
17. Thomas Huckins, 3d, seems to have been the only one of his father's family who perpetuated the family name. He owned the whole of the ancient Huckins estate, excepting the land on the wharf lane and in the common fields. He married in 1717 Rachell ———, who died March 22, 1765, aged 80. He died March 3, 1774, aged 86.

Children born in Barnstable.

23.   I.   Samuel, Sept. 29, 1718.
24.   II.   Thomas, Nov. 29, 1719.
25.   III.   John, May 12, 1721.
26.   IV.   Jabez, ⎫
27.   V.   Snow, ⎬ March 12, 1722-3.
28.   VI.   Joseph, June 24, 1726.
29.   VII.   A son, Feb. 7, 1727-8, died same day.
30.   VIII.   James, April 11, 1730, died June 25, 1818.
31.   IX.   Elizabeth, July 9, 1732.

James was the only one of this family that married.   He was the father of the late Capt. Samuel Huckins, the father of Joseph and James, the latter yet living.   The family has nearly run out. Celibacy has prevailed more in this family than any other, in Barnstable.

HAMMOND.

This is not a Barnstable name, it rather belongs to Yarmouth; but on account of its connection with the whale fishery, and for some other reason, it is introduced. The name has more *aliases* than any other. It is written Hammond, Hamon, Hamilton and Hambleton.

Benjamin Hammond was able to bear arms in Yarmouth in 1643. Mr. Farmer says he was a son of William of Watertown. Mr. Savage adopts his opinion, and Dr. Bond places the name of Benjamin among the children of William, but says he could not have been his youngest son, as stated by Farmer. William Hammond does not name him in his will. From this, and in the absence of other evidence, it may be inferred that he was not a son of William.

He came from London in the year 1634, probably in the Griffin, which arrived in Boston Sept. 18. Mr. Franklin B. Dexter, of New Haven, who takes an interest in the genealogy of this family, says that it is probable that his mother and sister came over with him in the same ship. Elizabeth Hammond, wife of William, came over in the Francis from Ipswich in 1634, bringing with her three children, Elizabeth aged 15, Sarah 10, and John 7.

Prior to 1643 there is little that is reliable respecting Benjamin Hammond. In that year he was a resident of Yarmouth, and constable in 1652. In 1655 he appears to have been a householder in Yarmouth. In 1669 he was a grand juror, and in 1672 served on an inquest at Plymouth. In 1673 he owned lands and resided in Sandwich, where he had probably resided the preceding ten years. In 1684 he removed to Rochester, and there died April 27, 1703, very aged.

It is reported that he married in 1650 Mary, daughter of Mr. John Vincent of Sandwich. This date is uncertain, for there was a Mary Hammon in Yarmouth in 1648. As there was only one family in town, I thence infer that she was the wife of Benjamin. I am indebted to Mr. Franklin B. Dexter for the following list of his children, probably not arranged in the order of their births: 1, Samuel, who married Mary Hathaway of Dartmouth, and died in 1728; 2, John, born Nov. 22, 1663, died April 19, 1749, aged 85, and his wife Mary (Arnold) died Aug. 3, 1756, aged 84; 3, Nathan, who married a Dexter; 4, Benjamin. He had also three daughters, two died young, and one named Rose Nov. 22, 1676, very aged.

This list of his children is imperfect. The William named in the following extract from the Boston Journal, was perhaps his oldest son:

"It may be interesting to our New Bedford and Nantucket friends to learn, as we do from an ancient chronicle before us, that the first person who killed a whale upon this coast, was named William Hamilton. He was born in Scotland, and in early life settled on Cape Cod, (place not stated) whence he removed to Rhode Island, he being persecuted for killing the whale by the inhabitants of the Cape, as one who dealt with evil spirits. Mr. Hamilton died in Connecticut in 1746, at the advanced age of 103 years. His children died at the following ages: Joseph, 86; David, 79; Benjamin, upwards of 90; Eliza, 93; Thankful, 102; Mary, 52."

HILLIARD.

TIMOTHY HILLIARD.

Timothy Hilliard was one of nature's noblemen—an honest man a scholar—a christian gentleman. He was born in Kensington, N. H., in 1746; graduated at Harvard College 1764; appointed chaplain of Castle William 1768, and the same year was elected a tutor of Cambridge College.* He was a member of the second church at Reading "1771, April 10. This day the Rev. Mr. Timothy Hilliard was ordained the pastor of this church, having been unanimously chosen to that office by the church and congregation.†" (Barnstable church records.) He was dismissed, at his own request, April 30, 1783, and on the 27th of Oct. following he was installed at Cambridge as colleague of Dr. Appleton. He died May 9, 1790, aged 43. Of his ancestry I know nothing.

He was married by the Rev. Simeon Howard in Boston, Nov. 7, 1771, to Mary Foster. His children born in Barnstable were:
Mary, baptized Oct. 16, 1772.
Joseph,   "   June 26, 1774.
Timothy,   "   July 21, 1776.
William,   "   July 12, 1778.
Charles,   "   Feb. 10, 1780.

Mr. Hilliard was pastor of the Barnstable church during one of the trying periods in our history. Violent political differences divided the members of the church, and for a long time many refused to unite with their brethren in its ordinances. Mr. Hilliard, though a very decided man in his opinions, by his discretion and

---

*The letter of Mr. Hilliard accepting the unanimous invitation of the East Church and Congregationalist Society to become its pastor, is on record. It is one of the best specimens of such letters that I have seen. It is too long to copy.

†I copy this entry as he wrote it in the records. Mr. Mellen, his successor, used nearly the same words in recording his own ordination. Afterwards Mr. Mellen erases "Rev. Mr." and interlines "Mr." This little matter, this straw, indicates the difference in the character of the two men. Mr. H. was very careful to give to every man the title which belonged to him by the usuages of sciety, and he claimed the same for himself. Mr. Mellen was a very modest man, and avoided all appearances or ostentation. Mr. H. kept a horse and rode. Mr. M. always went on foot, often to visit a sick parishioner five miles distant.

good management succeeded in reconciling the opposing factions. He held that when a man joined a church he retained all his civil rights, that a member was not subject to discipline on account of his political opinions, only for breach of covenant or immoral acts.

No pastor of the Barnstable church was ever more beloved and respected by his people than Mr. Hilliard. I have heard those who differed with him in politics speak as kindly of him as those with whom he agreed. No man was better qualified to perform the duties which Divine providence had allotted to him. He was discreet, courteous, affable in his manners, and candid in all his statements, never uttering a word to which the most censorious could object. His neighbor, the Hon. Edward Bacon, one of the deacons of his church, for a long time refused to attend church meetings on account of the violent political hostility of some of the brethren. Mr. Hilliard, by his prudent management, reconciled the contending factions, and restored harmony and good feeling.

Those who knew him will say, "he possessed an easy pleasant elocution and a devotional manner, and his discourses were plain in language, and replete with judicious sentiments, well arranged, instructive, and truly evangelical. While he was respected for his talents and acquisitions and made himself pleasing in social intercourse, he also possessed an amiable temper, kind and sympathetic feelings, and the genuine benevolence of the gospel." (Allen.)

While at Barnstable he published two fast day sermons in 1774, and after his removal to Cambridge, in 1785, a sermon at the execution of three persons; in 1788 a sermon delivered at the ordination of Rev. Henry Ware; in 1789, two, one at the ordination of Rev. B. Howard, and the other at that of Rev. John Andrews. In 1788 he published a Dudlean Lecture.

He left Barnstable on account of his health. The salt air he thought had impaired his usefulness, and that it would be imprudent for him to remain. At a parish meeting held April 30, 1783, a committee was chosen to confer with Mr. Hilliard, and endeavor to induce him to withdraw his request for a dismission. They were authorized to grant him leave to be absent for six or twelve months, to pay his expenses while absent, and that meantime his salary should continue and, if at the expiration of that time, he had not recovered his health, they would then grant his dismission if he so requested.

To this request Mr. Hilliard made a verbal reply through the committee that waited on him. He said he had several times travelled for his health, but on his return to Barnstable he soon found that the climate was hurtful to him. His physician had advised his removal, that the air of the Cape was hurtful to him, and that if he continued he could not be useful, and therefore he had decided that it was best for him to leave. He desired to thank the parish for its kind offers, but under the circumstances he could not accept them.

After the report of the committee was made, the parish voted to accept the request of Mr. Hilliard to be dismissed from his pastoral relation with the East Church and congregation in Barnstable.

At his ordination a settlement of £200 was granted to him in addition to his stated annual salary. After the vote had passed, granting his dismission, Mr. Hilliard proposed to give up one quarter of his settlement, £50, but the parish declined to receive it.*

These proceedings are alike honorable to Mr. Hilliard and to the Parish. At no time since the settlement of the town were the people poorer than in the spring of 1788. There was very little money in circulation, and to raise £100 lawful money at that time, was a more onerous tax for the Parish than $10,000 would be now. The love of the people for their pastor was greater than their love of money. To part with him was like parting with what they held as most dear on earth.

---

*Dea. Nathaniel Lewis, a man whom I well remember, was at that time clerk of the Parish. He was a shrewd business man, and at a public meeting there were few who could get the better of him in an argument. He was not a good clerk. I have not copied his entries verbatim, only the substance. The meaning and intention of the votes passed I have given.

HICKS.

Samuel Hicks was some time an inhabitant of Barnstable. He was admitted an inhabitant 3d Oct. 1662, but had then resided in the town several years. In 1670 he had removed to Yarmouth. He was the son of Robert of Plymouth, who came in the Fortune in 1621. His mother Margaret came in the Ann in 1623, bringing with her four children, Ephraim and Samuel, and Lydia, who married Edward Bangs, and Phebe, who was probably afterwards the wife of George Watson.

Samuel was able to bear arms in Plymouth in 1643, removed to Eastham, and in 1645 married Lydia, daughter of John Doane, had Dorcas 14th Feb. 1652, Margaret, 9th March, 1654, and probably others. In 1649 he was representative from Eastham; and not long after removed to Barnstable. His name appears in connection with some difficulties in the church after the death of Mr. Lothrop. He was engaged in promoting the settlement of Dartmouth, and removed to that town.

ISUM.

This name is uniformly pronounced I-sum, and in a receipt signed by him on the town records it is so written. The following anecdote is related of him. On a list of witnesses his name was written Isham. The judge noticed the odd name, and supposing it to belong to an Indian, said to the sheriff in a gruff tone, "bring that old Indian I-sham into court." Isum stepped upon the witness stand, and the judge to his surprise saw a well dressed, genteel man appear instead of the old dirty and ragged Indian that he expected. So great was the contrast that he apologized to Isum for his rudeness. The earliest notice of him that I find is in 1677, but he had been of Barnstable for some years previous. Dea. William Crocker gave him one right in the meadows, which indicates that Isum had lived with him when a boy, or perhaps it was in consequence of his marrying a daughter of his second wife.

John Isum was admitted a townsman March 4, 1692. He was entitled to a share in all the divisions of the common lands, and in the last he had 20 3-4 rights. He resided at Osterville. He married Jane, daughter of Robert Parker, 16th Dec. 1677. She was born March 31, 1664, consequently was not fourteen at the time of her marriage. The record of his death, Sept. 3, 1717, is erroneous, for his will is dated June 1, 1713, and was proved on the 10th of Oct. following. The will of the widow Jane Isum is dated April 13, 1715, proved 24th February, 1719-20. In his will he names his three sons and six daughters, showing that they were all living in 1713. He appoints his wife Jane and his son John executors.

Children born in Barnstable.

2. I. Jane, 7th Oct. 1679, married Michael Wilson 16th April, 1718.
3. II. John, 25th Aug. 1681.
4. III. Isaac, Feb. 1682-3. (See below.)

5. IV.   Sarah, Dec. 1684, married Joshua Lovell 9th May, 1717.
6. V.   Mary, June, 1687, married Abel Crocker 16th April, 1718.
7. VI.   Hannah, married Peter Blossom June 9, 1720.
8. VII.   Patience.
9. VIII.   Joseph.
10. IX.   Thankful, married Jos. Butler of Martha's Vineyard 1725.

Isaac Isum, son of John, married 3d May, 1716, Thankful Lumbert.

Children born in Barnstable.

11. I.   Isaac, March 21, 1718.
12. II.   Samuel, Oct. 26, 1716.
13. III.   John, Aug. 6, 1721.
14. IV.   Ebenezer, Aug. 25, 1723.
15. V.   Timothy, May 30, 1725.
16. VI.   Joshua, April 14, 1727.
17. VII.   Daniel, April 13, 1729.
18. VIII.   Abigail, Feb. 17, 1731.

This family has nearly run out in Barnstable, and whether there are any descendants in other towns I am unable to say. Mr. Savage thinks the name has been changed to Ishum. I notice that Isum's is so spelled in the records of marriages.

THE INDIANS.

2. Paup-mun-muke, Sachem of Massapee.
3. Sea-qu-uncks, Sachem of Scorton.
1. Iyannough, Sachem of Mattakeeset.

The Indians of Cape Cod seem to have been of a different race from those that inhabited the other parts of New England. They were peaceable, never engaged in any wars against the English, desired to have schools established, to be instructed in the doctrines of the christian religion, and in the arts of civilized life. Soon after the settlement a large proportion of their number could read, and many could write. They had religious teachers and magistrates, who held courts for the trial of small offences; but in the more important cases were assisted by Gov. Hinckley and others.

Notwithstanding this apparent prosperity, the attempt to civilize and christianize the Indians of Cape Cod was an utter failure. As long as they had such zealous men as Bourne, Cotton, Tupper, Treat and Hinckley, to advise them, to instruct them, to watch and guard all their interests, and to protect them against the cupidity of the whites, and that greater enemy of their race, the seller of strong waters, they prospered; but when those men were dead they relapsed into their savage customs and associated with the vilest among the whites and negroes whose vicious habits they adopted. They soon vanished away, and gave place to a more civilized, and a more enlighted race. To protect the South Sea Indians, as they were called, of whom Popmunnuck was the Sachem, Richard Bourne and other friends of the race, had the plantation of Massapee, a small portion of their territory, set off to them, which was to be an inheritance to them and their posterity. The Indian could not sell, and the white man was forbidden to purchase. Guardians were appointed to watch over and protect them; benevolent and charitable men provided funds for the support of ministers of the gospel and teachers of the young, and the poor had provision made for them. Notwithstanding all the labors of the benevolent, the care and expense that has been bestowed to preserve, civilize and christianize the race, they have perished ; for many years there has not been a pure blooded Indian in the County—all have vanished—the last of the Massapees is dead. Their plantation and their lands remain, claimed by a mingled race of negroes, Hessians and degraded English, in whose veins course a few drops of Indian blood, by virtue whereof, they claim the inheritance of the red men. All are not degraded. There are a few who are honest, industrious, temperate, but they are the exceptions.* A little time since the Selectmen of Massapee were in court. They managed their business carefully and well, were courteous and gentlemanly in their bearing, but the most casual observer would notice that the blood of the negro preponderated. Everywhere the black race adopts the habits and customs of civilization, more readily than the red. The Indian in his native wilds is tall, erect, of fine proportions and manly in his bearing, but when in proximity with the whites he seems, by a fatal necessity, doomed to fall, to become degraded and an outcast.

Hubbard, in the first edition of his history, made the remark, that the Indian must be civilized before successful attempts could be made to christianize him. All subsequent experience verifies the truth of that remark, yet the over-much zealous missionaries of that time caused the passage to be omitted in the subsequent editions.

Language. Though the Bible was translated into the Indian tongue, the number of primary or radical words in the language was comparatively few. The words were made up of harsh consonant sounds, very little modified by the vowel sounds. L and R, which smooth the harsher consonant sounds, did not exist in many dialects of the language. Beside the guttural and nasal sounds, they had a peculiar whistling sound which cannot be represented by any letters of the English alphabet, hence in words in which it occurred, no two persons would probably spell them in the same manner. To represent this sound Cotton used qu, or two o-o connected. The same word was also used in different senses. The accent affected the meaning, and so did the gesture. The word qunni or quinne as written by Cotton, others wrote cumma, cunne, cona, cono, &c. The primary meaning of this word is *long*, but the speaker when he so intended moved his hand horizontally—if he meant *high* or *tall* he raised his hand, and if *deep* he lowered it. A thing that is long is comparatively *narrow*, and therefore narrow things were qunni as well as long. A proud or haughty man was called qunni because he assumes a high position in society. The Indian name of Sandy Neck was *Cumma—*

---

*This statement was in a degree correct at the time it was penned. But at this period the Mashpee people have made a great advancement in morals and intelligence, and com pare favorably in social order with the communities around them.

or *qunni-quid*, that is a long point. The Indians often dropped one syllable of the radical words in the forming of compounds, and sometimes several letters were interposed. Cohasset,* sometimes written Conohasset, is a compound of *qunni* or *cono*, *hassum* a rock, and the terminal *et*, which is a contraction of the last syllable word *Ahteuke* which is variously written; thus, tuck, tuk, muck, ick, it, at and et, the form depending in some cases on the gender of the word to which it is annexed. *Ahteuke* may be defined as meaning soil, fields or lands, place or country. This word does not occur in Williams's vocabulary, but as he has a word of similar meaning not found in Cotton's, Sannukamuck he gives as a synonym of Auke, earth or land. Williams uses W in many words that Cotton spells with an M, also au for oh or oo. *Ohkee* (Cotton) *Auke* (Williams) the same word, a general term for earth or land. *Ahteuke* (Cotton) *Sanaukamuk* (Williams) are applied to smaller divisions. The latter word is a compound, for *kamuck* or *komuck* means home. It is used by Eliot, Cotton and Williams, and in compounds the first syllable, *ko*, is often omitted. In the names of places this word very frequently occurs. Sometimes the first syllable, but generally the last in some of its varied forms. Some Indian names are easily analyzed and defined; others it is extremely difficult, if not impossible, to ascertain with certainty the radical words from which they were compounded. This difficulty is increased by the different manner in which different persons write the same name. Cotton does not spell names uniformly, neither does Williams or Gookin. On the records there is a still greater want of uniformity.

The Indians had a name for every inlet of the sea, every point, every river, creek or brook; every pond and almost every swamp. Their names were all of particular places of small extent. They had no general names. The Indians of Barnstable, Plymouth, Nantucket and Dukes Counties, and a part of Rhode Island, were subjects of one prince. The other Indian nations called them Wampanoags—that is eastern, or white Indians. Gookin calls them Paw-kan-naw-cuts, because their prince or king resided at a place of that name, and if he had changed his residence the name would have changed.

SACHEMS or SAGAMORES. *I-yan-nough*, (captain or one who imitates) in 1620 was the Sachem of the *Mattakeeset* Indians. He was sometimes called Sachem of *Cam-ma-quid*, (Sandy Neck) because during some part of the year he resided there. His territory included what is now known as the East Parish in Barnstable, a part of West Barnstable, and the easterly part of Sandy Neck, South and West Yarmouth, and that part of Hyannis in

---

*Flint in his history of Cohasset says the meaning of the name is "a fishing promontory." He is mistaken. Namasket is a fishing place.

Barnstable which is situate east and northeast of Lewis' Bay.

SEA-QU-UNCKS,* or SE-CUNCKE, (Black Goose) inaccurately written on the Barnstable records SE-RUNKE, was the *Scauton* sagamore, and his territory extended into Barnstable and included the westerly part of *Scauton* Neck and Great Marshes.

PAUP-MUN-NUCKE appears, by his deeds dated in 1648 and in 1658, to have been the Sachem of the South Sea or Massapee Indians. His territory included all the south part of Barnstable, (excepting a small tract at Hyannis that belonged to I-YAN-NOUGH,) Massapee and Falmouth. He resided at a neck called *Cot-o-ches-et.*

NAMES OF PLACES. Some Indian names of place are obsolete ; others have been retained, and some have been changed into corresponding or other English names. The following list illustrates the practice of our ancestors, to which reference has been made :

INDIAN NAMES.	ENGLISH NAMES.
Mat-ta-kee-set,	Old or Common Fields.
Cum-ma-quid,	Sandy Neck.
Co-a or *Cotuit,*	The same.
San or *Sa-tu-ite,*	Cotuit Port.
Pey-me-chit,	The same.
Kok-a-cho-ise, (The Narrows,)	The same.
Cok-a-cho-ise, (Island)	Little Oyster Island.
Se-po-ese or *Seputt,*	The same.
Cot-a-che-sett,	Obsolete.
Sip-nes-set,	Obsolete.
Was-ko-tus-soo,	Obsolete.
Mis-tic,	The Indian Ponds.
Skon-ko-net,	The same.
Chun-ko-mug,	Oyster river.
We-qua-quet,	The same.
Tamahappaseeacon,	Tam's Neck.
Yanno's Land,	Hyannis.
Mos-keeh-tuck-qut,	Great Marshes.

By these names the principal places in Barnstable are yet known. Within the last quarter of a century attempts have been made to banish some of these old names, by giving to the Post Offices a different one, namely :

To Santuit,	Cotuit Port.
Oyster Island,	Osterville.
Mistic, or the Ponds,	Marston's Mills.
We-qua-quet,	Centreville.

If the new names are better than the old, then something has been gained by the changes. Most of them were effected by the action of a few persons. They signed petitions to have Post

---

*From Segut, black, and Wam-poh-tuk, goose, according to Cotton. As the name of the goose is a word in imitation of its cry, it is not surprising that they differ. Or the name may be from Se-quun-nock, the horse foot.

Offices established, designated by the new names. The Postmaster General took no interest in the matter, and granted the prayers of the petitioners. The people of these places never took action respecting the change. They are objectionable. They introduce confusion in the records and in legal conveyances. He that proposes a change of name should show some "sufficient season. The only reason I have heard urged is this, "the old names are Indian." In a critical point of view, nothing has been gained. In selecting names euphony or sound, I admit, should be regarded. Let any one who has a correct ear say whether Marston's Mills, or Pondville, is a more euphoneous name than *Mistic* though it be Indian; Cotuit Port than *San-tu-it*; Osterville than *Cot-a-cho-set*, *Skon-ko-net*, or even *Skon-ko-muck*; or Centreville than *Wee-qua-quet*. The Indian name of West Barnstable, if modified in form, so that it will apply to the village instead of the meadows, will be *Mos-ke-tuck-et*, a very pretty name. Associated with those old names, which have become household words, there are pleasant reminisences which endear them to every son and to every daughter of old Barnstable. Why ruthlessly sever them? Even the red man associated with the name the characteristics and the memories of the place. In all primitive languages there is a correspondence between the name, and the thing signified. Names were not arbitrarily given. Hebrew names always have a meaning that is significant. "And he named one Peleg." Why, because on the year that Peleg was born the Hebrews did that which was signified by Peleg—they "divided their lands." Indian names of places were descriptive. The names of their children were often records of events. When the child grew up, if he became remarkable for any particular trait, he assumed another which was more expressive, and better corresponded with his condition and station. Indian names are compounded of primitive words, occasionally extending to fifteen syllables, too long even for an Indian to pronounce, and he therefore contracted them, sometimes taking only a single syllable, and sometimes only a few letters of a primitive word.

Mattakeese is compounded from *matta*, not—in this connection, old or poor—*ohkee*, ground or fields; *ese* or *ise* the diminutive term, meaning less or little. *Mattakeset* is the same with the addition of the terminal *et*, which means "place" or "here is the place," which our Indians uniformly applied to places near the water. Our fathers translated the name literally, and called the Indian fields "Old Fields," a name that I have often heard the aged apply to them. In 1647 these Old Fields were enclosed by a common fence, and thereafter were called common fields because so enclosed. The eastern part was called the new, and the western the old common field, because that requiring only a few rods of fence, was enclosed the year the town was settled.

Within the common fields there are some localities of historical interest. Stony Cove (*Qus-suk-a-cup?*) and Stony Cove river, (*Qus-suk-tuck-gut?*) the boundary between the new common field and Yarmouth. Some of the fields in the vicinity are yet called Stony Cove lands. About half a mile west of Stony Cove, within the ancient bounds of Yarmouth, is a place known as Old Town. Here the Rev. Mr. Bachilor and his company attempted, in the winter of 1637-8, to form the first settlement within the present town of Barnstable. There is no recorded evidence that this name is connected with Mr. Bachilor's settlement; yet there is no reasonable ground for doubting that it is so connected. The changing of this boundary line explains the apparent error of Gov. Winthrop in stating that Mr. Bachilor attempted a plantation in Yarmouth, for it was Yarmouth at that time. The Colony Court ordered the line between Mattakeese and Mattakeset to be established. It was afterwards found that both names appertained to the same place, and that Stony Cove being the boundary between *I-yan-nough* and *Mas-am-tam-paine*, it should also be the town's. The old writers say Mattakeeset was partly in Barnstable and partly in Yarmouth. This is accurate, if reference is had to dates prior to 1642, but not to subsequent time, and therefore the statements in Davis' edition of Morton's Memorial, and in the publications of the Massachusetts Historical Society are inaccurate, because they refer to subsequent events. William Chase, always called of Yarmouth, the ancestor of the Chase family of this County, afterwards owned the Old Town lands, and in Mr. Lothrop's records, and the town records, he is named as having been at the settlement, a resident within the bounds of Barnstable though always an inhabitant of Yarmouth.

I-yan-nough's town. A little distance northwesterly from Old Town, was a swamp and fresh water pond, called by the Indians "*Mattakeese* swamp." On the borders of that swamp *Iyannough's* town was situated. It is named by Winslow, and it was there that he and his companions were so sumptuously entertained by *Iyannough*. This was the summer residence of the Indians, though they occasionally resided on the opposite side of the harbor at Sandy Neck. Here were their planting fields, and being near the sea shore, where at the last of May and beginning of June an abundance of the species of the crab known as the horsefoot and called by them *se-quun-nocks*, (black crabs) were taken and used to dress their corn fields, a practice that the English have continued. In the winter the Indians removed their wigwams to the forest, because it was less labor to remove the house than to carry the wood, of which they consumed large quantities. They usually removed to South Sea in the winter, selecting a sheltered place in the forest in which to erect their wigwams.

Many years ago the salt water broke into *Mattakeese* swamp, and it is now nearly overgrown with salt meadows, and is known as the Perch Pond, and its outlet is the Eastern Watering-place.

The West Watering-place, also called Bacon's Watering-place, is on the dividing line between the new and the old Common Fields.

Cum-ma-quid. (Long Point.) This was the Indian name of the eastern part of Sandy Neck, and of Barnstable harbor. It belonged to *Iyannough*, who at certain seasons of the year resided there, and hence, he is sometimes called Sachem of *Cum-ma-quid.*

Scauton, called by the English Scorton Neck, is the westerly part of Sandy Neck. This name is derived from squalk, the Indian name of an aquatic bird, and *o-tan*, town or village. Within the recollection of many living, thousands of these birds built their nests in the swamps and thickets on Scorton Neck. Their eggs were gathered up, and were considered as good an article of food as those of the duck. Scorton belonged to *Sea-qu-uncks*, (Black Goose) Sachem of the Scauton tribe. The extreme western portion of the Neck, is within the present boundaries of the town of Sandwich, and in that part the Indians, when they sold their lands, made a reservation yet known as the Indian fields.

Mos-keeh-tuck-qut, Cotton says, was the name of Sandwich. It was originally within the limits of the territory of the Scorton Sachem, and a small portion of it is now included within the boundaries of Sandwich. It is a compound from *Mos-ke-tu-ash*, hay and *tuck-qut*, a term which is sometimes applied to waters of a sufficient depth to be navigated by canoes—*Mos* is a contraction of *Moo*-che, much. The first settlers translated the name into Great Marshes, and it cannot perhaps be improved. It means a place where there is much hay ground or meadows, interspersed with creeks navigable by canoes. This is an exact description. If the village or residence of the Indians had been intended, the name would be *Mos-kee-tuck-et.*

Mis-teake or *Mistick.* In order to understand many Indian names, we must endeavor to adapt ourselves to his habits and mode of thought. The Indian saw and heard, he did not reason, and in giving a name he described what he actually saw or what he actually heard. He often used metaphor, never abstract terms. He would say "here is my hearthstone," "here I build my fire," or "here I sleep," meaning here is my house, just as the sailor says, "here I sling my hammock." The simple and effective oratory of the Indian depended on the skilful use of metaphor. To go to war was "to raise the hatchet," or "to draw the bow,"—to make peace was "to bury the hatchet." *To-too* in his will on the records of Barnstable, directs his executor to "bury me as near as you can to the feet of my mistress." The poetry and simple eloquence of this command can hardly be excelled.

In the naming of places, metaphor was seldom employed. The few radical words of their language admitted of so many different combinations, and changes in form, that it often is very difficult to decipher the meaning of names. They had some general rules for compounding, and when the form of the radical words is not essentially changed, the meaning can easily be picked out.

Mish-ee signifies *great* when applied to an animal—if to a man the first syllable was written *mis*, and if to an estate *mus*. It was sometimes written *mash* often *mas*. The name *Mash-pee* is from *mish-ee* and *sapee*, river. Mr. Holway who had a perfect knowledge of the Indian says, *Massapee* (great river) is the correct spelling. It is the same as Mississippi which we are accustomed to see in a French dress. To those species of fish that alternately live in the salt and in fresh water, the Indians prefixed to their names *mish*; that is, to the names of the herring, the trout, the salmon, and also to the sturgeon. The reason of this is, these fish come from the *Great* waters to the small streams and ponds. They are not natives, they are *mishee*-fish—and the places to which they resorted to spawn were *Mish-ee-ah-teake* lands. In forming the compound name, the "h" was dropped because it was applied to an inanimate thing of a different gender— and for the same reason teake is changed to tic. The two syllables "ee" and "ah" are dropped as unnecessary in the compound. It is thus that the name Mistic is formed. It is a common name, and is uniformly given to regions like that at the head of Oyster Island Bay or Inlet, the First Herring River and the Indian Ponds. It is applied to small streams and to still waters, particularly where the herring and the trout resort, and also to the places where the salmon, the sturgeon, and the bass are taken.

There is another reason, and perhaps the primary one. The Indian always noted the color of objects. *Mish-que* was red. The color of these fish is redish, especially after they are cured, therefore he called them *Mish-que*, that is "red-fish." The color of the water of all streams and ponds is not the same. In giving names to streams and ponds he had reference to the color of the water. Independent of other considerations, the First Herring Brook, on account of the color of the water, may have been called *Mis-tic.*

Co or *Coa-tu-it.* This name has been retained. It is derived from *quin-nee* or *co-no*, long—*ah-teuke* fields and the terminal *it* or *et*, place, meaning long fields. It appears by the records that when the purchase was made by the English, that there were strips of good land that laid parallel to the river and pond. These were the planting fields of the Indians, and in their sale they reserved a large portion thereof for their own use, calling them Coatuit or the Long Fields.

San-tu-ite or *Sa-ta-ite* is a different name. It is perhaps the same as *Se-tu-it* or *Sa-te-at*, afterwards Scituate, which Mr. Deane in his history says means "cold brook." The name is probably from *San-quoi*, cold, *Sa-pee*, river—and the common terminal *it* or *et*, and means "cold brook." This name was applied to the pond, and the river which issues from it—and probably to the country to the south of Cotuit, now called Cotuit Port and the High Grounds.

Pi-me-chit or *Pi-me-ter*. This is the name of an ancient landing place at the northwest extremity of Oyster Island Bay or Inlet. It is a name that does not appear in the records; but has been handed down from generation to generation. Probably the two last syllables are the same as M*is-teake*. The land in that vicinity was known by that name. The first syllable, *Pi* or *Pey*, is perhaps a construction of *pey-o-nat*, to come, that is a place where many come—or Mistic Landing. The strait or bay near this place tradition also says was called by the Indians *Brod-e-nuck*, probably *Paup-mun-nukes* whose residence was in that vicinity.

Po-po-mon-aucke is a word that resembles *Paup-mun-nucke*, the name of the Sachem. *Po* is long and narrow and refers to water—when repeated it means very narrow or shallow. M*on* is is an abbreviation of *Monan*, island, *aucke* is an abbreviation of *ah-teuke*, land, that is a tract of land surrounded, or nearly surrounded, by narrow shoal waters, that is an island or peninsula. It is descriptive of the place of residence of *Paup-mun-nucke* on the neck which is called *Cot-o-che-sett* in the records. It was a custom of Indian mothers to make the names of their children the record of events. They frequently removed from place to place, and it was customary to give the child the name of the place where he was born. This furnishes us with the origin and meaning of *Paup-mun-nuke*.

Wak-a-tass-so or *Was-ko-tas-soo*. Respecting this name my inquiries have furnished no results. It looks like a name given by the Indians to new grounds or lands recently cleared up, and that were in the vicinity of oyster-beds, but of this I am not certain. I am only certain of this, it was near *kok-a-cho-ise*, the name of the Narrows and of little Oyster Island, and as all the other places are provided with names, I infer that *Wak-a-tas-so* was the name of the larger or Great Oyster Island. It was a place where there was a small Indian village.

Cot-a-che-sett. This was the name of a neck of land containing thirty acre, southeasterly from Mystic Landing, and adjoining to Roger Goodspeed's houselot, that *Paup-mun-nuke* reserved

Se-po-ese or Se-pu-it is called "Little River," a literal translation of the name. It it situate northeasterly from San-tu-it or Cotuit Port. On its banks are many handsome country residences. It is not called by the old name, though the waters into which is empties and which separate Dead Neck from Oyster Island, still retain the name.

in his sale of land to the English in 1648, and the place of his residence. It was afterwards known as the Indian fields. This name is almost identical with *kok-a-cho-ise* and was the name of his Sachemdom, and the name of the small island ând narrows, a little distance to the southeast.

Se-paw-nes-is-set, *Se-pau-is-set*, or *Sip-nes-et*. This is the same word that Williams says is the superlative of *se-ip* river, and defines as "a little rivulet." The name is now obsolete. It was the little brook that flows into the bay at Oyster Island Landing.

Skun-ko-mug* or *Chun-ko-muck*. This name is derived from *Chun-koo*, the Oyster, and *ko* or *ka-muck*, home, or place of residence. In this connection the meaning of the name is "a bed of oysters," or reversed, "an oyster bed," or "a place where oysters abound." This was the name of the river or inlet on the east and southeast of Oyster Island village, and which is yet known as Oyster Island river. The inlet or bay on the southwest was sometimes called Oyster Island bay and sometimes Oyster river.

Ma-*nan* or *mo-nan* was the Indian for island; but in the In-

---

*Williams gives the Indian word au-cup, a little cove or creek, au-cup-waw-ese, a very little one. Cotton has not this word. He could have written it aw-qut—the broad sound of a he represented by aw. Williams, as I have before stated, represents the whistling sound of the Indian by C. Cotton generally by qu, never by cu—B, P and T, are interchangeable, sometimes the one is used and sometimes the other in the same word. Au-qut frequently occurs in the names of places on the coast, because it refers to inlets into which the tide flows. When a creek was intended, tuck in some of its forms was added, indicating that it was narrow, that there was land on each side; yet that there was sufficient water to paddle a canoe. Mug or muck in this case may be the same as qut, because the cove and not the land was the home or bed of the oyster.

However, it is a well establised fact; that, though like Sancho's island, it was on the main land, the Indians called it an island, and for nearly two centuries the whites called it so, and even to this day many call it an island. Geographically it is not surrounded by water; that howevei has nothing to do with the fact that for two centuries Oyster Island was the name of place or village. If we laugh at the absurdity of the name, that does not mend the matter or change the facts. It is not a particle more absurd than the present name. Oster-VILLE. "Ville" is French, meaning, as the dictionaries informs us, "town" or "city." Vill is an English word, from villa, Latin, and is applied to the divisions of a town, and is usually written village. Osterville is uniformly spelled with the "E" final, and is French and is to be defined as French. Is Osterville a town? If so, who are its Selectmen? If a city, where are its municipal officers? Where is its city hall? Who is its Mayor? Ash-u-woo-ham-itt was its last Mayor, while under Indian rule. Oster is still more absurd. It is neither Indian, French nor English. If it be Latin, it is like Mambrino's helmet, some rogue has cut off the front. I am aware that this is mighty small criticism; my answer is, it is in reply to much smaller---to that pseudo delicacy which turns up its wise nose at Oyster Island because it was a name derived from the Indian; but can with imperturbable gravity say Osterville! Suppose some wise-acre should undertake to criticise the name Barnstable, and say it is not a stable, therefore it is absurd to say Barnstable. If the baptismal name of a termagant be "Love," is she a lovely scold?

NOTE.---Since writing the above I have had an interview with Hon. Charles Marston, many years overseer of the Massapee Indians. He pronounced several of the Indian names of places at Oyster Island and vicinity, in the manner they were pronounced by Indians who could speak their native language. From the information received of Mr. Marston I am satisfied that the various or apparently various names applied to Oyster Island are from the same root, namely, Chun-koo, the Oyster. As he pronounced the name, there are no letters in English to represent the sound. The peculiar whistling sound I have named and a strong aspirate occurs in this name, thus, Skon-ko-net, Skun-ka-mug or muck, and Skunk-net, are all the same word, the third syllable being a separate word---thus, Sko-unk-koo or Chu-unk-koo---the terminal et or muck was used only when the land was intended, not when the river. He also informs me that the name of the tribe of which Paup-mun-nuke was Sachem, including the Mpssapees, was Cot-a-chese---the people, Cot-a-che-set, the place, which in pronouncing he gave to the first syllables the sound of Chuu-koo, the oyster, as above given.

dian names, that appertain to places in that vicinity, there is no reference to *mo-nan*. The Indian however made no discrimination between an island and a peninsula. The tract of country which has (Cotacheset) till very recently, been known as Oyster Island is a peninsula, bounded on every side except at the northwest by water, if Bumps' river, a branch of the Chun-ko-nuck, be considered its northern boundary.

At the division of the town in 1717 into two parishes, the *Skun-ka-mug* (Phinney's mill stream) was made a part of the boundary line. It now separates *We-qua-quet* from *Skon-ko-net* (town records,) *Skun-ka-mag* (Mellen,) or *Chun-ko-net* (Cotton.) These I consider to be only different spellings of the same name, all derived from *Chun-koo*, the oyster, *oh-kee*, land, and the terminal, which means place. The exact definition of the name is "an oyster bed." The terminal qualified the meaning. Instead of meaning the oyster bed itself, it implied a village or place near to the oyster beds.

Skun-ko-net, or rather Cot-che-set, is bounded on the south by the Vineyard Sound, called by our ancestors the south sea, southwest by, including Great and Little Oyster Island, by Oyster Bay, inlet or river, and northwesterly by *Mistic*. The early settlements made by the English were at *Sip-nes-set* and *Kok-a-cho-ise* in the south. In the north part few settlements have been made to this day, and excepting in the immediate vicinity of the mill privileges it is covered by an unbroken forest, and still retains the old name.

We-qua-quet. Several Indian names of Oyster Island have been given, apparently different; but on being analized and examined are found to be essentially the same. *We-qua-quet* is a different name. In this the change of a few letters makes a radical change in its meaning. The town records and the local pronunciation is *Che-qua-quet*,* with some unimportant variations not affecting the meaning. Bourne, Gookin, Cotton, and the colony records, change the first syllable to *We*, making another word of the name. The second syllable is quite uniformly written *qua*, though sometimes *koh*. The last syllable is written in almost every conceivable form, qut, quet, quette, quot, hut, hunt, &c.

After much time spent in the examination, my conclusion is that *We-qua-qu* is the best authorized spelling of the name of the river or harbor, and *We-qua-quett* of the village. Its deviation and meaning is plain. It is a compound of *we-ko-ne*, sweet, fair,

---

*In the Coleman article I gave the preference to this spelling. Che-qua-kwau, an intelligent Indian chief from the West, informed me meant "the edge of the forest," but among the great variety of spellings of the last syllable, I do not recollect one that precisely corresponds with this. Bourne and Gookin, who were familiar with the language, both write the name We. I remarked in that article that the authority of such men was not to be disregarded. I think they were right. The town records and the local pronunciation probably had the same origin, and we and che are not so dissimilar as to render it improbable that they have been confounded.

pleasant, delightful, &c., and of *au-qut*, a cove or inlet of the sea. As the water of the river or harbor is salt, the Indian, though he called it *we-ko-ne*, the prime meaning whereof is *sweet*, did not intend that the word should be so understood ; but in some of its many other meanings ; that is *fair* or *pleasant*. *Au-qut* has already been fully explained in a note. It means a cove, not so large and deep as to be called a bay or a harbor, yet navigable for canoes and small vessels. *We-qua-quet* in English would therefore be pleasant harbor or pleasant cove.

By adding the common terminal *et* or only *e*, we have the name of the place or village., *We-qua-quett*, which literally translated would be Pleasant Harbor or village or Pleasantville.

There is poetry in the name. The Indian did not erect his wigwam on the sea shore, but on the margin of the crystal waters of its ponds, and on the banks of the clear brooks that fall into the *We-qua-qut*, the name is sometimes written *We-koh-quet*. Here we have an additional word, koh, a contraction of *oh-ke*, fields, and without calling the imagination to our aid we may translate the name thus, "Sweet fields beyond the swelling floods." The only straining of the meaning of any of the radical words is that of *et*, it is rendered *beyond* instead of *here* or *on this side*. The unabreviated Indian words are *We-kone*, sweet, *oh-ke*, fields, *et*, here in this place, or on this side—*au-qut*, enclosed waters or swelling floods at the rise of the tides.

We-koh-quat, *fair weather*, Cotton, *We-kin-cau-quat*, Williams, are words that resemble *We-qua-quett* and may be the same. Cotton translates *We-ken-eauk-qut* warm weather. *Quot* or *quat* is a different word from *qut* or *quet*. It means weather and has no reference to a cove or to waters. I find the last syllable of the name spelt *hut*, *hunt*, *quutt*, but not with the broad sound of quot or quat.

There is another word from which the name may be derived, namely : *we-quash*, a torch or light—also the name of the swan. We-quash also has a meaning, to express which we have no corresponding word in English, it has therefore been anglicised. To we-quash, or we-quashing, is to spear fish by the light of a torch placed in the bows of a canoe. It is a good sport on a calm evening. The fish are attracted by the light, and fall an easy prey to the sportsman. Along the sandy beaches and in the clear waters of the We-qua-qut, the red man's torch often spread its flickering light over the surface, and the white men, spear in hand, often engages in the same sport. If the name is hence derived, its equivalent in English will be Torch Light Cove.

The Indians called the swan We-quash because it sits so *ightly* and *gracefully* on the water. Like the Torch Light Sportsman, it suddenly darts down upon its unsuspecting prey. If this bird gave its cognomen to the harbor, we have for its name Swan's Cove.

I have thus rapidly passed in review the radical words from which We-qua-quet may be derived. My own preference is clearly indicated. I may be wrong—and, if so, it will not be the first time. The name affords a practical illustration of the difficulties that environ the student of the analogies of an unwritten language. A misplaced letter changes the meaning of a radical word, and thus the inquirer is misled. Words phonetically the same have a widely different meaning, when differently accented, or when accompanied by a different gesture. Cotton and Williams' vocabularies are valuable aids; but they are collections of compounds and of phrases, not of the primary words of the language. Rasles dictionary of the Canadian dialects gives the radical words, and exhibits many of their combinations; but though printed in a splendid quarto, it is locked up in old Provincial French which the student has first to learn, and the work is therefore of little value to the general reader. Schoolcraft's five splendid folios, elaborately illustrated, is the best work extant on the history, the language and customs of the Indian tribes; but it is too expensive a book ever to become popular.

Whether We-qua-quet is derived from we-ko-ne, the Indian word for "sweet, delightful, consoling," &c.; from we-quash, light, or a torch, also the name of the "swan," and hence associated in his mind with "graceful" acts, and "aquatic sports," or from *Me-tuk-que*, (forming Che-tuk-quet) "an orchard," or from Wee-koh-quot, "fair weather" is of little importance, either is a good name.

Looking at the question from a business standpoint, We-qua-quett is better than Centerville, a vile compound of Latin and French, unmeaning, inappropriate and unconnected with the memories and the associations of the past. Commercially it is objectionable, leading to errors and mistakes. A We-qua-quett man is in a distant city—he writes to his family or to his employers, he omits to add after Centerville, "Massachusetts"—there are many post offices of that name—the postmaster cannot forward it out of the State in which he resides—he sends it to the dead letter office, and if it contains no valuable enclosures it is committed to the flames. If he forwards it to an office of the same name in his State, a like fate awaits it. Many such miscarriages occur, and so long as the present name is continued no ordinary care and precaution will prevent their recurrence. Return the old name, and the danger is lessened, if it is not entirely removed.

It may be asked, "of what use?" Of what use is the study of the Latin, the Greek, the Hebrew, the Chaldee or the Anglo Saxon?—the value consists mainly in the mental discipline the study incidentally affords. This is a sufficient answer to the first inquiry. But there is another use. An English, French, or German savan would be ashamed to confess that he was ignorant of the history and analogies of the words that he has daily occasion to use. Why should not Americans? It is not so. Go to Harvard College, inquire of the learned President "What is the meaning of the word Massachusetts?"—of the professors, of the tutors, and of the students—if you find two that can give you an answer, and the reasons for their opinions, you will find two more than there is any reason to expect. Ought this to be so. Men will spend hundreds of dollars to have their sons instructed in the barbarious idioms of the middle ages; but not to instruct them in *homespun* words, which they daily delight to repeat.

These are mercenary considerations; yet they are conclusive. In deciding such questions, utility is paramount; yet, if to the useful, we can conjoin the true or the beautiful, why should we seek to separate them. If a name is barbarous, difficult of enunciation, or has unpleasant associations, we ought to reject it—it should be doomed to oblivion. To such names as Mos-que-tuck-et, Mys-tic, San-tu-it and We-qua-quett, neither objection attaches, and no mercantile consideration has power to banish them from memory.

In Drake's History of the Indians there is an exquisite picture of the last of the Wam-pa-no-ags. A beautiful girl is seated in the shade, on the banks of the We-qua-qutt. Her pensive eye rests on the water—sorrow is depicted in her every lineament, she exclaims: "And will the white man still pursue?" Yes, he has pursued her race till all are gone—he claims her fields, her hunting grounds and her streams, he "still pursues," endeavoring to wrest from the Indian the names which he loved, to break the silver cord of affection which bound the red man to the home of his fathers, and our fathers to the country that opened its bosom to receive them.

The Indian demands our sympathy. In his character there are pleasant aspects. His erect form, his manly bearing, his courage, his fortitude, and his faithfulness in the performance of his vows, are the ennobling traits in his character. Inferior in the arts of civilized life, by the inexorable law of nature, he was destined to perish when he came in contact with a superior race.

Indian names of places are the connecting links between the present and the past—all that remains to remind us that another race once cultivated our fields, once roamed in our forests. Why ruthlessly sever those links? To save the barbarous, the uncouth, or those around which unpleasant associations are entwined, no one will plead. In other parts of our country, among our chief men, among those who have imperiled their lives in the defence of liberty and the right, a love for these old names and a desire to perpetuate them everywhere prevails.   Nearly all the States which have recently been admitted into the Union, many of our ships of war, our gun-boats, our monitors, and our steamships, have had Indian names bestowed on them.

I have only one more plea to enter for the old name.   To the Indian, *We-qua-quett* was a land of shady groves—of sweet waters—of pleasant streams—of manly sports ;   our fathers were well pleased with the name, they adopted it, their children cherished it, and their descendants have associated with it the memory of the olden time, of those good and true men who drank its sweet waters, and now rest beneath the green sod of its shady groves.   The Indian was their brother.   They knelt with him at the same altar, they prayed to the same God, and believed him to be a joint heir with them of a common salvation.   They called "Old Humphrey," the Indian teacher at We-qua-quet, their brother, they extended to him while living the right hand of fellowship, and they wept at his grave because a loved one of their Israel had departed.   Their affections were not circumscribed by race or color—the good and the true, he that strove to walk in the footsteps of the Master, they called brother.

JENKINS.

Several of this name came over early. Edward of Scituate, called a servant of Mr. Nathaniel Tilden, became a prominent man, and died in 1699. Henry, who settled in New Hampshire and, died in 1670. Joel of Braintree. John Jenkins, aged 26, took passage for New England, July, 1635, in the Defence, of London. In September, 1635, Elizabeth Jenkins took passage in the Truelove for New England.

The John Jenkins* who came over in the Defence was the man of that name who settled in Plymouth, and was admitted a freeman of the Colony January 3, 1636-7. At that date he was allowed to enlarge his grounds at Willingsley in Plymouth, showing that he had been an inhabitant of that town previous to the date of his being admitted a freeman. May 5, 1640, three acres of meadow between the south ponds and Eel River, forty acres of upland "thereby it," and six acres of land above Willingsley, were granted to him. Nov. 2, 1640, six acres in the Colebrook meadow were assigned to him. On the 29th of Dec. 1640, he bought for £16,10shs sterling, of Anthony Snow, a dwelling-house and eight acres of land on the south side of Willingsley brook.

In June, 1637, he volunteered as a soldier from Plymouth in the Pequot war, and in 1645 was a soldier in the Narraganset Expedition. He frequently was a juror, and in 1644 was constable of Plymouth, and was then called senior.

His early admission to the freedom of the Colony indicates that he was a man known to the first settlers, before he came over, and a member of an Independent Church. He was a large land owner and a house holder, facts from which it might be inferred that he had a family; but the records afford no evidence that he was then a married man.

In 1646 he removed to Eastham, his name appearing on the most ancient list of the freeman of that town which has been preserved. He did not remain long in that town. He was of Barn-

---

*Two men of this name came over early and settled in Plymouth. The elder was made a freeman soon after his arrival, and I am thus enabled to trace him in his wanderings. The other was a younger man, early joined the Quakers, and settled in Sandwich, where he died in 1684. Bishop has a long notice of him.

stable in 1652. His name is on the list of freeman in Barnstable in 1558, 1670, and in 1684.

June 7, 1659, the Colony Court granted liberty to Mr. Thomas Hinckley, Henry Cobb, Samuel Hinckley, John Jenkins and Nathaniel Bacon, "to view and purchase a tract of land at Saconesset, soe much as they can conveniently, and they are to have each of them a considerable portion thereof as the Court shall think meet, and the rest to be disposed of by the Court." Mr. Thomas Hinckley and Mr. Richard Bourne were authorized to purchase the said lands of the Indians. Subsequently others were added to the list of grantees or proprietors.

At the first division of the lands at Suckinesset,* Dec. 3, 1661, Samuel Hinckley signs for himself and John Jenkins. In 1668 he was admitted an inhabitant of the plantation, but he did not long reside there, for four years after he is called of Barnstable. June 4, 1686, Suckinesset was incorporated as a town. I presume by the name of Falmouth, but it is not so stated on the record. Previous to that date Suckinesset plantation was annexed to Barnstable, and it seems difficult to fix precisely the status of the residents thereon they had to bear arms in Barnstable, and the territory was in fact a part of Barnstable, as Maine was a part of Massachusetts before it was admitted to be a State of the Union.

In 1684 John Jenkins was a freeman of Barnstable. He had deceased in 1690, when his son John of Falmouth was made a freeman of that town. The settlement of his estate does not appear on the Probate Records. He probably died during the time of the usurpation of Sir Edmond Andros, when it was required that the estates of deceased persons should be settled in the Perogative Court in Boston. This was an arbitrary act, and unpopular with the people, and to avoid it, some divided their property by deeds, not by will. John Jenkins probably did so ; but as the records are burnt, it cannot now be verified. He was living in 1684 ; and probably died soon after, aged about 76 years.

John Jenkins married Feb. 2, 1652-3, Mary, widow of John Ewer of Barnstable, a young man who died early in 1652. Whether or not this was his second marriage, the records afford no evidence. His children are all recorded as born in Barnstable, though in 1668 he was admitted an inhabitant of Suckinesset. Tradition says he resided at West Barnstable on the estate now owned by his descendants, Dr. F. H. Jenkins, but this is very doubtful, in fact the records of the laying out of the lands furnish no confirmation of the truth of the tradition. He probably resided at first on the Ewer farm. In 1675 the town granted him an

---

*I prefer this spelling, because it accords better with the Indian words from which it is compounded. It signifies a place where black wampum is made. The quohaug, or round clam, was formerly abundant on the shores of Falmouth. From the dark colored portion of the shell the black wampum, or Indian money, was made. It was of half the value of the white. It was made in the form of beads, and strung, and was estimated by the fathom.

acre and a half of land at the head of his farm for his conveniency. No boundaries are given, and therefore its location cannot be fixed.

Children born in Barnstable.

2. I.   Sarah, 15th Nov. 1653.
3. II.   Mehitabel, 2d March, 1654-5, married Eleazer Hamblen 15th Oct. 1675, and had a family, was a member of the church, and was living in 1683.
4. III. Samuel, 12th Sept. 1657. This child probably died early. He is not mentioned afterwards on the records. There was a Samuel Jenkins in the Colony, but too old a man to have been the son of John.
5. IV.   John, 13th Nov. 1659. (See below.)
6. V.   Mary, 1st Oct. 1662, married Thomas Parker and re-removed to Falmouth, and had a large family.
7. VI.   Thomas, 15th July, 1666. (See below).
8. VII. Joseph, 31st March, 1669. (See below).

John Jenkins, son of John, resided a part of his life in Falmouth. In 1690 he was admitted a freeman of the Colony, and was sworn at the County Court in Barnstable June 24. The twenty admitted on that day were the last who were sworn freemen of the Plymouth Colony. About the year 1692 he returned to Barnstable, and settled on a small farm on the north of the Shoal pond in the East Parish. A part of this estate he bought of Joshua Lumbert, and a part was probably his father's. He inherited all his father's lands in Falmouth. He was a man of some note, entitled to be called Mister, a prominent member of the church, and though he resided in a small house, and in a retired spot, he inherited the aristocratic feelings of his English ancestry.

"He died very suddenly on the 8th of July, 1736," aged 77. His will is dated Dec. 15, 1730, and was proved on the third of Aug. 1736. He names his wife Patience, provides very scantily for her support, and if she married again she was to have £30 and no more, less than the one hundredth part of his estate. She did not marry again, but lived a widow till Oct. 28, 1745, when she died aged, according to the church records, "above seventy years."

To his three sons, John, Philip and Joseph, he bequeathed, and to their male heirs, in fee tail, "all my Waquoit land, that is all my lands east of the Mill or Five Mile river, so called, whether divided or undivided, to be an estate in fee tail ; saving that I give liberty to my sons and their said heirs to sell to each other, so that said lands and meadows go not out of the families of my said sons."

He orders that Dorothy, the widow of his son Samuel, deceased, shall be provided for at his house during her widowhood, or ''so long as she bears her deceased husband's name.''

To his eldest son, John Jenkins, he devised the dwelling house in which he then lived and the land adjoining, his lot of land to the westward of the Great (or Cooper's) pond, his cedar swamp near Shubael Davis', all his woodland in Barnstable, meadow, &c., &c.

To his daughter Sarah Basset £20, &c.,—to his daughter Ruth West £95 on her husband's bond of Jan. 20, 1729,—to his youngest daughter Patience Jenkins, £100; to his daughter-in-law Experience Paine £20; to his daughter Mary Studley £90, if his executors think she needs it; to his daughter Mehitabel Chapman £90, and to the poor of the East Church £5. In paying the legacies he ordered the ounce of silver to be valued at eight shillings. He appoints his wife Patience, son John, and Joseph Lothrop, Esq., executors.

To this will there are two codicils annexed. In the second, dated Dec. 15, 1732, he says, that whereas his son John became surety for his son-in-law James Chapman in a suit brought by Col. Bourne, commenced before he left the country, &c., therefore £48 to be deducted from legacy to daughter Mehitabel.

The inventory of his estate is dated 24th Aug. 1736. The apprisement was not probably made in silver valuing the ounce at 8 shs.; if so, he was the most wealthy man in Barnstable.

His personal estate apprised at   £738,11,11
House, homestead and all his real estate in Barnstable, 1,800
Lands in Falmouth,   600
                                            _____
                                             £3,138,11,11

And this the legal instrument gravely informs us did not include a pair of old money scales in the possession of Sackfield West.

He married for his first wife Mary, daughter of Robert Parker of West Barnstable; and 23d Nov. 1715, the Widow Patience Paine.

Children born in Falmouth.

9. I, John, 3d, born about the year 1687, baptized Oct. 8, 1695, was the ancestor of the Jenkins family at Falmouth. He married 3d Sept. 1708, Abigail Whetstone, or Whiston, of West Barnstable. She was a daughter of John of Scituate. His children born in Falmouth were: 1, John, June 27, 1709, married Oct. 30, 1734, Rebecca Green; 2, Joshua, June 5, 1712, married at 18, Aug. 20, 1730, Hannah Handy; 3, Abigail, March 27, 1715, married Benj. Crocker, Jr., May 15, 1738; 4, Mary, Feb. 10, 1717-18, married Sept. 5,

1739, Eben Swift. The fourth John Jenkins had James, born Dec. 9, 1735, died April 10, 1807, and a daughter Ruth. James Jenkins, son of the fourth John, married Oct. 18, 1762, Mercy Price. She died April 10, 1817. Children of James : 1, Zilpha, 1763 ; 2, Mary ; 3, John, May 7, 1766, died at sea Nov. 8, 1793 ; 4, Weston, Aug. 21, 1768 ; 5, Rebecca ; 6, Mehitabel ; 7, Thankful. Weston Jenkins married Oct. 28, 1795, Elizabeth Robinson, a descendant of Rev. John of Leyden. He died Feb. 13, 1834 ; she died Oct. 14, 1837. Their children were : 1, John, March 18, 1798 ; 2, Rebecca, March 19, 1800 ; 3, Hetty, May 3, 1802 ; 4, Charles, July 31, 1805 ; 5, Eliza, July 4, 1807 ; 6, James, June 24, 1809 ; 7, Eunice, July 23, 1812 ; 8, Harriet, Sept. 20, 1816. Of the family of Weston, the Hon. John Jenkins married twice, first Jan. 5, 1825, and second Chloe, who survives. He died Aug. 10, 1859. Rebecca married J. H. Parker, and second ——— Thompson. Charles died Oct. 29, 1862. Eliza married O. C. Swift, Esq. Eunice married Rev. J. D. Lewis. Harriet Rev. F. Morton.

10.   II.   Mary, born about 1789, baptized Oct. 8, 1695, married in 1725 Joseph Studley of Yarmouth.

11.   III.   Sarah, born in 1691, bap. Oct. 8, 1695, married Jan. 30, 1722-3, Wm. Basset of Barnstable, died Nov. 1, 1746, aged 55.—[Church Records.

Born in Barnstable.

12.   IV.   Mehitabel, 25th Sept. 1694, married James Chapman.

13.   V.   Samuel, 15th July, 1697, married Dorothy ———, and died early without issue.

14.   VI.   Phillip, 26th July, 1699, married Dec. 13, 1721, Elizabeth Clark, and had David born in Barnstable Sept. 22, 1722, his name thereafter disappears on the records.

15.   VII.   Joseph, 13th Aug. 1701, resided in the East Parish in Barnstable in the house that was his father's at Shoal Pond. He died Nov. 26, 1745, in his will dated four days before his death, he names his wife Dorcas, and his six daughters, Mary, Dorcas, Keziah, Experience, Rebecca and Patience. To the three first named he gives £30 each, old tenor, and to the others £60, to be paid when they should severally arrive at 21 years of age.

His personal estate was apprised	£322
Real Estate,	2502
	£2,824

A pound old tenor was less than half a dollar in silver money, £30 was $13.33 He had the tools of carpenter, and probably served an apprenticeship at that trade. Sept. 4, 1748, the Widow Dorcas Jenkins was dismissed from the East Church in Barnstable, and recommended to the first church in Wallingsford, Conn. Their children born in Barnstable were: 1, Joseph, Nov. 4, 1724; 2, Mary, June 11, 1729; 3, Dorcas, April 10, 1731; 4, Keziah, March 30, 1733; 5, Rebecca, Aug. 27, 1735, died Oct. following; 6, Experience, March 11, 1738-9; 7, Rebecca, Sept. 19, 1740; 8, Patience, Sept. 1, 1742.

16.   VIII.   Ruth, —— 1704, married May 7, 1729, Dr. Sackfield West of Yarmouth. After the death of his father-inlaw he removed to Barnstable, and occupied a part of the Jenkins homestead at Shoal Pond, which he afterwards owned. It is now known as Dr. West's field. The Dr.'s controversies with the church occupy much space on the records. As a physician he had but little practice. His oldest son Samuel was born in Yarmouth March 4, 1730. When a boy he was employed in husbandry on the Jenkins farm at Shoal Pond. Traits of genius were discovered in the lad by some gentlemen of influence, and he was sent to Harvard College, graduated in 1754 one of the most distinguished of his class. Afterwards the honorary degree of D. D. was bestowed on him. He was settled in the ministry at New Bedford, and died at Tiverton, R. I., Sept. 24, 1807, aged 77. He was a giant in intellect; able to cope with Edwards in divinity and in politics with the most renowned. He was an ardent patriot, a member of the Convention for forming the Constitution of Massachusetts and of the United States. Being awkward and ungainly in his person, negligent in his habits, and grossly defective and careless in the tones and inflections of his voice, his genius, his profound learning, and his great intellectual power, failed to give him popularity. Men of his character are rarely popular. The late Dr. Samuel Savage was as rough as Dr. West; yet, being a good story teller and a very witty man, he was popular. Dr. W. was not, however, always dry and logical. His wife Experience was a very tall woman, in reply to a question desiring his opinion of early marriage, he said: "I have found by l-o-n-g E-x-p-e-r-i-a-n-c-e that it is good to marry." There is genuine wit in this reply; but it is the wit of the logician, not of the comedy.

17.   VII.   Patience, bap. Oct. 6, 1717. Mr. Jenkins calls her his youngest daughter.

        (7.)   Thomas Jenkins, son of John, born 15th July, 1666, resided at West Barnstable. In his will dated Nov. 9, 1737, proved Feb. 15, 1745-6, he names his wife Mercy to whom, in ad-

dition to thirds, he gives his best bed and £40. To his son Ebenezer he gives the east end of his house then occupied by him, and
other property. To his son Samuel land at Skonkonet, and to his
son Josiah other property. To his grandson Thomas, son of
Ebenezer, land at Skonkonet. To his daughter Thankful he bequeathed £10, to Mary £10, Hope £10, Experience £20, Sarah
£20. He signs his will with his mark, not always evidence that
the testator can not write ; but this will having been made seven
years before his death, he was probably in good health at the
time, and this fact indicates that his education had been defective.

His estate was apprised at £3,849,16,10. Among other matters a negro woman is apprised at £100. The currency had then
became much depreciated and to reduce these sums to lawful
money two-thirds at least must be deducted. 80 bushels of corn,
wheat and other grain, in the inventory, is apprised at £49, four
times its value fifty years earlier. However, calling his estate
£1000 in lawful money, he was wealthy for the times.

He was in the eightieth year of his age when he died. He
married 24th Aug. 1687, Experience, daughter of James Hamblen,
Jr. It appears by his will that he married a second wife named
Mercy ——— .

Children born in Barnstable.

18. I.   Thankful, 19th May, 1691, married (Isaac ?) Taylor.
19. II. Experience, 28th March, 1693, married John Pope Oct.
          3, 1717.
20. III. Mercy, 5th Jan. 1695-6, married John White 23d
          Dec. 1718.
21. IV. Ebenezer, 5th Dec. 1697. He died June, 1750, and in
          his will dated June 19, 1750, proved on the 5th of July fol-
          lowing, he names his wife Elizabeth and all his children.
          His estate is apprised at £357,19,4 in lawful money. He
          resided at West Barnstable in a part of his father's house,
          situate on the estate now owned by Chipman W. Whelden.
          He married 9th Nov. 1721, Judith White. She died April
          25, 1729, leaving an only child Thomas. He married July
          25, 1732, Elizabeth Tupper, who survived him. His children
          were : 1, Thomas, born March 8, 1725-6, married Thankful
          Wing of Harwich April 23, 1752 ; 2, Ebenezer, July 6,
          1736 ; 3, Nathan, Oct. 21, 1734, married Dec. 9, 1762,
          Rachel Howland, (father of Asa and grandfather of the
          present Nathan) ; 4, Martha, Friday Nov. 4, 1737 ; and 5,
          Elizabeth, Friday May 9, 1740.
22. V.   Samuel, 7th Jan. 1699-10. (See below.)
     VI. Josiah, 16th April, 1702, married in 1737 Mary Ellis
          of Middleboro', and resided at West Barnstable. His will

is dated 29th Dec. 1749, and was proved in the following February. He had no children, and he seems to have loved his brothers and sisters more than his wife, for he is not liberal to her in his will. The principal part of his estate he gave to his brothers Ebenezer and Samuel, and legacies to his sisters Thankful Taylor, Mercy White, Hope White, Sarah Nye, and his cousin Nathan Jenkins. He had a splendid wardrobe, and appears to have been a fashionable man in his day.

24. VII. Hope, 5th July, 1704, married —— White.
25. VIII. Sarah, 1st Dec. 1706 married 1737 Lemuel Nye.

(8.) Joseph Jenkins, son of John, resided at West Barnstable. He had lands at the "New Bridge" in 1690. His will is dated Jan. 1733-4, and proved Nov. 8, 1734. He appears to have been a man of good estate, and provides most liberally for the support of his wife "Lidia." To his daughter Abigail Hinckley he devises £10; to Lidia Crocker £25; to Prudence Baker 10 shs., and to his unmarried daughter Hannah £60. To his two sons, Joseph and Benjamin, he devised all his estate, they providing for their mother and paying the legacies to their sisters. He died in 1734, aged 65, and his wife Lydia survived him.

Children born in Barnstable.

26. I. Abigail, July, 1695, married Benj. Hinckley Nov. 2, 1716, and had eleven children.
27. II. Bathshua, July, 1696, died young.
28. III. Ann, May, 1701, married Oct. 19, 1721, Joseph Lothrop, and did not survive long.
29. IV. Joseph, 29th Feb. 1703. This Joseph is called 3d on the records—his father was Joseph 1st, son of John 2d. After the death of his father in 1734 he is called junior. He was published to Martha Phinney in 1728. July 15, 1736, he married Mercy Howland. He died Jan. 15, 1749. His children born in Barnstable were: 1, Mercy, May 25, 1737; 2, Joseph, May 3, 1739, married Hannah Foster of Tisbury Oct. 2, 1787; 3, Bathsheba, Oct. 22, 1741; 4, Mary, March 13, 1742; 5, Abigail, Sept. 6, 1745; 6, Bethia, bap. June 14, 1747; 7, Zaccheus, 8th Feb. 1748; 8, Sarah, bap. Nov. 26, 1749.
30. V. Lydia, 30th June, 1705, married Nov. 9, 1727, Cornelius Crocker. (See Crocker.)
31. VI. Benjamin, 30th June, 1707. He resided at West Barnstable on the estate formerly owned by Rev. Mr. Shaw, now owned by Dea. David Parker. He married Oct. 29, 1730, Mehitabel Blush, and had: 1, Ann, Oct. 3, 1731, married Isaac Goodspeed Oct. 17, 1754; 2, Hannah, Jan. 25, 1734-5, married Job Howland Dec. 6, 1753; 3, Lydia,

March 16, 1735-6, married Joshua Nye 1756 ; 4, Mehitabel,
Feb. 24, 1737-8 ; 5, Benjamin, April 12, 1740 ; 6, Southworth, Nov. 29, 1742 ; 7, Timothy, Jan. 28, 1744 ; 8, Bethia, June 4, 1747 ; 9, Sarah, March 1, 1750-1 ; and 10,
Tabitha, March 31, 1753.

32.   VII.   Reliance, 6th April, 1709, died young.
33.   VIII.   Prudence, bap. April 6, 1718, married Samuel Baker
         May 30, 1732, removed to Windham, Conn.
34.   IX.   Hannah, bap. April 6, 1718, married Stephen Free-
         man Oct. 22, 1736.

   (22.)   Samuel Jenkins, son of Thomas, born 7th Jan.
1699-1700, resided at first at Skonkonet on the estate given him
by his father and now owned by Lemuel Lumbard.   When Ichabod Hinckley removed to Tolland, Conn., Samuel Jenkins purchased Hinckley's farm, which is now owned by Dea. Braley Jenkins.   His wife being half sister to Ichabod and a daughter of
Ensign John Hinckley by his second wife.   Widow Mary Goodspeed (a daughter of John Davis, Sen'r) had lands adjoining
which she owned in her own right.   Samuel Jenkins married Nov.
9, 1721, Mary Hinckley, and had born in Barnstable,

37.   I.   Experience, Dec. 4, 1722, married April 12, 1739, Lewis
         Hamblen.
38.   II.   Mary, Sept. 7, 1725, died June 7, 1727.
39.   III.   Samuel, Oct. 20, 1727.   (See below.)
40.   IV.   Nathaniel, Dec. 6, 1728, married March 30, 1752,
         Maria Ellis of Rochester, and had Alvan.
41.   V.   Simeon, Sept. 8, 1733, married March 25, 1762, Ho-
         diah, daughter of Dea. John Hinckley, and had Simeon,
         John, Prince, Perez, Braley, born 1775, now living, Hodiah
         and Lucy.
42.   VI.   Lot, March 13, 1737-8, married Oct. 21, 1761, Mercy
         Howland.

   (39.)   Samuel Jenkins, Jr., married March 11, 1749-50,
Mary Chipman, daughter of Dea. Samuel, and had,

I.   Josiah, Sept. 30, 1750.
II.   Deborah, Feb. 2, 1752.
III.   Abiah, Jan. 21, 1754.
IV.   Samuel, Nov. 23, 1755.
V.   Mary, Jan. 16, 1758.
VI.   Joseph, June 6, 1760.

   This family removed to Gorham, Me., and the following family letters, furnished by Charles H. Bursley, Esq., of West Barnstable, will be of interest.   They are good specimens of the correspondence of the times.   Mrs. Jenkins writes the better letter.
Women always do.   They go straight forward, writing just as
they converse, which is the true art of epistolary writing.
These letters prove that Samuel Jenkins and his wife had re-

ceived a good common school education. Scarce an instance of bad spelling occurs in either. Mrs. Jenkins writes her name Genkins, the husband Jenkins. At that time J was called I consonant, and they were formed alike. Mrs. Jenkins' capital I's are identical in form with her small g's, and the G which she used in writing her name she probably called J, or I consonant. No post offices had then been established, and letters had to be transmitted by private conveyance.*

GORHAM, July ye 26, 1778.

DEAR SISTERS: This with love to you, hoping through Divine goodness it will find you all well, as it leaves us, that is the small family I have with me. None of my children but Abiah are with me. All my sons are, if living, in the army, and Molly (Mary) is married away, and lives about a mile from me.

I hear there are several accidents happened at Barnstable, write me the particulars. If you have heard from my brothers in Connecticut, let me know it. There was here a brother of one of my neighbors from Stratford last winter, who informed me of the death of my brother John (Chipman). I questioned him about it, and told him he had moved to Middletown. He said he knew it, and he was acquainted with him—he had lost his fingers in a mill, he had a son at Stratford, and I might depend upon it, he had been dead as much as three or four years. May God sanctify this stroke of his providence for good, and may we be ready also.

I am afraid what I may hear concerning my sons, but I hope I may be prepared, let it be as it will.

I should write more, but it is the Sabbath. Give my love to your children, and my duty to mother *Genkins* and the brothers and sisters. Tell sister Hamlen that Lewis and Perez were here an hour or two; and Phebe's sister Young came to town last Sabbath, and was taken very sick on Monday. Yesterday she was very low with the pleuresy. Write me everything you know worth a writing by the bearer of this letter. I suppose he will stay only a few hours, being on business. I conclude with love to you and yours and all friends.

MARY GENKINS.

Abiah gives duty to you, and love to all cousins.
This for Hannah and Elizabeth Chipman.†
"For Mrs. Elizabeth Chipman at Barnstable." "Pr favor of Mr. Hanscon."‡

GORHAM, Jan. 29, 1781.

LOVING SISTER: These come with our love to you and children, hoping you are well, as through Divine Goodness we are, except my wife who has been poorly ever since last March; but is a little better. We rec'd yours by Mr. Lovell,—was glad to hear from you. And now a short account of my family. Our children are all except one married. We have seven grand-children, Josiah one daughter, Sarah; Deborah

---

*My great grandfather Delap was in Nova Scotia during the Revolution, and two years elapsed, during which he found no opportunity to send a letter to Barnstable.

†Hannah Chipman was the eldest sister of the writer of this letter. Elizabeth Chipman was the wife of her brother, Dea. Timothy Chipman. She was a Basset from Sandwich.

‡Hanscon. Two of this name settled in Gorham. Mr. Pierce says they came from Scarborough.

three children, Hannah, Elizabeth and Ebenezer; Abiah two, Josiah
and Prudence; and Mary one daughter Abiah. It seems to me that
they are the prettiest children I see anywhere. They all live near us
except Abiah, who resides eighteen miles distant. Mr. Lovell* informs
us that sister Hannah would be glad to come and live her sister. Were
she here we should be glad; but as times are, it would be difficult for
her to come, either by land or water. For me to come by land for her
would cost more paper dollars than a few, and to come by water is
hazardous. If there could be some way found out for her to come with
Lovell's family I esteem it best. As for my coming at present, it is not
practicable.

As to news, we have none. Old Capt. John Phinney,† formerly of
Barnstable, the first settler in Gorham, died not long since almost ninety
years old. Let us hear from you as often as possible—we will do the
same.

I am dear sister, your loving brother,

SAM'LL JENKINS.

N. B.—My wife has this moment started a notion, that you did not
know who Sam'll married—it was Lydia Dier from Truro.

GORHAM, November 22, 1783.

DEAR SISTER: This with love to you and yours, hoping it will find
you all well, as, through Divine Goodness, I and mine are at present.
I have not heard from you since Major Lewis came. I then received
gladly what you sent me that was my sisters. You cannot think how
greatly rejoiced I was to see one of my old neighbors, who could tell me
everything I wanted to know concerning my own family. Your
brother‡ had had a long fit of sickness last spring, was very low, and
has been able to do but a trifle this summer. He is better this fall, but
not so well as before. He intends, with submission to Providence, to
go to Barnstable this winter. The twentieth of June last we had the
sorrowful and heavy news of our son Joseph's death. He died that
day, two months. He had been in the service two years, and died with
consumption near West Point—a loud call to us all. He was carried
into the country and was comfortably provided for during the last
month or six weeks of his life. What most contributes to my comfort
is, God was pleased to give him a time of consideration. He sent us
word not to mourn for him, but to prepare to follow him, for he trusted
the eternal estate was secured. You are not a stranger to my grief,
though I have been to yours.

> Not from the dust afflictions grow,
>   Nor troubles rise by chance,
> Yet we are born to care and woe,
>   A sad inheritance.
>
> As sparks break out from burning coals,
>   And still are upward borne,
> So grief is rooted in our souls,
>   And man grows up to mourn.

The rest of my children that are here are well. Josiah has gone to

---

*I am not informed that either of the Lovells removed to Gorham; but it appears by
this correspondence that one of them did.

†Capt. John Phinney was born April 8, 1796. He died in Gorham, Dec. 29, 1780, and
was 84 years, 8 months and 11 days old, allowing ten days for difference between old and
new style. Mr. Pierce, in his history of Gorham, says he was 87 at his death. His wife
Martha (Coleman) died Dec. 16, 1784, aged 86 years, 9 mo., 2 days, if the date of her birth
on the records is in new style.

‡Named Basset from Sandwich.

"*Bagaduce.*"* Phebe hath two sons about six months old, Samuel and Jacob. Prude (Prudence, wife of Josiah) a daughter the same age, named Polly (Mary.) Abiah lives a little way off. Sam'll has a daughter about three weeks old named Lidia. Molly (Mary) one five weeks, named Elizabeth—making fourteen grandchildren I have living.

You know not how much I want to come and see all my old friends and relatives. Give my love to all brothers and sisters, cousins and friends. Tell cousin James Smith's wife† I never forgot what she said to me, that I must write concerning religion; but I was loth to write that I did not well like my minister, though when I came home, the first time I heard him, I thought I could not be content to sit under him, and it came to my mind, "Despise not small things," which made me to think I did not well to be uneasy. He has been dismissed two years.‡ We had a minister ordained this month one (not legible) a fine man.— I hope he will prove a blessing, and that decayed religion will revive uuder his ministry.

It has been very much the practice of the place for parents to own the covenant and have their children baptized. There are counted to be near a third of the people to be Separate Baptists, and some of that party are become what is called Shaking Quakers. I think they are a most monstrous deluded set of people. The performances at their meetings consist in dancing, hideous howlings like wolves, standing on their heads, pretending to speak in unknown languages, and the like ridiculous behavior. I take them to be the people that Christ warns us of when he saith, "Take heed that you be not deceived. Then if any man shall say uuto you, lo here is Christ or there believe it not: for there shall arise false Christs and false prophets, and show great signs and wonders, if it were possible deceive the very elect. Behold I have told you before, if they say behold he is in the desert, go not forth, or in the secret chamber believe it not."

Dear sister, I could write till morning, but being very late must break off abruptly, begging you to send me a letter by Mr. Lewis,§ and so conclude, very tired, with love to you and children.

M. GENKINS.

To Mrs. Elizabeth Chipman, Barnstable.

John Jenkins, the second, appears to have been a resident in Plymouth in 1644, and probably earlier. In 1648 he became an inhabitant of Sandwich. He married a daughter of one of the prominent Quaker families in that town. His daughter Elizabeth was born in Sandwich April 30, 1649, and he had two sons, Zachariah and Job. He died in 1684, but his estate remained un-

---

*Mrs. Jenkins wrote a very legible hand, but this name I cannot make out. Capt. Josiah Jenkins was an officer in the Revolution, was in an engagement on Lake Champlain and at the battle of Monmouth. He married Prudence Davis and had Saiah, two Marys, Aurelia, Nancy, Josiah and Katharine. He died in 1831, aged 81.

†James Smith married Hannah Barlow of Sandwich. His mother was a Hinckley, and perhaps hence the relationship—cousin to Samuel Jenkins.

‡Rev. Josiah Thacher of Lebanon, Conn., graduate of Princeton College, and a decendant of Antony of Yarmouth, was dismissed in 1781. Rev. Caleb Jewett was ordained pastor of the Con. Society in Gorham, Nov. 5, 1783. Jewett gave no better satisfaction than Thacher and his predecessor, Lombard.

§Major George Lewis of Barnstable removed to Gorham. His second wife, Desire Parker, was a neighbor of Mrs. Jenkins before she removed from Barnstable.

settled till April 2, 1708, when an inventory thereof was made.

His house and lot were apprised at,	£8,00
A piece of land lying between the lands of Israel Garrett,	20,00
Lands above John Bodfish's,	16,00
Meadow adjoining Town Neck,	35,00
do.	37,00
	£116,00

All the real estate was assigned to Zachariah, he paying to the heirs of his brother Job Jenkins, deceased, £46, and to his sister, Elizabeth Jenkins, £52.

Zachariah married and had a large family. Job also married and had issue. Elizabeth had not married in 1708. She was then 59 years of age.

As this is not a Barnstable family I omit details. In the Cudworth article I referred to this John Jenkins. His history is an exceedingly interesting one. He was fined £19,10 shillings for refusing to take the oath of fidelity, attending quaker meetings, and other acts, involving no violation of the public peace, or any immorality. The law requiring all able to bear arms, to take the oath of fidelity, was an old law that had not, in 1658, been enforced for several years, but as Gen. Cudworth, Isaac Robinson, and others among the best men in the Colony averred, it was revived and used as a trap in which to catch some persons who had conscientious scruples against taking it. I reverence the character of the Pilgrim Fathers ; but I will not therefore palliate or excuse their faults. Their proceedings against Norton and other Quakers at Plymouth are justifiable in law, because the Quakers were the agressors. Norton would fare no better in a court of justice to-day, than he did in 1658. The Quakers at Sandwich were not generally the agressors. They asserted their rights as citizens, and subjects of the British realm. In ecclesiastical matters they adopted the same broad and tolerant views that the Pilgrim Fathers had always asserted and always maintained. They held that the conscience was free ; that man was not responsible to his fellow men in matters of faith, but to God alone. The fundamental principles of the Congregational or Puritan polity was, that a church should consist of as many members as could conveniently meet together to worship, and that when they had so met they had a right to elect their own teachers, elders and other officers. Those rights were denied to Sandwich Quakers. The history of John Jenkins, as found in the Colony records, in Bishop and other writers, exemplifies the persecuting spirit which had crept into the Colony in 1658, defacing the fair record of our fathers.

To pay the fines which Jenkins conscientiously believed to be

levied unjustly, and in a persecuting spirit, Barlow seized two
cows and one steer, valued at, sterling, £11,10,00
Money in the hands of James Skiff, due him for work, 8,00,00

£19,10,00

And the pot in which he boiled his victuals. When Barlow
took the pot Mrs. Jenkins threw down a piece of new cloth of
twice the value of the vessel, and begged him to take that, for, if
her kettle was taken, she could not cook for her family. Barlow
refused. In levying his warrant, he maliciously took such articles as would cause most distress in the family—the cows which
gave milk for the children, and the only iron vessel in the house.
At that time the local traders did not sell iron ware—a pot could
not be purchased without sending sixty miles to Boston. About
eighteen months after she bought one, meantime some kind neighbor lent her a kettle.

Aug. 17, 1658, a special term of the court was held at the
dwelling-house of Mr. Richard Bourne in Sandwich. Gov.
Prince, and Capt. Thomas Willet, Capt. Josias Winslow and Mr.
Thomas Hinckley, assistants, presided. Sundry of the ancient
inhabitants had petitioned the court that a special term be held in
Sandwich to inquire into and redress their grievances. It was
alleged that John Jenkins and eight others, all Quakers, had not
been legally admitted inhabitants. In reply John Jenkins plead,
"That though he had lived at Sandwich about ten years, and had
three children; and the very first year he came he was made a
Freeman, and had his voice in town meetings, and had Common
Privileges; yet he was now denied his share in Whale Oyl, which
as a Freeman fell to him." Barlow the constable interfered and
said, "He must not speak for he was no Freeman."

Jenkins in fact was not a freeman. He claimed to be a townsman, though in his defence, as reported by Bishop, he uses the
word freeman. The decision of the Court was that Jenkins and
the eight others "shall henceforth have noe power to vote in any
towne meeting till better evidence appear of their legall admittance, or to claime title or interest into any town privileges as
townsmen," according to an order of the Court dated third of
October, 1639. It was also ordered that thereafter no one "shall
be admitted an inhabitant of Sandwich or enjoy the privileges
thereof, without the approbation of the Church and of Mr. Thomas
Prence," or of one of the assistants.

By this decision about one-half of the Quakers in Sandwich
were disfranchised. Bishop refers to this meeting, and represents
it as very disorderly and turbulent. He however mixed up the
proceedings at two Courts, that of Aug. 27 and of Oct. 2, 1658.
He says Major Winslow "showed much Vehemence and Fierceness
of spirit against them; (the Quakers) sometimes starting up and

smiting the Table with his Stick, then with his Hand, then stamping with his Foot, like a Madman, saying he could not bear it,—Let them have the Strapado." The Court was governed in their decision by milder measures, yet more severe than the occasion required. Nine were disfranchised, and sixteen fined £5 each at the October Court, three of whom in addition were sentenced to imprisonment.

The authorities represented that the Quakers were not then the peacable and respectable people that they have been for the last century and a half; that they were disturbers of the public peace; and that they entered into the churches and claimed a right to bear testimony against the worshipers as corrupt and antichristian.

A careful analysis of all the facts, which I have not the time to make, will place the matter in its true light. Some few years since a friend sat as magistrate to try similiar cases. The accused were defended by able counsel, all the facts were clearly established by testimony, there was no controversy in regard to them, and the law applicable to the cases was clearly stated. At the conclusion of the trial, which continued two days, several were fined two dollars each and costs. They would not pay a cent. "They would sooner rot in jail." The friends of some of them paid their fines, others went to prison, one of whom was a mother with an infant child.

A censorious writer like Bishop might take the Barnstable case and magnify it, with as much apparent truthfulness, into one of extreme intolerance, persecution and cruelty. The question at issue in the Court held in Sandwich on the 29th of August, 1658, and at the Court held in Barnstable, were precisely of the same character, and involved the same principles of law. The Quakers at Sandwich justified their breaches of the peace by pleading conscientious scruples, and the liberty of speech. So did the Comeouters at Barnstable. The decision was acquiesced in by the prisoners and the people, and to this day, if the presiding magistrate wanted a favor, there are none to whom he could appeal with more confidence than to those whom he fined and sent to prison.

The decision at Sandwich was a fire-brand thrown into the community, stirring up the worst passions of the human heart, setting brother against brother, the son against the father, and the daughter against the mother.

The reason of this is apparent. Gov. Prince and Mr. Winslow were irritable; they could not patiently hear the enthusiastic, overbearing and ill-advised "testimonies" of the Quakers. They lost their temper, and with it the power to act prudently and discreetly. The imfamous Barlow at that time had an influence, and his taunting speeches irritated the Quakers and induced them to utter severe things against the Governor and Mr. Winslow. During the trial Capt. Willett and Mr. Hinckley, associate justices, sat quietly and took no offence. If the other gentlemen had done the same, it would have been better for themselves and for the people for whom they acted.

Mr. Winslow was an honorable man, and as soon as the irritation of the moment had passed, his good sense resumed its sway. Of those who had taken part in the proceedings against the Quakers, he was among the foremost to condemn the decisions of the Court and to restore those noble men who had been disfranchised because they resisted the intolerant spirit that spread through the Colony in 1657 and 8.

Many charge the churches with being the authors of the intolerant proceedings in Sandwich. Members of the churches as individuals acted, but not under the authority of the churches or as members. The Plymouth church does not appear to have acted, the Barnstable, Yarmouth and Eastham, certainly did not, and there is no recorded evidence that Mr. Leveridge's, at Sandwich, did. The presumption, however, is that the latter church did take action. There is evidence, however, that a portion of the members were opposed to the persecutors, and the factious spirit in his church compelled him to leave Sandwich.

That renegade Episcopal minister, the drunken and vile Barlow, soon lost his influence over the members of the Sandwich church, to which by pretended piety and zeal for its interests he had surreptitiously obtained admittance. After Mr. Leveridge left, the church, though divided into two factions, the Bourne and the Tupper, discarded the intolerant policy for which some of its members had become notorious. From one extreme they perhaps ran into the other. After several had preached on trial, Mr. John Smith of Barnstable, whose Catholic and tolerant principles had rendered him obnoxious to the majority in 1658, and who for the same cause in 1669 sold his estate in Barnstable and removed to New York, returned in 1671 and was soon after invited to become the pastor of the church in Sandwich, and was ordained. Thus in a term of less than twenty years, a complete revolution was effected in public opinion, and that town became one of the most quiet and orderly in the Colony.

The history of Sandwich from 1657 to the settlement of Mr. Smith is one of unsurpassed interest. Mr. Balies hardly refers to the Quaker troubles there, and Mr. Freeman after giving a few extracts from Bowden, a second hand authority, and not always accurate, slurs over the whole matter with the stale remark, "We weary by such recitals."*

---

*It would be difficult to decide which is the more objectionable, the bad grammar or the bad taste of this remark.

JONES.

———

Ralph Jones, the ancestor, was able to bear arms in Plymouth in 1643. He was of Barnstable in 1654, and settled at Scorton. His house stood on the main land within a few feet of the bounds of Sandwich. He was a farmer and owned lands with the Fuller families, with whom he was connected by marriage. In 1657 he was fined for not regularly attending meeting, not a very henious offence for a man who resided six miles from the place of worship. He afterwards became a zealous member of the Quaker society in Sandwich, and suffered persecution on that account. He does not appear to have been an early member, for in 1657 he took the oath of fidelity, which the Quakers uniformly declined to do. His absenting himself from the Barnstable Church, however, indicates that he early favored the Quakers, some of whom resided in his immediate vicinity.

In the Postscript to Bishop's New England Judged George Keith, in a reply to the marvels of Cotton Mather, tells a story about Ralph Jones, which is not entirely apochryphal. He says, "I shall only add one passage more, which I was informed of, and had it writ from some of the people of *Barnstable*, how that from an honest man, a *Quaker*, in the Town of *Barnstable*, were taken four cows, with some 'calves, the *Quaker's* name being *Ralph Jones*, who is yet alive; and these Cattle were taken away by the Preacher of that Town, his son-in-law, who had married his Daughter, and returned to the Priest as a part of his Wages. The Priest sent to *Ralph Jones* to tell him, *He might have two of his cows returned to him if he would send for them.* But he never sent, and so the said Priest used them and disposed of them as his own, killed one of the calfs, and sent a part of it to his Daughter, that lay in child-bed; she no sooner did eat a little of the Calf, but fell into great trouble and cryed, *Return home the man's Cows, I hear a great noise of them*; and so died in that Trouble. The Priest alledged, the *Quakers* had bewitched his Daughter, although it cannot be proved that ever they had any business with her. But to what evil construction will not Malice and Hypocrisie and Covetousness bend a Thing? Some time after the said Preacher killed some of these Cows to be eat in his house saying, *He would try if the Quakers would bewitch him* ; and not long after he died, even before the Flesh of these Cows was all eat. This passage is so fresh in that Town that it is acknowledged by divers of the neighbors to be true."

It is stated in a note in the margin that this "passage" was first published in London in 1693, and by Bishop in 1702, the date of the imprint of the edition from which I quote. Ralph Jones died in 1692, and as he was living at the time, it must have been written as early as that year. The facts are not clearly stated. At first reading, I understood the "passage" to mean that the "Priest" married a daughter of Ralph Jones, which was not the intention of the writer. He intended to say that Ralph Jones a quaker resident in Barnstable, had four cows and some calves taken by the constable to pay his ministerial tax. The officer was the son-in-law of the minister. The latter offered to give up two of the cows ; but Jones refused to send for them. Afterwards the minister killed one of the calves, and sent a part of it to his daughter, then lying in child-bed. She eat a little and fell into great trouble and desired her father to return the cows, and soon died in consequence of the eating of the veal. The minister charged the Quakers with having bewitched his daughter and caused her death. Some little time after the minister killed one of the cows to be eat in his house, saying, he would try if the Quakers could bewitch him. Before he had eaten all the flesh of the cow he fell sick and died.

This is the meaning of the "passage." It is in reply to the marvles recorded by Cotton Mather. The intention of the writer was to make it appear that the death of the daughter and of the father was a judgment of God.

Excepting the name of Ralph Jones, neither dates or names are given. This omission is ominous of evil intent, and if the story is a fabrication it is difficult, two centuries afterwards, to bring satisfactory evidence to prove it untrue, or that the circumstances in the case have been exaggerated.

After careful examination I am satisfied that the cows were taken in payment for taxes due from Ralph Jones by Dea. Job Crocker, son-in-law of Rev. Thomas Walley, and constable of the town of Barnstable in 1676. I regret that a man so excellent in all the relations of life as Dea. Crocker was, should have such things laid to his charge. As constable, he was obliged to serve the process and take the cows, and to that extent no blame attaches to him. The story says that his wife, who then laid on her death bed, requested that the cows should be returned, and her father, the Rev. Mr. Walley, offered to give up the two that legally belonged to him, the other two legally belonged to the country, and the constable had a right, I presume, to surrender those also.   Now if these are the facts, the refusal or neglect of Deacon Crocker in returning the cows is a blot on his fair fame.

The daughter died that year, and the father two years after. That their deaths were, as it is pretended, a judgment of God, to punish them for their guilt in being accessory to the taking of the cows is nonsense—as stupid as any of the marvels of the unseen world related by Cotton Mather—and in reply to which this and other equally absurd stories are printed by Bishop in his appendix to New England Judged.

There is another side to the story, I will not say the right side ; but it was this that had the support of the best legal talent of the times.   The lands in the Old Colony were granted to the churches, on the express condition that a learned and orthodox minister should be maintained in each town.   The ministerial tax was a lien upon the land, and the civil authorities, until that condition was changed, were bound to enforce it.   The rental of the Cape Cod fisheries was devoted to the maintenance of a free school, and he that hired a right to seine on the shore, might with the same show of equity refuse to pay the tax, because the school was established at Plymouth, and he was thus deprived of his share of the benefit.   The original owners of the lands and of the fishing privileges in the sale or lease imposed certain taxes on them, and the right of a Quaker or an Orthodox to complain is not apparent.   The policy of such taxation is another question.

Ralph Jones was as stiff-necked as Dea. Crocker.   When Mr. Walley informed him that he would not insist on his legal rights, and that he could take the two cows to which he was entitled, Jones said, "No, your son-in-law drove them away, now let him drive them back, I wont go after them."   Perhaps he was right, but a more conciliatory course would have exhibited a better spirit.

If four cows and their calves were taken to pay the tax, it was an exorbitant sum.   The market value at that time was about £4 sterling, or $20 for each or $80 for the whole.   Deducting one-half, the fine for not paying voluntarily, left the sum taxed $40 in silver money, equal to $120 at the present time.   Ralph Jones was not a man of wealth, and a part of his estate was taxable in Sandwich.   There were about one hundred tax payers in town at that time, and Jones' proportion of the gross sum raised to support the ministry would not be over the one hundredth part.   If his tax was £8 sterling the gross would be £800, a sum equal to the gross amount of Mr. Walley's salary during the sixteen years he was minister of Barnstable.   It is preposterous to believe that Jones was so taxed, yet this is a part of the story, and as much entitled to credence as the rest of it.

To aver that the death of Mr. Crocker and of Mr. Walley was a judgment of God, in punishment of a particular sin, is a palpable absurdity. The amount of the tax is exaggerated. It probably included his town and colony tax, and had probably been in arrears for a considerable time. Jones refused to pay, as others* at that time did because all the taxes were put on one list. Both parties were in the fault, and the one was as stubborn as the other was stiff necked.

None of the descendants of Ralph Jones have been distinguished in church or state, or for their great wealth. Like their ancestor, they belong to the middling class of honest, industrious farmers and mechanics.

In his will dated the 11th of the 3d month, 1691, and proved April 20, 1692, he says, "I, Ralph Jones, of ye town of Barnstable in New England, being aged and weak in body," disposes of his estate to his children. He does not name his wife, and the presumption is she had then deceased. He says, "My mind and desire is, that after my decease my body be decently buried by ye advice and assistance of my dear Friends ye people of God called Quakers at their burying place in Sandwich." He refers to meadow which his father Capt. Matthew Fuller bought of John Freeman, and names his seven sons, Shubael, Jedediah, Ralph, Samuel, Matthew, John and Ephraim, and his daughters Mercy, Mary and Mehitabel. He appoints his son-in-law John Fuller, the younger, and Edward Perry, the Quaker, overseers. The witnesses were Capt. Thomas Fuller, John Isum, and his daughter Mehitabel Fuller, wife of John Fuller, Jr. He signs with his mark, showing that though he might be able to read, he could not write. His daughter Mehitabel also signs "M," "her mark."

Ralph Jones being himself an unlearned man, and residing several miles from schools or churches, his family had no opportunity for acquiring even the rudiments of a good education. Among his neighbors there were, however, men of intelligence. The brothers Samuel and Matthew Fuller, the wayward Mr. Thomas Dexter, and Robert Harper, the stalwart Quaker, resided at Scorton, and their families were well educated for the times. Edward Perry and several of the early Quakers, earnest men of some intelligence, were also his neighbors.

Ralph Jones married April 17, 1650, Mary Fuller, daughter of Capt. Matthew Fuller, then of Plymouth. His older children were probably born in Plymouth, the earliest date on the Barnstable record being 27th Aug. 1654. I have carefully examined only the Barnstable records. From the Probate and the Sandwich records much information may be obtained by those who

---

*For particulars of the proceedings in collecting ministerial taxes see "Bourman Family." Soon after this time the laws were modified and made more liberal.

take an interest in the genealogy of the family. One peculiarity will be noticed. They remembered the cow story, and for several generations bore no love to the ministry, and very rarely invited the clergyman to solemnize a marriage.*

Children of Ralph Jones.

3. I. Mehitabel, born about the year 1651, probably at Plymouth. She married John Fuller, Jr., removed to East Haddam, Conn., had a large family, and have many descendants.
3. II. Matthew. (See below.)
4. III. Shubael, 27th Aug. 1654. He was living in 1692, and is named by Mr. Fessenden as resident in Sandwich.
5. IV. Jedediah, 4th Jan. 1656. (See below.)
6. V. John, 14th Aug. 1659. He was living in 1692. Removed from Barnstable.
7. VI. Mercy, 14th Nov. 1666.
8. VII. Ralph, 1st Oct. 1669. (See below.)
9. VIII. Samuel. (See below.)
10. IX. Ephraim.
11. X. Mary.

Matthew Jones, son of Ralph, owned Mr. Nathaniel Bacon's Great Lot at Cotuit, Oct. 16th, 1690, he exchanged this land for thirty acres on the west of John Dunham's land near Santuit.

He married 14th Jan. 1694-5, Mercy Goodspeed, a daughter of John, who resided at Mistic. She was then only fifteen years of age and was his second wife, if the records of the births of his children are accurately recorded. As he had children born in 1690, I call him the oldest son of Ralph, though he may have been younger than John. Early marriages were common in those times, yet better evidences than the arrangement of the names in the father's will is required to authorize stating that Matthew married at 18, and at 22 took a second wife who was only 15.

Children born in Barnstable.

12. I. Benjamin, 5th Jan. 1690, married Hannah Gifford Aug. 30, 1721. No record of his family appears. He was living in 1743, because Benjamin, son of Samuel, was then called the younger.

---

*Down to the present time this feeling has not been entirely eradicated, especially among the males. Simeon Jones, son of Isaac, born in 1728, resided in the high single house just within the bounds of Sandwich. Lemuel, son of Ralph, lived on Scorton Hill. When both had been drinking freely they resolved to swap estates, and deeds of exchange were drawn up and executed. This exchange made Simeon a Barnstable man, and liable to pay taxes to Mr. Shaw, though he pretended to be a Quaker. Simeon inherited the old family grudge against ministers, and could tell the cow story with some embelishments of his own. He was on friendly terms with Mr. Shaw, but would not attend his meetings. One year a few days before the annual Thanksgiving he dressed a fat turkey, which he took to Mr. John Bursley's and said send Heman with that turkey to Mr. Shaw. Tell the boy to ask Mr. Shaw if he wanted the turkey. He did so. Mr. Shaw said he did not wish to take it. But, said Herman, Mr. Simeon Jones. Oh, that alters the case, said Mr. S. Tell Mr. Jones I am very much obliged to him—and here my boy is a penny for you.

13. II. Ralph, 5th Jan. 1692, married Abigail Linnell March 17, 1721.
14. III. Experience, 1st March 1697.
15. IV. Josiah, 14th June, 1702.
16. V. Ebenezer, 6th June, 1706, married Hannah Jones March 1, 1732.

Jedediah Jones, son of Ralph, married Hannah Davis 18th March, 1681-2.

Children born in Barnstable.

17. I. Shubael, 17th July, 1683. Jan. 12, 1744, a Shubael Jones, Jr., married Mary Allen. This indicates that Shubael, son of Jedediah, was then living. He had a daughter Catharine May 19, 1744.
18. II. Simon, 5th April, 1685. Dr. Simon Jones married Hannah Atkins March 3, 1735.
19. III. Isaac, April, 1790, married Patience ———, and had Lydia Feb. 24, 1711-12; Jedediah, April 1, 1714, married Mary or Mariah Fuller of Sandwich, April 14, 1737, and had Nye and other children; Patience, Feb. 10, 1717-18; Isaac, June 16, 1720, married Mercy Goodspeed Feb. 22, 1751-2, and had Timothy, Patience, Susannah, Abner, Goodspeed and Lydia; Sarah, Oct. 1, 1724; Simon, Ap. 11, 1728, married Hannah 1751, and had Joseph, Mariah, Jedediah, Simon, Asa and Hannah; and Micah, Aug. 30, 1732.
20. IV. Timothy, May, 1692, married Elizabeth Jones, June 9, 1720.
21. V. Hannah, Sept. 1694.

Ralph Jones, son of Ralph, had,

22. I. Deborah, March, 1696.
23. II. Elizabeth, 25th Nov. 1698.
24. III. Thankful, 12th April, 1701, married May 23, 1745, Timothy Hallett of Yarmouth.
25. IV. Bethia, 9th April, 1706.
26. V. Cornelius, 30th July, 1709. He was of Sandwich and married July, 1736, Hannah Percival of Barnstable.

Samuel Jones, son of Ralph, married Mary Blish 26th June, 1718.

Children born in Barnstable.

27. I. Joseph, June 9, 1719.
28. II. Benjamin, July 14, 1721, married Grace Hoxy of Sandwich Nov. 17, 1743, and had Saul Jan. 16, 1743-4; Mary, June 19, 1745; David, Aug. 6, 1747; and Joseph, July 14, 1752.
29. III. Samuel, April 4, 1723.
30. IV. Mary, April 13, 1727.

In addition to the above there was a Reuben Jones who married July 26, 1739, Sarah Percival, then of Sandwich, and had Deliverance Oct. 6, 1736, and Ephraim June 20, 1745.

An Adams Jones married Mary Baker Oct. 26, 1699. Ebenezer Fuller married Martha Jones Jan. 1, 1725. David Smith married Abigail Jones Aug. 13, 1726. Ebenezer Jones married Hannah Jones March 1, 1732. (Abigail and Hannah were married by Mr. Russell, and are the only ones of the name of Jones that I find on record who were married by a clergyman.) Reuben Meigs married Rebecca Jones Oct. 10, 1732. John Jones, Jr., married Thankful Jones, of Sandwich, Sept. 22, 1733. Michael Hammet married Hannah Jones Dec. 1, 1737.

These records indicate that there were several families of the name, to which no reference is made in this genealogy.

JACKSON.

Was one of the first settlers in Barnstable. Mr. Deane says that he removed from Plymouth to Scituate. He joined Mr. Lothrop's church Feb. 25, 1637-8, and came to Barnstable in October, 1639. He built his house on the second lot east of Calves Pasture Lane, which contained eight acres, and is now owned by the heirs of Thomas and Benjamin Allyn. On his removal from Barnstable in 1647, he sold his houselot to Capt. Samuel Mayo who resold it to Mr. Thomas Allyn, whose descendants are the present owners.

Feb. 23, 1644-5, he was "excommunicated and cast out of ye church for Lyeing and sundry suspitions of stealing, as pinnes which were John Russell's and divers other things from others."

Jan. 31, 1646-7, "he acknowledged his evils, renewed his covenant, and was again received into church fellowship."

Feb. 10, at night, 1646-7. Removed from Barnstable "to live at Scituate beeing necessitated thereunto."

He married twice ; his first wife died of consumption at Scituate March 4, 1638. He married Nov. 20, 1639, Hester, daughter of Dea. Richard Sealis of Scituate, and a niece of Mr. Timothy Hatherly. After the death of his father-in-law "he succeeded to his residence." His son Jonathan was a soldier in Phillips' war, and received a grant of land for his services. Jonathan had an only son Jonathan born in 1685, and daughters Sarah and Hannah. The second Jonathan married twice and had a daughter Sarah born in 1730, and Jonathan born in 1733. Jonathan third married in 1757 and had several children, among whom was the late Roland of Scituate, and Dea. Ward of Boston.

Samuel Jackson was a freeman of the Colony in 1644, and died in 1682, aged 72 years.

His children were:

I. Ann, baptized in Scituate March 25, 1638, that being the first day of the year old style. It is stated in the record that she was then two or three years old, and if Mr. Deane is accurate she was probably born in Plymouth.

Born in Barnstable.

II.   Bethia, bap. March 14, 1640-1.
III. Hester, bap. Feb. 5, 1642-3.
IV.   Samuel, bap. Feb. 7, 1646-7.   Samuel was born in 1645 or
      6, during the time his father was an excommunicant.   In the
      church records the death of Samuel is entered as having oc-
      curred soon after his baptism.   This is probably the fact,
      though the entry is crossed out in the record.
V.   Jonathan.   This son was probably born in 1647 at Scituate,
      and is the only child named by Deane who survived the
      father.

As short as this family sketch is, it is perhaps the fullest and most accurate of the series.   For four successive generations there was only one male in each.   Eleven names occur in the four generations.   In the Crocker genealogy 143 persons are named in the corresponding number of generations ; and the list is probably incomplete.

LEWES.

George Lewes, the ancestor of the Barnstable family, came from East Greenwich, in the County of Kent, England. He was by trade a clothier, and though called of East Greenwich, circumstances make it probable that he was for a time a resident in London and a member of Mr. Lothrop's church in 1632. He married about the year 1626, Sarah Jenkins, a sister of Edward, who afterwards was a resident in Scituate. He probably did not come over till after the church in London was broken up, and the imprisonment of Mr. Lothrop in 1632. He was of Plymouth in the following year, and though a member of the church there, his name does not appear on the tax lists of 1633 or of 1634. Though not a man of wealth, he was liable to pay at least a poll tax. The omission of his name can be accounted for only on the supposition that he was taxed as one of "Mr. Hatherlies men." That gentleman was benevolent and assisted many worthy men to come to New England, and, after their arrival, he assisted them in procuring employment and comfortable homes. Goodman Lewis' name is often associated with Mr. Hatherly's on the records, and he was probably indebted to that gentleman for assistance.

George Lewes was one of those who were dismissed from the church in Plymouth in 1634, "in case they join in a body at Scituate." He became a member at Scituate Sept. 30, 1635, eight months after the organization of the church. It is presumed that those who were thus dismissed on the arrival of Mr. Lothrop, had been members of his church in London and were desirous to reunite with their former brethren in church-state, and again listen to the teachings of their aged and revered pastor.*

Before October, 1636, Goodman Lewes had built a house on Kent street, in Scituate, so named because the residents thereon

---

*The Rev. Hiram Carleton examined this subject with much care. He consulted our early church records, Neal, Crosby, and other reliable authorities. He made out a strong case, showing that the leading members of the London, Scituate and Barnstable churches were the same persons. The records of the London church cannot be found. The London church was broken up as I have stated—the Scituate church was not a continuation, or removal of the London. Mr. Lothrop certainly was of this opinion when he declined to partake of the sacrament with the Boston church, giving as a reason that he did not at the time of his arrival consider himself a member of a particular church.

came from that county, and were known as "the men of Kent."
His lot was the first south of Meeting House Lane and contained
five acres, and his house built thereon stands No. 18 on Mr. Lothrop's list of the houses built in that town.*

On the removal of Goodman Lewes in 1639 to Barnstable, he
sold to Richard Willis of Plymouth, his dwelling house and lot
containing five acres, one acre and three-fourths of swamp, and
three acres of marsh ground, and his right to commonage ("to be
procured by all good wayes and meanes, suite of law excepted")
for the sum of £19 sterling. Willis sold the same to Thomas
Robers, for £21,10s sterling. The memorandum of these two
trades is embodied in one instrument dated Jan. 9, 1639-40.
Prior to this date formal deeds were rarely executed, a memorandum of the sale was made on the records, and the same was held
to be binding in law. Rev. John Lothrop's deed of his estate in
Scituate, dated in 1640, is one of the earliest formal deeds on
record.

George Lewes's home lot in Barnstable was the second west
of the Hyannis road. The lands on the south side of the highway, between that road and Freeman Hinckley's or old Court
House Lane, was divided into five houselots of eight acres each,
or four between Hyannis Road and the Railroad Avenue. Mr.
Nathaniel Holmes and his sons are the present owners of the
Lewes lot. He also owned an acre of meadow on the opposite
side of the highway, with the high hill on the north, still known
as Lewes hill. He had ten acres of land in the old common field,
now owned by Solomon Hinckley and Alvan Howes, and four
acres of marsh at Sandy Neck.

His lots were as good planting lands as any in the east parish. "Ulti ma die Januarii, 1654"-5, he sold these four parcels
of real estate in Barnstable, with his dwelling-house, to Samuel
Mayo for £28 5 shillings sterling. His deeds, recorded in the
town records, has an historical interest. Mayo conveyed the
property to John Phinney, and he to Elder Henry Cobb, and
other members of the church for a parsonage, and to induce Rev.
Wm. Sergeant to make Barnstable his permanent place of residence. As these conveyances are quoted in full in the account of
Mr. Sergeant it is unnecessary to repeat them in this connection.

He owned three acres and a half of meadow at Mystic Landing granted to him by the town July 26, 1654. This he sold May
27, 1661, to John Thompson.

His great lot is thus described on the records: "Sixty acres
of upland more or less lyeing by ye pond commonly called Rowley's pond, at ye easterly end thereof, running 80 rods easterly,

*There were two of the name of Lewes in Scituate, George and John. Mr. Deane calls
them brothers. Mr. Lothrop distinguished them as Goodman Lewis senior, and Goodman
Lewis junior. In these extracts I have presumed that George was the elder.

and 120 southerly and northerly, that is to say, from outside to outside."

This tract of land he sold to his sons Edward and John in 1652 and some part of it is yet owned by his descendants. Whether George Lewis ever resided on this land I am not informed. His son Edward's house stood on the northeast of the pond, called at first Rowley's, then Lewes's, and now Hathaway's pond.

In 1654, before the sale of his estate to Samuel Mayo, Goodman Lewes had "let and farmed for some certain years" the estate of Mr. Dimmock, whose health was feeble. It appears that he occupied for a number of years the ancient fortification house, of which an account has been given. Mr. Dimmock owned another estate at West Barnstable, a short distance east of Anthony Annable's, where he probably resided at that time.

George Lewes was admitted a freeman of the Colony Jan. 14, 1636-7. His early admission shows that he was a man in good standing and had been known by the colonists before he came over. At that time there were few flocks of sheep in this colony, and in no town was there sufficient business to give employment to a clothier. Necessity compelled him to become a planter. Being poor, a servant's share of five acres was allotted to him in the division of the lands at Scituate—a quantity insufficient for the raising of stock product for which there was a good demand at remunerative prices. Elisha, the prophet, had twelve yoke of oxen hitched to his plow, when Elijah met him as the bearer of a mission from the Most High. He must have had a more ample field in which to turn than our fathers allotted to their servants.

However industrious and prudent a man may be, the income to be derived from five acres of land, in a new country, would be insufficient to furnish a family with the necessaries of life. In a country where land was so abundant it would seem a short sighted policy thus to limit the quantity allotted to settlers. They had been accustomed to live in villages, and the force of habit had an influence, and many circumstances peculiar to the times demanded that the settlements should not be too widely extended. Compact settlements could be more readily defended against hostile attacks of the Indians, and all would be nearer to "the mill, the market, and the meeting."*

Passages like the following from the Colony records are often read with incredulous eyes:

January 1, 1637-8, Mr. Timothy Hatherly, Rev. John Lothrop, and others of Scituate, "complained that they had such small proportions of land there allotted to them that they could not sub-

---

*I find this expressive alliteration in the Yarmouth Records.

sist upon them," and the Court on their petition granted them the lands between the north and south rivers, on the condition that they make a township there, settle all differences between them and Mr. Vassal, and maintain a ferry over the north river. These conditions were not complied with. It seems singular to have a complaint of want of room at that early period. The same territory now supports ten times as many people, and we have no complaint that "the place is too straite for them."

The raising of stock, as above remarked, was then the most profitable business of the farmer, and they required much land for pasturage, and extensive salt meadows, from which to procure forage for their cattle. It was the extensive salt meadows, and the facilities for raising stock, that induced Mr. Lothrop and his church to remove to Mattakeese, rather than to Sipican as they first proposed.

Goodman Lewes was seldom employed in public business. In 1648 and '50 he was surveyor of highways, in 1649 a juryman, and in 1651 constable of the town of Barnstable.

He wrote his name Lewes. On the Colony records it is sometimes written Lewes, sometimes Lewis. His sons and grandsons spelled their name with two e's, and it is so uniformly written in the early town and church records. After 1700 some wrote the name Lewis, and during the last century that has become the uniform orthography. In this article I spell the name as I find it.

There was a George Lewes at Casco in 1640. Mr. Willis supposes he was a son of George of Barnstable. Mr. Savage, however, shows conclusively that he was another man. In 1649 there was a George Lewes and a Richard Foxwell at Scarborough. Mr. Deane supposes they were Barnstable men. Foxwell certainly was not. George Lewes, Senior, was an inhabitant of Barnstable June, 1655, and in 1661. There is no evidence that he left Barnstable. It is possible that he may have been of Scarborough in 1659, but it is not probable that so aged a man removed to the eastern country. His son George was an inhabitant of Barnstable in 1659. I am of the opinion that George of Casco was afterward of Scarboro', and the records decidedly favor that opinion.

Mr. Deane says George Lewis had sons Nathaniel, 1645, and Joseph, 1647, born in Barnstable. These names do not occur in the town or church records, nor in the will of Goodman Lewes, though he names all his other children. He also says that Thomas, son of George, removed from Barnstable to Swansey, and there had Samuel 1672, and Hepsibah 1674, and that Joseph of Hingham was son of George. These errors have been copied and perpetuated by the many who have undertaken to write the genealogy of the Lewis family.

The identity of the names in the families of George Lewes of

Barnstable, and Edmund Lewes of Lynn, misled Mr. Deane*; and, subsequent writers, with the exception of Mr. Savage, adopted his errors, without a critical examination. However careful a writer may be, mistakes cannot always be avoided. The records are imperfect, and the entries are not always reliable, and in every generation there will be some Sarahs and some Methuselahs who set at defiance the general laws of life. For assistance in correcting the errors of Mr. Deane, I am largely indebted to Hon. Solomon Lincoln of Hingham, and to Hon. James Savage of Boston, to the latter for facts obtained by him since the publication of his Dictionary.

George Lewes was not one of the distinguished men of his times. "He was an honest *Goodman*, and got his living by his labor." He was a sincere christian, and his constant purpose seems to have been to live in peace with all men—to avoid suits at law, to yield rather than contend with his neighbor. He was not a shrewd business man, and perhaps not so careful a manager as many. He did not hold that "the chief end of man is to gather up riches"; but to do good, to train up his children in the way they should go, to be useful citizens—honest and industrious men. His son James was a man of more energy of character, of more business tact, and became a distinguished man. Thomas was in some respects like his brother James. The other sons, George, Edward and John, were like the father—good, honest men—quiet and respectable citizens, and their descendants to this day inherit the same good qualities.

George Lewes, clothier, from East Greenwich, County of Kent, England, married first in England Sarah Jenkins, who came over with him, and here died. He married second Mary† ———, living in 1670, whose family name is not known. He died in Barnstable in 1662 or 3. His older children were born in England, and no record of their births having been preserved, the arrangement of their names is problematical.

1. I. Mary, born in England about the year 1623, married Nov. 16, 1643, John Bryant of Scituate, and died before 1657, leaving a family of seven children.

3. II. Thomas, born in England, married June 15, 1653, Mary Davis, daughter of Dolar. Thomas removed to Falmouth, was proprietor's clerk, and a prominent man there.

4. III. George, born in England, perhaps the older of the family, married Dec. 1, 1654, Mary, daughter of Barnard

---

*It is not easy to establish a negative proposition; but he that carefully compares the genealogy of the families of Edmund Lewes of Lynn, and of George Lewes of Barnstable, will be satisfied that Mr. Deane erred in the particulars I have referred to.

†A deed of George Lewes dated in 1654 is signed by "Mary," his wife. I do not know that this justifies me in calling her a second wife. In early times many names were held to be synonyms—thus Sarah and Mary—Elizabeth, Eliza, Betsey—Abigail, Nabby, Abiah. Some names were applied to males or females, namely: Love, Experience, Hope, Melatiah, Abiel, &c.

Lumber, died 20th March, 1709-10.

5. IV. James, born in 1631, in England, married Oct. 31, 1655, Sarah Lane, daughter of George of Hingham, died Oct. 4, 1713, aged 82 yrs.

6. V. Edward, probably born in England, married 9th May, 1661, Hannah Cobb, daughter of Elder Henry. He died March 29, 1703. She died Jan. 17, 1729-30, aged 90 years, 3 months, 12 days.

7. VI. John, born in Scituate March 2, 1637-8, baptized March 11, 1637-8, an inhabitant of Barnstable 1670, killed at the Rehobeth battle March 26, 1676.

8. VII. Ephraim, born in Barnstable July 23, 1641, baptized July 25, 1641. He was living in 1663, but there is no notice of him after. He was probably dead in 1670.

9. VIII. Sarah, born in Barnstable Feb. 2, 1643-4, baptized Feb. 11, 1643-4, married 1st James Cobb, 26th Dec. 1663, and 2d Jonathan Sparrow, Esq., of Eastham. She died in Barnstable "Feb. 11, 1735, in the 92d year of her age," as recorded on her grave stones, according to the town records 92 years and 9 days.

Mr. Deane says he also had Nathaniel 1645, and Joseph 1647. Neither the town colony or church records, confirm this statement. Mr. Savage rejects this addition but gives him a son Jabez, who died unmarried. His authority I do not find.

(3.) Thomas Lewes, son of George, was born in England about the year 1628. He came over with his father when a child of four years, residing about three years in Plymouth, then removed with his father to Scituate, and from thence to Barnstable in 1639. His education was obtained in the new settlements, before public schools had been established. Generally the children of the first comers were better educated than the succeeding generations. The ministers of religion had, at that time, small parishes and smaller salaries, and necessity compelled them to resort to other employment. Many of the early pastors were physicians, and nearly all of them taught a school in the winter, and cultivated their farms in the summer. All of George Lewes's children excepting George were well educated for the times.

In the investigation of the history of Thomas Lewes, I have been aided by Thomas Lewis, Jr., Esq., and S. P. Bourne, Esq., of Falmouth. The colonial records, the town and church of Barnstable and of Falmouth, the Probate and the records of the proprietors of Suckenessett have been carefully examined. The result of the investigation is this, he was a son of George Lewes, married and lived in Barnstable as stated, and died in Falmouth after 1703, but these records fail to show where he resided from 1670 to 1677. This gap covers the period when Mr. Deane says he was at Swansea, was Selectman, &c., and had by wife Hannah, Samuel, 23d April, 1673, and Hepsibah 15th Nov. 1674. Mr. Deane's statement of his removal to Swansea is apparently right; but there are other records and other conflicting facts. Thomas Lewis of Lynn, son of Edmund, whose wife was Hannah Baker, removed to Swansea about 1670. I have not space to state all the facts. The evidence in my judgment is conclusive, that Thomas Lewis of Swansea was a son of Edmund of Lynn. The subsequent history of his family is known—he was not a son of George of Barnstable.

Thomas Lewis, son of George, resided in Barnstable till 1662, and probably till 1668, for he was in June that year qualified as one of the surveyors of highways. In 1654, the year after his marriage, he owned the easterly part of his father's houselot, adjoining the lot of John Davis. "Quinque Die, April 1656," he bought for £20 the ancient tavern and twelve acre houselot of Thomas Lumbart, Senior, bounded westerly by the lot of Mr. Robert Linnell, northerly by the harbor, and easterly by the lands of Thomas and Joseph Lothrop. This old tavern, the first built in Barnstable, stood on the houselot now owned by the heirs of Ezra Crowell, deceased. He had not sold this estate in April, 1661. June 1, 1658, he was admitted a freeman of the Colony, and his name is on the lists of the freemen of Barnstable, up to June 4, 1686, when Suckenesset was incorporated as a town.

He was not one of the original proprietors of Suckenesset, and was not admitted an inhabitant resident in that plantation till 1668.* He was clerk of the proprietors from July 1685 to March 26, 1691, and probably for a much longer period. July 23, 1677, he had lands alloted to him at Little Neck, near Wood's Hole. On that lot he had a dwelling-house, which he sold with the land Feb. 25, 1689-10, to Jonathan Hatch, Senior, of "Sacknesset," for "ten shillings in silver money." The deed is in the handwriting of "Thomas Lewes, Senior," witnessed by "Samuel Ganson and Matthew Price," and was acknowledged before Col. John Thacher of Yarmouth, justice of the peace, Dec. 17, 1703, nearly fourteen years after it was dated. The lot is described as No. 4 of the Little Neck lots, and as extending "across the Neck to the Great Horbour, so called."

The handwriting indicates that he was a ready penman, and it can be easily read by persons familiar with manuscripts of that date. Few errors occur in the spelling, and the conditions of the grant are clearly stated. The small sum named as purchase money, perhaps

---

*Since writing this I find some evidence that he was of Barnstable in the early part of the year 1668, consequently removed that year. All the original proprietors at Suckenesset were not residents. At least one-half of the original grantees were non-resident proprietors. Before Suckenesset was incorporated, June 4, 1686, strictly speaking, all the inhabitants were townsmen of Barnstable, and by admitting an inhabitant at Suckenesset, strictly speaking, was only an admission that the party had become a proprietor by purchase or otherwise.

indicates that it was deed of release or exchange, but there is nothing in the terms of the sale that justifies that conclusion.*

Thomas Lewes, son of George, born in England, married June 15, 1653, Mary, daughter of Dolar Davis.

Children born in Barnstable.

10. I. James, 31st March, 1654. (See No. 10.)
11. II. Thomas, 15th July, 1656. (See No. 11.)
12. III. Mary, 2d Nov. 1659.
13. IV. Samuel, 14th May, 1662. Samuel Lewis resided in Falmouth—a prominent man of his time—a surveyor of lands—moderator at town meetings, Selectman, &c., &c. I do not find that he married and had a family, neither do I find when he died. He probably removed from Falmouth.

Benjamin,† probably a son of Thomas, married Sept. 8, 1702, Elizabeth Crow of Yarmouth, resided in Falmouth, and had Judah, June 4, 1703; Elizabeth Jan. 17, 1705. His wife Elizabeth died March 8, 1706-7, and he married 2d June, 1708, Hannah, daughter of Ensign John Hinckley of Barnstable, and had Samuel June 4, 1709, and Bethia Feb. 11, 1710-11. After this date his name disappears. The ages of his two wives make it probable that Benjamin was born before 1670.

Cornelius Lewes of Falmouth, married Sarah [Green] Jan. 19, 1726-7, and had Micajah Oct. 25, 1727; a daughter Feb. 25, 1729; Elijah, May 14, 1730. Who this Cornelius was I cannot determine.

George Lewes, son of George, was a planter, and resided in the East Parish in Barnstable. He was not so well educated as others of the family, and had not the active business capacity of his brother James or Thomas; yet he was honest and industrious, a good neighbor, and a worthy member of the church. His house stood on the south side of the highway, on the lot of land recently owned by Mr. Daniel Cobb, deceased. His houselot, containing five acres, with a barn standing thereon, he bought Sept. 10, 1656, of Barnard and Joshua Lumbard. It was bounded north by the highway, east by the great lot of Thomas Lumbard, south and west by the land of Barnard Lumbard. This was originally the land of Joshua Lum-

---

*In this deed he writes his name Lewes, and his son James, and Benjamin of Falmouth, in a deed dated Oct. 17, 1700, spell their names in the same manner.

†There is scarce room for doubt that Benjamin Lewes was a son of Thomas. I do not give him a serial number, because there is no recorded evidence that he was such. His age, the ages of his wives, and the names of his children, indicate that he was. Thomas' descendants appear to have removed from Falmouth before 1720. The present families trace their lines of descent from three if not four different branches of the Barnstable family. 1, Lothrop; 2, Ebenezer; 3, David; 4, Robinson. The descendants of Nathan, Isaac and George, who removed to Falmouth earlier, seem to have disappeared.

Truth also seems to require me to give Hannah Hinckley in marriage to Benjamin Lewes of Falmouth instead of the man of the same name in Barnstable. Such mistakes are unavoidable, and in this case it destroys all the pretty stories I have told of the honorable descent of Liza Townhill the reputed witch.

bard and the lot contained six acres, one acre in the sale to Lewes (where Nathaniel Gorham's barn now stands) being reserved.

His farm was on the north side of the road. In 1654 he had sixteen acres bounded west by the road to the new common field, north partly by the land of Goodman Wells, and the Indian reservation, and easterly by the land of Thomas Huckins, at the "Horse Prison," so called.

May 19, 1656, he bought for £20 the dwelling-house and sixteen acres of land of Robert Shelly, bounded east by the road to the new common field, south by the highway, west by the Dimmock farm, and north by the land of Goodman Isaac Wells. By the purchase of the Shelly estate his farm extended on the County road from a point a little east of the present dwelling-house of Mr. W. W. Sturgis to the Horse Prison, which stood near the dwelling-house of Edward Gorham, deceased.

Beside the above he owned two lots of three acres each at Sandy Neck, and his share in the common lands. Jan. 16, 1683, he sold one-half of one of the above lots at Sandy Neck to his brother James for one good cow, meadow then being more highly valued than at present.

Dec. 1, 1654, he married Mary, daughter of Barnard Lumbard, a girl of 14 years. He died 20th March, 1709-10, aged about 80 years.

Children born in Barnstable.

14.   I. George, Sept. 1655, married Elizabeth ————. (See No. 14.)
14.   1-2.   Mary, 9th May, 1657.
15.   III.   Sarah, 12th Jan. 1659-60.
16.   IV.   Hannah, July, 1662, died 1667.
17.   V.   Melatiah, 23d Jan. 1664, married Edward Gray of Yarmouth, July 16, 1684, his second wife.
18.   VI.   Bathshua, Oct. 1667, married John O. Kelley 10th Aug. 1690.
19.   VII.   Jabez, 10th June, 1670. (See No. 19.)
20.   VIII.   Benjamin, 22d Nov. 1678. (See No. 20.)
21.   IX.   Jonathan, 25th July, 1674. (See No. 21.)
22.   X.   John, 1st Dec. 1676.
23.   XI.   Nathan, 26th July, 1678. (See No. 23.)
24.   XII.   Thankful, bap. 17th Sept. 1683, married Samuel Look Oct. 19, 1704.

(5.) Lieut. James Lewes, son of George, was born in England in 1631. He was a boy of eight years when he came to Barnstable. James appears to have improved every opportunity for acquiring knowledge. The boy was the father of the man ; honest, intelligent and industrious. At that time no public schools had been

established ; but a majority of the first settlers were well educated,
and intelligent—men of large and varied experience in the business
of life. The duty of educating their children, they held to be second
only in importance to their duty to their God. No town in New
England was settled by a more religious, a more virtuous, or a more
intelligent population than Barnstable. In such a community, the
boy who desired knowledge, had ample opportunities to acquire it.
He had to toil early and late, but the long winter evenings he devoted to learning. Around the spacious kitchen fireplace, brilliantly
lighted by pine torches, the village youth would often cluster, with
their books and their slates, eager in the pursuit of knowledge. The
parent, or perhaps the pastor of the church, was their teacher. In
this manner many acquired an education sufficient to fit them for the
business of life.

When a lad James was bound an apprentice to a blacksmith,
and in after life, when he had become a distinguished man, he
thought it not derogatory to his character to blow the bellows, or
swing the hammer. He was industrious and frugal. When he
could not earn a shilling he was content if he earned a penny which
he put to a good use. By careful management he accumulated, a
good estate.

In the Goodspeed article there is a diagram of his houselots.
In 1655 his houselot, containing twelve acres, was the lot on the
west of Taylor's lane, now owned by the heirs of F. W. Crocker,
Esq., deceased. To whom this lot was assigned at the settlement of
the town I am unable to state. It remains very nearly in the same
condition that it was in 1655. The successive owners have been
James Lewes, his son George Lewes, who bequeathed it to his
daughter Mercy Taylor, and she to her daughter Alice, wife of the
late Capt. Isaac Bacon. From him it passed into the hands of Mr.
——— Williams of Boston, in payment of a debt of Isaac Bacon,
Jr. Williams sold it to the late David Crocker, Esq,

In 1655 this lot was bounded on the west by the Wid. Mary
Hallett, and in 1668 by her son-in-law John Hathaway who had
bought of his brother-in-law Josiah Hallett. John and Josiah
started in life about the same time that James did, and imagined
they were born to be rich. They frequented the taverns, acquired
bad habits, and to pay their bills sold from time to time their paternal estates. James, by his industry and frugality, laid aside sufficient to purchase all their uplands, meadows, and rights to the commons. In 1678 he was the owner of all the lands between Taylor's
lane and the Hyannis road, excepting the lands of John Davis on the
southwest corner.

In 1655 he owned three acres of planting land in the old common field, and three acres of meadow at Sandy Neck. January 29,
1667-8, three acres of land on the south of his houselot was granted
to him by the town. Subsequently he purchased other real estate.

At the division of the common lands in 1703, he was entitled to 48 3-4 shares, considerably more than an average. He had then distributed a large part of his estate to his children.

In 1655 his house was on the lot adjoining Taylor's lane. By the purchase of the Hallett lands he became possessed of John Hathaway's house, which stood on a cross road now discontinued, and the ancient Roger Goodspeed house. This house is now standing, if it be justifiable so to speak of a building that has suffered so many transformations. In the record of the laying out of the County road in 1686 the record says, after passing the house of John Davis, Sen., "up ye hill called Cob's hill, by the house and shop of Lieut. James Lewes, on south side of sd way, too narrow at his barn three foot, and so sd road lying near ye house of Wid. Bacon on ye north side of sd way." The obvious meaning of this passage is that Lieut. James Lewis' house was near Cob's hill and west of the Wid. Bacon's ; if so, he then occupied the Goodspeed house, and his shop stood on where the Custom House now stands, on the corner of the old way connected with the road called Goodspeed's outlet.

No man in Barnstable brought up his family better than Lieut. Lewes. All of his ten children were well educated for the times, and all became useful and respectable men and women. The secret of his success in life is quickly told—he never neglected his business. Every year he added a field to his estate, and though one of the most generous of fathers, he ranked among the wealthy in 1703. His son Ebenezer, to whom he had transferred the old Goodspeed estate, was equally wealthy, and for his other sons he had liberally provided.

Jan. 18, 1699, Capt. Joseph Lothrop, aged about 75, Mr. John Howland, aged about 77, and Lieut. James Lewes, aged 68, old men, all June 18th, saith the record, joined the church in Barnstable.

He was admitted a freeman of the Colony June 1, 1658. His name often appears as a juror, and surveyor of highways. He was lieutenant of the military company of Barnstable many years, and probably a soldier in Philip's war, for his heirs were proprietors of Gorham town. He was one of the Selectmen in 1679, '81, '89, and '90.

The will of Lieut. James Lewes, Sen., is dated May 8, 1713, proved Oct. 17, 1713. To his son George Lewes he gives "one-half of my dwelling-house and barn, and one-half of lands thereunto adjoining," and he confirms his former deed of gift of the other half. He also names his sons Ebenezer, Samuel, James, John and Joseph, and his four daughters, Sarah Waterman, Susanna Beals, Mary Linkhorn, and Hannah Lumbard. He appoints as his executors his four sons, Samuel, James, George and Ebenezer.

Lieut. James Lewes, son of George, married Oct. 31, 1655,

Sarah Lane, daughter of George of Hingham. He died Oct. 4, 1713, aged 82.

Children born in Barnstable.

25. I. John, Oct. 29, 1656, baptized by Mr. Hobart of Hingham. (See below.)
26. II. Samuel, 10th April, 1659. (See 28.)
27. III. Sarah, 4th March, 1660-1, married Jan. 6, 1685, Thomas Lincoln, and 2d Robert Waterman.
28. IV. James, 3d June, 1664. (See below.)
29. V. Ebenezer, 20th Dec. 1666, admitted an inhabitant of Barnstable, 1691. (See 29.)
30. VI. George, 1673. (See 30.)
31. VII. Joseph, born 1676. (See 31.)
32. VIII. Susannah, married Lazarus Beals of Hingham.
33. IX. Mary, married Benjamin Lincoln Jan. 17, 1694.
34. X. Hannah, married Jediah Lumbard Nov. 8, 1699.

(6.) Edward Lewes, son of George, resided at Rowley's pond, now known as Hathaway's pond. His house stood in the field near the northeast corner of the pond. Jan. 12, 1662-3, George Lewes, Sen., and Geo. Lewes, Jr., had the great lot of the father, by a joint deed to Edmund Lewes and his brother John Lewes. Edmund had the northerly part, containing 27 1-2 acres. No house is named in the deed, and the presumption is that it was built by Edward. In 1697 Edward Lewes and his sons Ebenezer, John and Thomas, are called South Sea men, and their proportions of the common meadows in the first and second divisions thereof were set off to them in the easterly part of the Wequaquet meadows. The families of Edward Lewes, Dolar Davis, (son of John) and John Linnel, were connected by intermarriages, and their lands and meadows at the South Sea adjoined. In consequence of the destruction of the records of deeds it is difficult to trace the ownership of real estate. I find by the tax lists* of 1737 and 8, that although these families were called South Sea residents, they were assessed as belonging to the district on the north side of the town, not with Hyannis or Wequaquet. I am inclined to the opinion that some of these families resided at the farm owned by John Dunn in 1720, and now known as Dunn's field, or on the other clearings in that vicinity, subsequently

---

*Twenty of the name of Lewes are found on the Barnstable tax list for 1737, namely: Seth, son of Benjamin, who resided at Israel's Pond, on Dimmock's lane; Ebenezer, 3d, son of Samuel, in a house that stood where Joseph Cobb's now does, his brother schoolmaster Joseph Lewes was exempt that year; Mr. George Lewes, Senior, lived near Taylor's lane; Ebenezer Lewes, Esq., son of Lieut. James, and his sons James, Jr., Ebenezer, Jr., Nathaniel and George, Jr., and Capt. James Lewes, son of Lieut. James, in the vicinity of the Meeting House; Dea. John Lewes, son of Edward, and his sons John, Jr., Shubael and James, 3d, at Cooper's pond; Jonathan, son of the second George, and his sons George 3d, and Jonathan, Jr., at Hyannis; Isaac and Thomas, sons of Edward, and Thomas, Jr., and Jesse, sons of Thomas, at Wequaquett. Seth's descendants removed to Cooper's Pond with this exception. The Leweses of the present day reside where their father's resided in 1737, and most of them where their ancestors did two centuries ago. The Lewes are fond of home.

owned by the Colemans. This view of the matter affords a satis-factory explanation of the apparent incongruities of the town and as-sessors' records. No more barren land than George Lewes' great lot was cleared in Barnstable, and though Edward Lewes may have resided there for a time, it is certain that he did not remain long. It is probable he settled in the vicinity of Dunn's field, because the meadows allotted to him were near that field.

His house at Rowley's pond was afterwards owned by the eccen-tric and witty Matthew Lumbert,—afterwards it was occupied by his son-in-law Joseph Cob, and therein the curious gymnastic feats of his bewitched daughters were performed. (See Cobb.)

Edmund Lewes was occasionally employed as a surveyor of lands, was on important town committees, and sustained a good character.

Edward Lewes, in his will dated 22d Feb. 1702-3, proved on the 6th of April following, gave all his real estate to his sons Shu-bael and Isaac, on the condition that they support their mother Han-nah Lewes, who survived till Jan. 17, 1729-30, and then died aged 90 years, 3 months, 12 days. He also names his sons Ebenezer, John and Thomas, and daughter Hannah, and names his wife and sons Isaac and Shubael executors of his will. Samuel, Jabez and Ebenezer Lewes were the witnesses; and James and Jabez Lewes apprised his estate at about £200.

Edward Lewes married 9th May, 1661, Hannah, daughter of Elder Henry Cobb. He died March 28, 1703, aged nearly 70 years. The town record of his family is incomplete. The names of his younger children are found in the probate records.

Children born in Barnstable.

35. I. Hannah, 24th April, 1662. Living in 1703, unmarried.
36. II. Eleazer, 26th Jan. 1664. Admitted a townsman in 1689, his father and brother John had meadows at South Sea allotted to them in Eleazer's right. He died before 1703, un-married.
37. III. John, 1st Jan. 1666. One of the South Sea men 1697. (See No. 37.)
38. IV. Thomas, March, 1669, one of the South Sea men 1697. (See No. 38.)
39. V. Eleazer. He is named as living at the death of his father in 1703. He is not named as one of the South Sea men in 1697, and being entitled to a share in the common lands only as an heir to his father, he must have been born after 1673, and was not married in 1697. He died or removed soon after 1703, perhaps to Falmouth, for an Ebenezer Lewes was a land holder in that town 1716.
40. VI. Shubael, married Dec. 8, 1703, Mercy, daughter of Joshua Lumbard. He probably died early, as his name does

not appear on the town or probate records. His widow married Nathaniel Baker 5th Jan. 1719-20, and died Dec. 7, 1768, aged 84.

41. VII. Isaac. He is not named as a proprietor; but had his share with Shubael and Ebenezer as the heirs of Edward. He joined the church in 1743, died Jan. 25, 1761, aged above 70 —(church records.) (See No. 41.)

(7.) John Lewes, son of George, born in Scituate March 2, 1737-8, bap. March 11, was a townsman of Barnstable in 1670. His father conveyed to him Jan. 12, 1662-3, the southerly half of his Great Lot at Rowley's Pond. In 1675 there was a John Lewes in Sandwich, probably the same man. He was a soldier in Capt. Gorham's company, and was killed at Rehobeth March 26, 1776. He does not appear to have had a family. James Haddeway afterwards owned his lands at Rowley's Pond. There was an ancient house on the southeast of the pond, probably built by a Lewes.

(8.) Ephraim Lewes, son of George, born in Barnstable July 23, 1641, is named as living in 1663. After that date his name disappears on the records. He probably died unmarried soon after his father. His name has been kept in the family to this day.

THIRD GENERATION.

(10.) James Lewes, son of Thomas, born 31st March, 1654, removed with his father to Falmouth, Mass., and there married March 27, 1679, Eleanor Johnson.* James Lewes is named as a land-holder in Falmouth in 1704.

Children born in Falmouth.

42. I. John, Feb. 5, 1680.
43. II. Eleanor, Aug. 3, 1682.
44. III. Remember, Dec. 26, 1684.
45. IV. Deborah, Aug. 20, 1686.
46. V. Ebenezer, Aug. 22, 1690.
47. VI. Thomas, Feb. 22, 1691-2.
48. VII. Hannah, Oct. 14, 1694.
49. VIII. Sarah, Sept. 1696.
50. IX. Benjamin, June 13, 1698.
51. X. James, 20th July, 1700.

(11.) Thomas Lewes, son of Thomas, (3) removed from Falmouth to Eastham. He was born in Barnstable July 15, 1656.

---

*Of this family I know nothing. There was a Thomas Johnson of. F., early. Mary, wife of Mr. Johnson, admitted to the Barnstable church Nov. 5, 1704, and had daughter Mary baptized Sept. 1, 1706.

The following is a copy of the inscription on his grave stones in the ancient burying ground in Eastham :

HERE LYES YE BODY
OF THOMAS LEWES
DIED MARCH YE 19, 1718,
IN YE 64
TH YEAR OF HIS AGE.

This date is old style—March 19, 1719, N. S., the two records corresponding precisely. The age is right—the names of his children are old family names, except a few borrowed from the Bangs or Freeman family. His will is dated Jan. 15, 1712-13, proved April 23, 1718-19. He appoints his wife Jane Lewes sole Executrix, names oldest son Thomas, sons John, George, Nathaniel and Benjamin, and his four daughters. The widow's estate was settled in the Probate Office April 25, 1720-21, showing that she survived her husband about two years.

Thomas Lewes, Jr., married Jane ———, who survived him. The names of his three older children are obtained from the Probate records. They were probably born in Falmouth ; the other seven in Eastham. In 1691 he is named as a landholder in Falmouth ; but not subsequently.

52. I.   Thomas, married Judith Smith of Harwich, 1722. He died in 1728, leaving several small children. His widow married in Yarmouth Isaac Taylor, Nov. 30, 1733.
53. II.   John.
54. III. Joseph.
55, IV.   A daughter. A Dinah Lewis of Harwich, married Oct. 1727, John Savage of Tiverton.
56. V.   George, May 6, 1691.
57. VI.   Nathaniel, March 31, 1696.
58. VII. Rebecca, March 17, 1697-8.
59. VIII. Benjamin, Oct. 8, 1700.
60. IX.   Sarah, June 2, 1702.
61. X.   Apphia, May 9, 1704. In a petition to the Judge of the Probate Court, dated April 2, 1726, she says she is 22.

(13.) Samuel Lewes, son of Thomas, (3) resided in Falmouth. He was a prominent man—a surveyor,—often selectman, moderator of town meetings, &c. I have no account of his family. A Benjamin Lewes of Falmouth married Sept. 8, 1702, Elizabeth Crow of Yarmouth, and had, as already stated, a family. He was a land holder in 1704, moderator of a town meeting 1710. This man may have been son to Samuel. There were several Lewes families in Falmouth of which I have no account—only know that there were such.

(14.) George Lewes,* son of George, (4) born Sept. 1655,

*I have mislaid my memoranda respecting this family, and I give it as I find it noted on my book. As I am unable to trace the family, I do not feel confident of the accuracy of the above.

married Elizabeth ———. He died in 1683, and his three children are named on the Probate records.

62. I. Hannah.
63. II. George.
64. III. Samuel.

(19.) Jabez Lewes, son of George, (4) born in Barnstable 10th June, 1670, married 20th Feb. 1695, Experience Hamblin. His son John is recorded as born in Barnstable 27th Aug. 1696. In 1702 he had removed to Yarmouth, where he had three children whose births are recorded, and the same were baptized in the church at Barnstable of which his wife continued to be a member all her long life. He had other children, Eleanor named in his will and Jabez of Harwich, probably his son. In his will dated Jan. 19, 1737-8, proved 1738, he names his wife Experience, eldest son John, sons Elnathan and Antipas, and daughter Eleanor Robbins. Jabez of Harwich died April 6, 1732, and for that reason it is probable he is not named. Jabez the elder was not a prominent man, though on the Probate records he is called Mr., a mark of distinction in those days. He died in 1738, aged 68, and the widow Experience July 26, 1766, aged 92 years and 3 months.

Children of Jabez Lewes.

65. I. John, born in Barnstable 27th Aug. 1696. (See No. 66.)
Jabez married Sarah Lincoln Feb. 27, 1723—had born in Harwich Thomas, Dec. 22, 1724; Sarah, March 4, 1727-8, and perhaps others.
Eleanor married ——— Robbins.
66. II. Elnathan, born in Yarmouth Aug. 27, 1702. (See No. 67.)
67. III. Antipas, born in Yarmouth Feb. 3, 1704-5. (See No. 68.)
68. IV. Naomi, born in Yarmouth July 1, 1708, married Jesse Lewes March 8, 1731-2.

(20.) Benj. Lewes, son of George, (4) born in Barnstable 22d Nov. 1675, married 10th Feb. 1696-7, Margaret Folland of Yarmouth. In 1691 the town agreed to raise £30 to assist in defraying the expense of procuring a new charter for the colony of Plymouth. To raise this sum parcels of the common lands were sold. George Lewes bought for £5 twelve acres of land at Crooked Pond, of late years known as Lampson's Pond. This tract of land he gave to his son Benjamin, who built his house thereon. It was in a solitary spot in the midst of the forest, about equally distant from the settlements on the north and south side of the Cape. The great Indian trail between Hyannis and Yarmouth passed near his house.

In his will dated 20th May, 1725, proved April 30, 1726, he names his wife, sons Seth and Benjamin, and daughters Mary Pitcher, Elizabeth and Mercy Lewes. He appoints his brother Nathan Lewes his executor. In addition to his estate at Crooked Pond, he had bought the estate of Israel Hamblin at Israel's Pond in an equally solitary spot in the forest. He had conveyed the latter, and some other property, equal to two-thirds of his estate, to his son Seth, on the condition that he would support his parents during their natural lives. Such conveyances often lead to trouble, and this was not an exception to the general rule. The final settlement of his small estate occupies much space on the records.

That a man of common sense should select such a place for his residence is surprising, and perhaps more so that his children should follow in his footsteps. For some little time Seth resided at Israel's Pond, Benjamin at Crooked Pond, and Elizabeth at Half-way. Connected by straight lines their house would stand at the angles of an equilateral triangle, and a mile distant from each other. Elizabeth married at sixteen Wm. Blachford, who came from Tower Hill, London, and all her life was known as Liza Tower-hill, and a reputed witch in the times when the folly of witchcraft had its firm believers. The solitary residences of the members of these families had an influence over the minds of the superstitious, and gave origin to many of the thousand and one marvellous tales that were told of them. Notwithstanding, Benjamin Lewes and all the members of his family were, as I have shown in another article, honest men and women and worthy members of the church of Christ.

Children of Benjamin Lewes born in Barnstable.

69. I.   Mary, 5th July, 1698, married Joseph Pitcher 1719.
70. II. Seth, 1st Aug. 1704. (See No. 70.)
71. III. Elizabeth, 17th Jan. 1711-12, the reputed witch, married Nov. 12, 1728, Wm. Blachford. She died July, 1790, aged 78, (Church Records.) In the two articles which I have published respecting her, I said that no stain rested on her character as a member of the East Church in Barnstable. I was mistaken. Recently on looking over the church records I found that a complaint was made against her Oct. 28, 1771, by Thankful Gilbert, the wife of Samuel, for abuse. Elizabeth readily confessed her fault, and "her confession being read, was voted to be satisfactory, by a large majority" of the church.
72. IV. Mercy, 3d March, 1712.
73. V.   Benjamin, 14th July 1716.
     And another son that died April 22, 1721.

(21.) Jonathan Lewes, son of George, (4) born 25th July, 1674, married by Justice Allen of Martha's Vineyard, to Patience Look. He was one of the first settlers at West Yarmouth, and Lewes Bay, on the borders whereof he settled, received its name

from him.   He removed to Hyannis in 1711, and the small bay at
that place was also named in honor of him.   Tradition calls him
the first white settler at Hyannis.   The Colemans and some
others were there before him.   He died Dec. 11, 1743, aged 67,
and his widow Patience July 4, 1767, aged over 80.

In his will dated Dec. 8, 1743, proved 4th January following, he names his three sons Jonathan, Melatiah and Lemuel;
and his daughters Thankful Bacon, Bethia Jean and Patience
Lewes, and his wife Patience.   To his daughter Bethia, then 36
years of age, he gave "his great chamber, over his great room,"
showing that one of the first houses built at Hyannis was a two
story building.   His grand daughter, Mrs. Rachell Cathcart, says
that the Ben. Hathaway house was her grandfather Jonathan's.
His oldest child, Thankful, was born in Barnstable, Bethia,
George and Jonathan in Yarmouth, and the other six in Barnstable.

74.   I.   Thankful, 22d Nov. 1704, married Gershom Lumbard
17th March, 1725-6, he died 1729, leaving a daughter Hannah born 25th Jan. 1726-7.   She married 2d Nathaniel
Bacon 1730; 3d, Augustine Bearse, Sept. 7, 1744.   She
died a widow Nov. 1774, aged 70 years.

75.   II.   Bethia, 27th Oct. 1706.   She survived, unmarried till
Oct. 1806, and at her death lacked only three weeks of being 100 years of age.

76.   III.   George, 15th Oct. 1708, married and removed to the
Vineyard.

77.   IV.   Jonathan, 30th Nov. 1710.   (See No. 77.)

78.   V.   Jean, 28th April, 1713, married Bays Hawes July 1,
1744, removed to the Vineyard.

79.   VI.   Lot, 6th May, 1715, probably died young.

80.   VII.   Lois, 22d Sept. 1718, Levi on Church Records, died
young.

81.   VIII.   Melatiah, 6th Feb. 1720.   (See No. 81.)

82.   IX.   Patience, 23d May, 1723, died aged, unmarried.

83.   X.   Lemuel, 28th Sept. 1725, married March 7, 1750, Temperance Bearse, and had a large family, one of whom Rachel, born Aug. 22, 1771, is now living—a great-grand-
daughter of George Lewes, 2d, who came over about the year
1630.   (For a notice of this family see No. 83.)

(23.)   Nathan Lewes, son of Geo. (4) born 26th July,
1678.   He removed to Falmouth before 1733.

He married Aug. 24, 1705, Sarah Arey.   She died in Falmouth, March 17, 1733-4, and he married 2d Experience ———.
He and his wife were admitted to the church in F. in 1742, and
dismissed to East Middletown, Conn., in 1749.

Children born in Barnstable.

84. I. Hannah, 13th Feb. 1706.
85. II. Daniel, 24th June, 1708.
86. III. Mary, 11th Sept. 1710.
87. IV. Sarah, 24th June, 1713, married Benoni Gray Sept. 1, 1732.

88. V. Nathan, 29th Oct. 1715. He was a mariner and re-moved with his father to Falmouth; married June 27, 1737, Ann Weeks of F. Children: 1, Isaac, Nov. 1738; 2, Sarah, Jan. 25, 1741; 3, Amasa, March 5, 1742, baptized in 1743 as the child of Nathan, Jr.; and 4, Frederick, March 17, 1745, the latter married in 1768 Deborah Cush-ing of Hingham. Nathan Lewis, Jr., married. He died in 1747, and his estate was rendered insolvent. He and his wife Ann were admitted to the Falmouth church in 1741, and Nathan Lewis, the father I presume, and his wife Expe-rience in 1742.

89. VI. George, son of Nathan, born 18th March, 1718-19. In 1744, Bartlett, son of George and Bathshuba Lewis, was baptized in Falmouth and in 1747 their son George. I have a memorandum that George, son of Nathan, married April 22, 1741, Susanna Pope. This Susanna was probably the wife of another George.

(25.)   John Lewes, son of Lieut. James, (5) born Oct. 29, 1656, and baptized by Mr. Hobart in Hingham where he was probably born, married Nov. 17, 1682, Hannah Lincoln, daughter of Daniel of that town. His wife died Oct. 30, 1715, and he died Nov. 5, in the same year, aged 59. This John has been con-founded with John, son of George, who was killed at the battle of Rehobeth March 26, 1676.

Children born in Hingham.

90. I. John, Oct. 13, 1683, married Deborah Hawke May 2, 1716.

91. II. Daniel, Sept. 29, 1685. He graduated at Harvard Col-lege in 1707, married Elizabeth, daughter of James Hawke, Dec. 11, 1712. After graduating he taught the Grammar School in Hingham until 1712, when he was invited to settle in the ministry at Pembroke, and was ordained there Dec. 3, 1712. He died in Pembroke June 29, 1753, and his widow died there June 11, 1755.

92. III. Hannah, Jan. 10, 1687-8, married Martin Hopkins.

93.   IV.   Sarah, July 12, 1690, married Jacob Loring Feb. 1708-9.

94.   V.   Susanna, Jan. 5, 1692-3, died Feb. 26, 1692-3.
95.   VI.   Rachel, June 19, 1694, married David Cushing.
96.   VII.   Susanna, Dec. 9, 1697.
97.   VIII.   Mary, June 2, 1700, died young.
98.   IX.   Isaiah, June 10, 1703, graduated at Harvard College 1723, taught school in Hingham and Marshfield, and preached on the Sabbaths.   He married June 25, 1730, Abigail, daughter of Reuben Winslow of Marshfield.   In 1730 he was settled in the north parish of Eastham at £110 yearly salary and £200 settlement, and the parsonage lands. In 1747 his annual salary was *increased* to £75, new tenor. In 1750-53, 6s 8d, in 1754 £70, and thereafter £50 sterling. In 1785 Rev. Levi Whitman was settled as his colleague. He died Oct. 3, 1786, aged 83 years.

(26.)   Samuel Lewes, son of Lieut. James, (5) born 10th April, 1659, married Dec. 1690, Prudence Leonard.   Widow Prudence Lewes died March 31, 1736, aged 60.

Samuel Lewes resided in the East Parish, owned the estate which his uncle John bought of Joshua Lombard, next east of Elder Henry Cobb's great lot.   He died Dec. 1726, aged 67, intestate.   Letters of administration on his estate were granted to his widow Prudence Lewes Jan. 25, 1725-6.   The Inventory of the estate by Shubael Dimmock, James Cobb and Samuel Bacon, amounted to £1,551,04,0 in the depreciated Bills of Credit then current.   The homestead which contained about ten acres, and the dwelling-house thereon, was apprised at £644.   Mr. Samuel Lewes' house. it appears, was the second built on the lot, for in the division the cellar of an old house is named.   He also owned a house and land at South Sea.   In the division, the widow had the improvement of one-third of the estate.   The other two-thirds were one-half to Samuel, the eldest son, who took the South Sea property ; one quarter to Joseph, who had the easterly part of the homestead ; and one quarter to Ebenezer, who had the western part, adjoining the Cobb land.   The rest of the estate was divided in the same proportions to the sons.   The two daughters, Thankful and Hannah had each £146,12,8 "in good bills of credit."

Children born in Barnstable.

99.   I.   Samuel, 22d June, 1700.   He resided at South Sea, married Reliance ———, and had born in Barnstable : 1, Susanna, Jan. 19, 1722 ; 2, Nehemiah, July 4, 1704 ; 3,

Samuel, April 13, 1726 ; 4, Leonard, Oct. 25, 1728 ; 5, Solomon, May 31, 1730 ; and 6, Barnabas, April 12, 1734.

100. II. David, ⎱ died 3d Jan. 1706.
             ⎰ Twins, 12th Dec. 1702.
101. III. Joseph, ⎰ graduate of Harvard College 1724, and for more than sixty years taught school in Barnstable. The town was divided into four districts, and he taught alternately in each. He studied theology, and preached on the south side of Barnstable during the winters of 1727-8, and 9. For his services the first winter he had £5, 2s the amount assessed on the South Sea people, and on the 3d £10. Thereafter he does not appear to have preached. He was learned, a good neighbor and a sincere Christian ; but wanting in energy of character, he never exerted much influence. In his old age he married Martha Davis, a twin daughter of Stephen Davis, born 1731, had no children. He died Feb. 1788, aged 86.

102. IV. Ebenezer, 9th Aug. 1706. He does not appear to have married. In his will dated 22d Aug. 1752, he is called 3d, and names his brothers Samuel and Joseph, and his sisters Hannah Bacon and Thankful Lewis. He appoints his kinsmen, Robert Davis and Jonathan Lewis, his executors.

103. V. Thankful, 22d Jan. 1708.

104. VI. Hannah, 1st July, 1710, married 1738, Oris Bacon, five years younger than herself, and had no issue.

(28.) James Lewes, son of Lieut. James, (5) born 3d June, 1664, married Nov. 1698, Elizabeth Lothrop, 2d, Mercey Sturgis of Yarmouth. She died Dec. 7, 1745, aged 64. He died June 18, 1748, aged 84. In his will dated March 25, 1747, proved June 29, 1748, he names his daughter Mary Dunham, wife of Gideon ; his grand-daughters Susanna and Elizabeth, daughters of his son James, deceased, and his son Jonathan, to whom he gives nearly all of his estate, apprised at only £2,300,09, old tenor. He names his nephew Nathan Lewis. As five are not named in the father's will it is probable they died young.

Children born in Barnstable.

105. I. Mary, 16th Aug. 1700, married Gideon Dunham.

106. II. Elizabeth, 8th May, 1702. Not named in her father's will.

107. III. James, 9th July, 1704, probably married Abigail Taylor of Yarmouth March 5, 1727, and had two daughters, Susanna and Elizabeth. He was a mariner and died in 1730, when he was called 4th, leaving an estate apprised at £150.

108. IV. Barnabas, 17th March, 1706, not named in father's will.

109.   V.   Solomon, 26th June, 1708, not named in father's will.
110.   VI.   Jonathan, baptized May 10, 1713.   (See 110.)
111.   VII.   Sarah, baptized April 14, 1714, not named in will.
112.   VIII.   John, baptized July 19, 1719, not named in will.

(29.)   Ebenezer Lewes, Esq., son of Lieut. James, (5) born Dec. 20, 1666, was a man of wealth and one of the most active and intelligent business men of his time. He was judge of the Court of Common Pleas, and held many municipal offices.

He married first Anna Lothrop, daughter of the Hon. Barnabas, April, 1691, and second Rebecca Sturgis of Yarmouth, Feb. 28, 1728. The latter died April 10, 1734, aged 65. Ebenezer Lewes, Esq., died ———.

Children born in Barnstable.

113.   I.   Sarah, 13th Jan. 1691-2, married Eben. Hinckley June 11, 1711.
114.   II.   Susannah, 17th April 1694, married July 24, 1712, James Allyn.
115.   III.   James, 4th Aug. 1696, married 1733 Rebecca Hatch, daughter of Capt. Moses Hatch, of Falmouth, by whom he had Rebecca born Aug. 5, 1734, married Isaac Baker Oct. 6, 1754; Abigail, baptized Dec. 19, 1736, and James May 4, 1740, his wife died July 5, 1740, aged 30. He married 2d Dorcas Baker Sept. 3, 1745, and had Elizabeth baptized June 7, 1747. His wife Dorcas died July 5, 1748, aged 35. He married for his third wife, April 12, 1750, Joanna Howland. (This James I presume was the one of the name that was insane, and had a guardian appointed May 13, 1756.)
116.   IV.   Ebenezer, 9th May, 1699, married Nov. 1736, Mary Coree of Long Island, and had : 1, Mercy, Nov. 22, 1732; David, Jan. 19, 1739-40; Ebenezer, Jan. 5, 1742-3; Martha, Oct. 21, 1745.
117.   V.   Hannah, 14th Feb. 1701.
118.   VI.   Lothrop, 13th June, 1702, graduated at Harvard College 1723, died 1773. Respecting Mr. Lothrop Lewes, I can obtain no information. His father gave him 20 shillings in his will.
119.   VII.   George, 5th April, 1704.   (See 119.)
120.   VIII.   Nathaniel, 12th Jan. 1706-7, married Feb. 19, 1736, Fear Thacher, and had : 1, Elizabeth, July 21, 1737; 2, Abigail, Dec. 24, 1740, died young; 3, Abigail, Sept. 2, 1742; 4, Hannah, Oct. 16, 1744; and 5, Nathaniel, June 5, 1745, the latter a man of note in his day. Nathaniel, the father, died July 7, 1751, aged 43.

121. IX. John, 15th July, 1709, married Thankful Crowell, of Yarmouth, July 21, 1718, had born in Yarmouth: 1, Lydia, March 23, 1718-19; 2, Temperance, Feb. 7, 1721; 3, Experience, all of whom died in Oct. 1724; born in Barnstable, 4, Jabez, Aug. 30, 1725; 5, Thankful, March 18, 1727; and 6, Deborah, Feb. 19, 1728-9.

122. X. David, ⎱ 8th Nov. 1711.
123. XI. Abigail, ⎰ married Solomon Sturgis Aug. 2, 1732.

(31.) Mr. George Lewes, son of Lieut. James, born in 1673, married by Col. John Otis to Alice Crocker, daughter of Josiah Crocker, 14th June, 1711. She died 23d Feb. 1718, aged 39. He died Nov. 1769, in the 96th year of his age, and is buried in the old burying ground where he has a monument. His death is also recorded in the church records, and he is there called nearly 96 years of age. He owned the dwelling-house which was his father's, and in his will divides his estate between his daughters Mary and Anna. He gave his dwelling-house to his daughter Mary, reserving a room which he called his "study," which he allowed his daughter Anna also to occupy. Her husband, Hon. Peter Thacher, occupied it as his office during the sessions of the Courts. It appears that Lieut. James and his sons bought out John Hathaway and the Halletts. The meadow and beach near the Raft-dock recently claimed by the town, it clearly appears, was the property of George Lewes, not the town's, and that matter is now forever set at rest.

Mr. George Lewes was an intelligent man, of studious habits, and associated with the most influential. His name does not often appear as a public officer, though he was well educated for the times, and capable of performing duties to which he did not aspire.

Children born in Barnstable.

124. I. Sarah, 5th April, 1712, died June 13, 1713.
125. II. Mary, 9th March, 1713-14, married Eben. Taylor, Aug. 16, 1733.
126. III. Anna, 3d Feb. 1715-16, married Peter Thacher Oct. 24, 1735.
127. IV. Josiah, 19th Feb. 1717-18. April 20, 1742, George Lewes was appointed administrator on the estate of his son Josiah, mariner. He was then 24 years of age, and it is not named that he had a family, in the settlement of his estate or in that of his fathers.

(32). Joseph Lewes, son of Lieut. James, born in 1676, removed to Hingham. He married Feb. 3, 1702-3, Sarah Marsh, daughter of Thomas Marsh of Hingham. She died Jan. 5, 1717-18, and he married for his second wife Elizabeth Dixon of

Hingham, a daughter of George Vickory of Hull. She died Sept. 1, 1736, aged 45. Joseph Lewes died in Hingham Aug. 22, 1767, aged 91. Like his brother, he had sixteen children, the larger part married and died in Hingham.

Children of Joseph Lewes born in Hingham.

128. I.   Sarah, Dec. 15, 1703.
129. II.   Joseph, Dec. 1, 1705, graduated at Harvard College in 1725. After he had completed his education he resided in Boston, where he was a merchant. He afterwards returned to Hingham, and taught school many years. He was not a prominent citizen. He died Jan. 14, 1786, aged 81.
130. III. Thomas, Sept. 30, 1707, graduated at Harvard College 1728. He studied divinity and preached occasionally. He was not very successful in life, owing to his habits. He died in Hingham April 4, 1787. He married Mary Lawson in 1736. and had a large family of children. Some of his descendants are very respectable citizens of Hingham.
131. IV.   Paul, March 25, 1710.
132. V.   James, Sept. 9, 1712, graduated at Harvard College 1731. He removed to Marshfield, married Lydia Rogers of that town, had five sons and one daughter. He was a school master in Marshfield many years and was worn out in the service, and died in that town.
133. VI.   Jonathan, Dec. 3, 1714, married Lydia Stodder 1740.
134. VII. Mary, Sept. 6, 1717, married Knight Sprague 1735.
135. VIII. Elizabeth, July 14, 1719, married David Beal, Jr., 1739.
136. IX.   George, July 23, 1721, married Susanna Hall.
137. X.   Samuel, June 28, 1724, died Aug. 17, 1724.
138. XI.   Samuel, Oct. 28, 1725, married Sarah Humphrey 1750.
139. XII. Israel, April 19, 1727, died July 31, 1727.
140. XIII. Ebenezer, July 21, 1728, married Hannah Hersey Nov. 1751.
141. XIV. Lucy, Oct. 23, 1730, never married.
142. XV.   Hannah, Dec. 3, 1731, married Elisha Lincoln.
143. XVI. Eunice, May 11, 1736, died Sept. 1744.

(36). Eleazer Lewes, son of Edward, was a townsman and proprietor in 1697. After that date his name disappears on the records.

(37). Dea. John Lewes, son of Edward, resided at Cooper's Pond, born January, 1666, married Elizabeth Huckins June 4, 1695. He died March 8, 1738-9, aged 73, and his widow Elizabeth Lewes July 12, 1741, aged 70.

Dea. John Lewes' will is dated Aug. 5, 1736, proved April

25, 1737.   He names his wife Elizabeth and all his children.   He gives his real estate to his sons James and Shubael, to Edward £20 in money, to John 5 shillings and one-third of dock at Cooper's island, he having already received most of his portion ; and to his son Gershom and daughters Elizabeth Snow and Thankful Lewes, legacies.

Children born in Barnstable.,

144. I. Edward, Sept. 6, 1697. He was not taxed in Barnstable in 1737. He married May 14, 1719, Rebecca Lothrop, and had : 1, Mehitabel, March 4, 1720-21 ; 2, Solomon, Dec. 22, 1722 ; 3, Isaac, Sept. 27, 1724. The latter married Feb. 10, 1747-8, Martha Bearse, a member of the church, and used her tongue more freely than the other members desired, had : 1, Lydia, Aug. 14, 1748 ; 2, Solomon, April 10, 1750 ; 3, Lothrop, Dec. 21, 1757, (ancestor of several respectable families at Falmouth) ; 4, Isaac, April 4, 1758, (also of Falmouth) ; 5, Martha, July 13, 1761 ; and Rebecca April 5, 1763. This family removed to Rochester and afterwards to Falmouth.

145. II. Thankful, Dec. 6, 1698.

146. III. Elizabeth, Aug. 28, 1701, married Jabez Snow of H. April 2, 1724.

147. IV. James, June 4, 1703, married 1st Abigail Taylor, of Yarmouth, March 5, 1727 ; 2d, Bethia Hathaway April 2, 1742. This I think was the James Lewes who was insane in the latter part of his life.

148. V. Gershom, Dec. 30, 1704.

149. VI. Shubael, Dec. 29, 1705, married widow Mary Snow, of Harwich, June 5, 1735, dismissed to the East Church March 28, 1738-9, and had Samuel baptized Sept. 11, 1737 ; Elizabeth born Feb. 2, 1739 ; Sarah, Dec. 8, 1741. Shubael and his brother John were of Harwich for a little time.

150. VII. John, April 28, 1706, married Mary Hopkins, a member of the Harwich Church Oct. 6, 1726, and had : 1, Timothy, July 25, 1727 ; 2, Hannah, April 17, 1729 ; 3, John, May 29, 1731 ; 4, Mehitabel, Sept. 13, 1733. These four baptized in Harwich Sept. 5, 1735. 5, Bethia, Dec. 25, 1735. John Lewes, Jr., was dismissed to the third church in Windham, Conn., July 3, 1743, and his wife Nov. 8, 1747.

(38). Thomas Lewes, son of Edward, born March 1669, married 28th Sept. 1699, Experience Huckins. He died Feb. 9,

1754, aged 74, and his wife died Dec. 23, 1733, aged 55 years, 4 months, 25 days.

Children born in Barnstable.

151.   I.   Experience, 15th Aug. 1699.

152.   II.   Thomas, 1st Aug. 1702.

153.   III.   Jesse, 11th March, 1705, married 1st, Naomi Lewes March 8, 1731-2 ; 2d, Feb. 26, 1735-6, Mercy Crosby of Harwich, and had : 1, Mary, Dec. 23, 1736 ; 2, Anner, March 13, 1738 ; 3, Naomi, Jan. 12, 1740, 4, Thomas, baptized July 31, 1743 ; 5, David, baptized July 20, 1746 ; 6, Sarah, baptized June 18, 1749. Children of Thomas of this family were remarkable for longevity—averaging 80 years.

154.   IV.   Desire, 14th May, 1707, married Stephen Davis, Sen., Nov. 12, 1730. She died Feb. 29, 1784, aged 77.

155.   V.   Ephraim, 8th April, 1710, married Sarah Hamblin Oct. 7, 1736, and had : 1, Thankful, June 5, 1739, married Shubael Davis, April 30, 1752 ; 2, Rebecca, Oct. 13, 1741 ; 3, Jacob, Jan. 4, 1743-4 ; 4, Esther, baptized April 3, 1748. Sarah Lewes, wife of Ephraim, died June 16, 1764.

156.   VI.   Abigail, baptized 24th Nov. 1717.

(14).   Isaac Lewes, son of Edward, married Experience Hamblin 13th Sept. 1732, perhaps his second wife. He died Jan. 25, 1761, aged the church records say "*above* 70," probably nearly 80. His wife Experience died July 24, 1749, aged 64.

Of Ebenezer, son of Edward, I find little.

(42 to 51).   These are Falmouth families of whom I have no information.

(52 to 61).   Eastham and Harwich families.

(65).   Jabez Lewes, son of Jabez, married Feb. 27, 1723-4, Sarah Lincoln of Harwich. He joined the Harwich church July 23, 1727, died April 6, 1732. Children : Thomas, Dec. 22, 1724 ; Sarah, March 4, 1727-8 ; and Jabez, baptized June 23, 1730.

(66).   Elnathan Lewes, son of Jabez, born in Yarmouth Aug. 27, 1702, married Oct. 16, 1735, Priscilla Lewes. He died June 19, 1782, aged 80. (Yarmouth Records.) He resided at West Yarmouth, and had :

157.   I.   Benjamin, Sept. 19, 1737, married Sarah Crowell Dec. 3, 1767, and had Priscilla Oct. 26, 1768 ; Betty, July 2, 1770 ; Benjamin, April 12, 1772 ; Sarah, March 6, 1774 ; Sarah, Dec. 17, 1778 ; Lydia, May 16, 1781 ; Ruth, Sept. 23, 1783 ; Edward, Sept. 29, 1785 ; and Nathan, Oct. 12,

1788. He died March 26, 1793, and his wife Sarah same year.

158. II. Mary, July 20, 1739.

159. III. Thankful, April 16, 1741.

160. IV. Priscilla, April 16, 1742.

161. V. David, July 16, 1744, by wife Phebe had Susa July 24, 1776; Phebe, July 5, 1778; David, May 22, 1781; Elizabeth, April 19, 1783; Temperance, June 2, 1789; Priscilla, Jan. 24, 1791; Mary, March 19, 1793; Sally, Oct. 13, 1795; Richard, Aug. 15, 1798. He married 2d Temperance Lewes, daughter of Lemuel, and had 5 other children. He removed to Kennebec.

162. VI. Elnathan, June 3, 1746. By his wife Thankful he had Mary, May 21, 1777; Thankful, March 2, 1779; and Elnathan May 19, 1781.

163. VII. Antipas, Dec. 25, 1751.

164. VIII. Naomi, Feb. 27, 1754.

165. IX. John, July 23, 1756, married Desire and had Mehitabel, Nov. 26, 1786; Isaiah, Sept. 10, 1788; John, Nov. 30, 1791; and Simeon, Dec. 9, 1794.

(68). Antipas Lewes, son of Jabez, born in Yarmouth Feb. 3, 1704, married Oct. 15, 1730, Martha Bearse. Antipas Lewis, of Yarmouth, in his will dated 17th April, 1740, proved June 11, 1746, he names his wife Martha, his sons Timothy and Jabez, and his daughters Naomi, Elizabeth, Martha, Ruth and Experience, the birth of the latter not on the town records. He died Feb. 11, 1783, aged 79. He resided at West Yarmouth and had:

166. I. Timothy, born Sept. 6, 1731.

167. II. Martha, June 1, 1733.

168. III. Naomi, Aug. 6, 1734.

169. IV. Sarah, June 24, 1736.

170. V. Elizabeth, June 28, 1730.

171. VI. Ruth, April 24, 1741.

172. VII. Jabez, July 8, 1743.

173. VIII. Sarah, Aug. 25, 1746.

Jabez Lewis of this family married Jerusha ———, and had Timothy May 12, 1768; William, Aug. 6, 1771; Naomi, Jan. 27, 1773; Jabez, Dec. 2, 1775; Martha, Sept. 30, 1778; Keziah, Oct. 10, 1781; Jerusha, Sept. 23, 1784; James, April 22, 1787; William, Feb. 20, 1790.

Timothy of this family had fourteen children, many of whom are yet living. Benjamin, son and grandson of Benjamin, had five children.

I have traced the descendants of Jabez who settled in Yarmouth down to the present time.

On the Yarmouth records I find some families, probably descendants of Jonathan, who settled at Hyannis. A George

Lewis, by his wife Susannah, had Betty May 17, 1777; Lydia, Nov. 17, 1780; and Susanna Jan. 15, 1783.

A Jonathan Lewis by his wife Hannah had: Clement, Nov. 15, 1788; Watson, Nov. 4, 1789; Rodman, Sept. 10, 1791; Sophia, Aug. 31, 1793; Asenath, June 14, 1795; and Laura, Dec. 9, 1796.

(70). Seth Lewes, son of Benjamin, born Aug. 1, 1704, married by Joseph Doane, Esq., Oct. 22, 1724, to Sarah Revis. His early residence was at a house built by Israel Hamblin, near a pond, on Dimmock's lane, known as Israel's pond—a solitary place surrounded by the forest, and more than a mile from a neighbor.* He probably did not reside there many years. I think he owned the estate at Cooper's pond, where his son Benjamin afterwards resided. Seth Lewes died in 1751, aged 47.

The births of his children I do not find on the town records. The baptisms of his children are recorded in the church records.

174. I. Elijah, bap. Sept. 27, 1730.
175. II. Thankful, bap. Sept. 27, 1730.
176. III. Sarah, bap. May 9, 1731.
177. IV. Temperance, bap. April 7, 1734.
178. V. Mercy, bap. Aug. 29, 1736.
179. VI. Desire, bap. April 15, 1739.
180. VII. Lovey, bap. May 17, 1741.
181. VIII. Benjamin, bap. Oct. 16, 1743, married for his second wife Desire Bacon, Jr., Jan. 22, 1795, and was the father of the late Capt. Seth, and the present Benjamin and Elijah, and the late Capt. Robinson Lewis of Falmouth.

(77). Jonathan Lewes, Jr., son of Jonathan, Senior, of Hyannis, married Elizabeth, daughter of Thomas Cobb of Barnstable, Oct. 13, 1737, aged 22 years. He was a shoemaker and resided on the north side of the town after his marriage. His wife was a member of the East Church, and died May 31, 1751, aged 36 years. Jonathan Lewes, 3d, was of about the same age as Jonathan, Jr., and both had Elizabeths for their wives, and it is difficult to distinguish their families.

Children of Jonathan Lewes, Jr., and Elizabeth Cobb.

182. I. Jonathan, bap. Sept. 9, 1739.
183. II. Elizabeth, bap. June 27, 1742.
184. III. Rachel, bap. Dec. 9, 1744.
185. IV. Lot, bap. March 15, 1746-7.

---

*In turning over the leaves of the church records my eyes rested on the following: "1777, June 2, Edward Hawes departed this life aged about 37, suamanus;" a modest manner of recording a suicide. Mr. Hawes hung himself on a tree standing at the corner of the road that leads to the spot where Seth Lewis' house stood. It long remained as a monument of the act. Mr. Hawes sold his valuable estate, bought of the Paine family, to the late Dr. Samuel Savage, and received in payment continental money. It soon after depreciated, Hawes suddenly became poor, and in consequence committed suicide.

(81). Melatiah Lewes, son of Jonathan, married Abigail Bearse Oct. 1, 1742. He died insolvent in 1767.

Children born in Barnstable.

186. I. Theodale, March 16, 1743, married Oris Cobb Dec. 6, 1764.
187. II. William, Sept. 18, 1745.
188. III. Levi, Nov. 27, 1746.
189. IV. Melatiah, July 27, 1752.

(83). Lemuel Lewes, son of Jonathan, born 23d May, 1723, resided at Hyannis, had a family of eleven children, many of whom were distinguished for their longevity, one of whom, Rachell, is now living at the advanced age of 94. He married March 7, 1750, Temperance Bearse.

Children born in Barnstable.

190. I. Richard, Nov. 26, 1750. He was a soldier in the Revolution, 33 years one of the selectmen of Barnstable, and a man much respected. He married Molly Lovell and has children now living. He died in old age.
191. II. Elizabeth.
192. III. George, Sept. 14, 1754, a soldier in the Revolution, and during the latter part of the life of Col. James Otis, he was the Colonel's waiters, and was with him wherever he went. He related many anecdotes of Col. James, and his son James the patriot, the latter he called "young Jim," the common appelation by which he was distinguished by his neighbors in Barnstable. George Lewes lost $1400 by the depreciation of the continental money. He died in 1850, aged 96.
193. IV. Temperance, April 3, 1757, married her relative, David Lewes of Yarmouth, removed to Kennebec, where she has children living.
194. V. Lydia, May 30, 1759, married Nathaniel Bunker of Nantucket.
195. VI. Lemuel, Sept. 17, 1761, married Puella Lovell.
196. VII. Bethia, Sept. 23, 1764, married 1st Rowland Hallett, and was the mother of the late Seth Hallett, Esq. She married 2d, Dea. Sylvanus Hinckley.
197. VIII. Jonathan, Sept. 25, 1766, married —— Hallett, removed to Cincinnati. He carried with him a large family of small children—lost one out of his wagon, and did not miss it till he had travelled nearly a day, went back and found it.
198. IX. Anna, July 4, 1768.
199. X. Rachel, Aug. 22, 1771, married John Cathcart, and is

now living. She is the last survivor of the professional midwives of Barnstable. She does not profess to have been so successful, or so skillful as old madam Killey; but she shows a good record, few of the present practitioners of the obstetic art can show a better—200 children—never lost a child or a mother. She retains all her faculties, and few would call her a woman of over 75. She hears common conversation, but speaks loud and strong herself, using many gesticulations, and makes frequent quotations from the scripture and favorite hymns. She has been a hard worker all her days. She has met with several severe accidents in her life. Several years ago she was run over by a wagon, from the effects of which she yet suffers. She remembers when there were only three dwelling-houses within the present limits of the village of Hyannis.

200. XII. Jean, born March 25, 1774, was the youngest daughter of Lemuel Lewes.

(110). Jonathan Lewis, 3d, son of James, bap. May 1, 1713, married Elizabeth Corey of Southold, L. I., Dec. 13, 1735. The wife was a member of the church in Southold; but is not named in our records till Jan. 31, 1747-8.

Children born in Barnstable.

206. I. James, Jan. 25, 1740.
207. II. Barnabas, Oct. 7, 1743.
208. III. Joshua, Jan. 9, 1747-8, bap. Jan. 31,1747-8.
209. IV. Jonathan, May 25, 1750.

(119). George Lewes, son of Ebenezer Lewes, Esq., born April 5, 1704, married Sept. 12, 1737, Sarah Thacher of Yarmouth. He resided in the ancient dwelling-house of Ebenezer Lewes, Esq., yet standing. He was a hard working, industrious man, not distinguished in public life. His children perhaps inherited that energy and decision of character from the mother. In his time the garden and grounds of Frederick W. Crocker, deceased, in front of his house, was a thick and almost impenetrable swamp. He was called junior all his life; his uncle George outlived him twelve years. In his will dated July 19, 1757, he names his daughters Anna Gorham, Sarah Loring, Temperance Lewes, and Susanna Lewes, and sons John, (executor) George, Josiah and James; his wife Sarah and his father Ebenezer Lewes. The inventory of his estate amounted to £284,60,2. His widow Sarah died April 30, 1762.

Children born in Barnstable.

210. I. Annah, Dec. 9, 1728, married Nathaniel Gorham Oct. 3, 1752.
211. II. Thankful, Jan. 10, 1729, died 16th March, 1729.

212. III. John, Oct. 5, 1731, married Deborah Phinney Oct. 19, 1752, and had David* Aug. 10, 1753, (father of the late Capt. William Lewis, the well-known ship builder) ; Peter, June 7, 1756, David and Peter lived in the old house ; Ebenezer, March 30, 1759, removed to Waquoit; John, Aug. 4, 1763, removed to Waquoit; Deborah, June 4, 1766, married Thomas Dimmock ; Elijah, March 23, 1769, removed to Boston ; Thacher, May 3, 1772, removed to Falmouth ; Joshua, Dec. 17, 1775.

213. IV. Thankful, April 6, 1734.

214. V. Sarah, July 31, 1737, married Otis Loring Feb. 20, 1755, died June 23, 1785.

215. VI. Temperance, Aug. 25, 1739, died Sept. 4, 1739.

216. VII. George, April 9, 1741, married Mary Davis Oct. 12, 1760. She died Feb. 1782, aged 41, and he married 2d Desire Parker. Major Geo. Lewis was one of the most distinguished of the family. He removed to Gorham, Maine, where he died July 24, 1819, aged 78 years. (See No. 196.)

217. VIII. Temperance, June 13, 1743, died Jan. 4, 1744.

218. IX. Josiah, April 29, 1745, (father of the late Josiah Lewis.) He was a ship-carpenter. He, with others, during the Revolution, got off the British ship of war Cumberland cast ashore at the Cape. In attempting to bring her into Barnstable harbor, she caught on the tongue of the Yarmouth flats where she remained. The place has since been known as the old ship.

219. X. Temperance, Oct. 20, 1747.

220. XI. Susanna, Sept. 5, 1749, married Jonathan Davis of Barnstable. She was born a few hours before midnight Sept. 26, 1749 ; he a few after, on the 27th. He died Sept. 22, 1840, aged 91 ; she died Sept. 25, 1841, aged 92.

221. XII. James, Aug. 1753, the youngest child, was drowned Oct. 17, 1773.

(196). Major George Lewis, son of George, born April 9, 1741, was one of the most distinguished men of the family. He married Oct. 12, 1760, Mary Davis, daughter of Hon. Daniel Da-

---

*David Lewis and his brother Peter resided in the ancient Lewis house. He married twice, and died in a fit when alone in his house. He was found in the morning lying dead on the floor of his room, apparently having died without a struggle. Josiah Lewis, a brother of David, was a shipwright, and was killed by a tree falling on him. His children were the late Josiah Lewis, Joseph Green Lewis, Harvey Lewis, and Hannah Lewis, wife of Sylvester Baker. Josiah Lewis, William Lewis, and Joseph G. Lewis, ship carpenters, bought about the year 1742 the American ship Astrea, cast away at Billingsgate. They got her off, and in attempting to bring her into Barnstable to repair she caught aground on "the tongue" of the Yarmouth flats, where portions of her timbers remained more than fifty years.

[In Mr. Otis notes, in his own handwriting, is the endorsement on the margin, "This is not right." It probably refers to the ship-wrecked vessel. It conflicts with the statement made in the paragraph 218, IX, but as the editor has no means of ascertaining which is correct, both are allowed to stand for what they are worth.] S.

vis. She died Feb. 1782, aged 41, and he married second Desire Parker, daughter of Samuel of West Barnstable. He died in Gorham July 24, 1819, aged 78.

Children born in Barnstable.

222. I. Mehitabel, July 21, 1762, married —— Crocker.
223. II. Lothrop, Feb. 13, 1764. Of Col. Lothrop Lewis, Josiah Pierce, Esq., in his history of Gorham, says: "Probably no Gorham man ever stood higher in the estimation of his fellow-citizens than the Hon. Lothrop Lewis. His morals were pure, obliging and courteous in manner, prudent in words and action, and distinguished for sound common sense. His mind was not brilliant, nor its operations rapid, but clear and persevering." When young he was much engaged in surveying lands. He was often a referee in important and difficult cases. He held many civil and military offices, and discharged their duties with fidelity. He was Colonel of a regiment of cavalry, Justice of the Peace, Deputy Sheriff, Selectman, Representative to the General Court, member of the board of war from 1812 to 1815, and land agent of the State of Maine. He died in Bangor Oct. 9, 1822, while in the discharge of his official duties. Col. Lewis was twice married, first to Tabitha Longfellow, by whom he had Stephen L. 1795, and Mary 1796. His second wife was Wid. Mary J. Little, a daughter of Judge Prescott of Groton, Mass., by whom he had Annah, Catharine and Elizabeth.
224. III. Sarah, Jan. 13, 1766, married Capt. Eben'r Peabody.
225. IV. Annah, March 21, 1768, married John Darling.
226. V. James, Aug. 21, 1770. Mr. James Lewis was a man of ability, character and property. About the year 1803 he became a convert to Methodism, and soon after an earnest and zealous preacher. His great fluency of speech, powerful voice, and evident sincerity, drew together large audiences. He travelled extensively, and when past eighty years of age visited his relatives at the Cape. To the last his physical and intellectual vigor remained almost unimpaired. He died in Gorham Aug. 20, 1855, aged 85, highly respected by men of every shade of religious belief.
227. VI. Ansel, Feb. 2, 1773. A surveyor of lumber in Portland.
228. VII. George, March 28, 1775. He was a farmer at Bridgton, Me., and major in the militia.
229. VIII. Daniel Davis, July 22, 1777. A Baptist clergy-

man, settled in Patterson, N. J., where he died a few years ago.

230.   IX.   Mary, Sept. 29, 1779.

231.   X.   Robert,   } twins Jan. 12, 1782.

232.   XI.   Abigail,   } married Capt. William Prentiss and was the mother of the distinguished orator, Sargent S. Prentiss.

I have drawn out this article to a great length without exhausting my materials. To tell the truth I got wearied before I had finished, and have not written the latter part with that care that I did the first, I could not do it—it would have occupied me for a year, and would have made a volume. There were eleven John Lewis's born within a century ; to trace their families without mixing them is a Herculean task.

LINNEL.

When I commenced writing the history and genealogies of the Barnstable families, I was aware that the arrangement of the articles was objectionable. They were written, as newspaper articles usually are, to be read, thrown aside and forgotten. The width of the colums of a newspaper is not sufficient for the systematic arrangement of the genealogies without a smaller type, or many abbreviations are used. In regard to these articles, my present opinion is, that I shall at some future time revise them and publish them in a book form. If I do this, I shall print the genealogies and the histories of the families as separate articles. The genealogies few will read, they are tables for reference, and it is important that they be printed in the best possible form for that purpose. The histories of the families, separated from the genealogies, will be more interesting to the reader, who takes no special interest in the family.

In the Linnel genealogy I have no special interest to gratify. I have carefully collected and arranged all I could find respecting the early generations to No. 31, after that number only a part of the families are given ; to do otherwise would extend the article to a greater length than is desirable.

ROBERT LINNEL.

Descendants of Mr. Robert Linnel born in Barnstable.
1.   Robert Linnel, married 2d Peninah ———.
2.   I. Sarah, born 1607, and married 1, Thomas Ewer. 2d, Thomas Lothrop Dec. 11, 1639.
3.   II. David, 1627.
4.   III. Hannah, married John Davis March 15, 1648.
5.   IV. Mary, married Richard Childs Oct. 15, 1649.
6.   V. Abigail, married Joshua Lumbard May 27, 1651.
7.   VI. Shubael, (or Samuel).
8.   VII. Bethia, bap. Feb. 7, 1640-1.
     3 David Linnel, married Hannah Shelley March 9, 1752-3.
9.   I. Samuel, born 15th Dec. 1655.
10. II. Elisha, born 1st June, 1658.

11. III. Hannah, 15th Dec. 1660, married Dolar Davis 3d Aug. 1681.
12. IV. Mary, married John Sergeant.
13. V. Abigail, married Ralph Jones 17th March, 1721.
14. VI. Experience, married Jabez Davis 20th Aug. 1689.
15. VII. Jonathan, born 1668, died Sept. 8, 1725.
16. VIII. John, born 1671, died 9th Feb. 1747.
17. IX. Susannah, 1673, married Eben. Phinney 14th Nov. 1695.

15 Jonathan Linnel of B. & Eastham, married Elizabeth, born 1667, died 26th July, 1723.

2, Rebecca.
18. I. David, 28th Jan. 1693-4.
19. II. Elizabeth, 17th April, '96, died May 17, 1714.
20. III. Hannah, 17th April, '96, married —— Mayo.
21. IV. Abigail, 1st July, '99, married Samuel King.
22. V. Jonathan, 4th Aug. 1701.
23. VI. Thomas, 12th Oct. 1703.
24. VII. Elisha, 15th Feb. 1706-7.

16 John Linnel of Barnstable, married Ruth Davis 1696, died 8th May, 1748.
25. I. Thankful, 12th Nov. 1696, married James Bearse 12th Nov. 1726.
26. II. Samuel, 16th Nov. 1699, died Sept. 12, 1770.
27. III. John, 15th June, 1702.
28. IV. Bethia, 14th May, 1704, married Augustine Bearse 3d June, 1728.
29. V. Joseph, 12th June 1707.
30. VI. Hannah, 10th July, 1709.
31. VII. Jabez, 31st July, 1711.

32. Jonathan Linnell, Jr., of Orleans, had a son Josiah, father of the present Jonathan L., aged 80, and other children, but I have no record of the family.

23. Thomas Linnel married and had a family, but I have no copy of the record. He had several children.
33. I. Jonathan, born 1720, died June 7, 1794.
34. II. Thomas, born 1731, died Aug. 27, 1817.

26 Samuel Linnel, married Wid. Hannah Scudder.
35. I. Elizabeth, Oct. 8, 1726, married Benjamin Blossom of Sandwich 1750.
36. II. Hannah, born 1st Feb. 1728, married Simeon Jones, Jr., April 4, 1749.
37. III. Abigail, born 14th Jan. 1730, married Seth Goodspeed March 13, 1753.
38. IV. Samuel, born 9th April, 1733.
39. V. John, 10th Nov. 1735.
40. VI. Bethia, 17th April, 1744.

27 John Linnel, married Mary Phinney Oct. 28, 1734.

29 Joseph Linnel, married Dorcas Smith Nov. 26, 1747.

41.   I.   Levi, 6th Feb. 1749, O. S.
42.   II.   Thankful, 30th July, 1750, O. S.
43.   III.   Dorcas, 27th July, 1752, O. S.
44.   IV.   Lydia, 21st Feb. 1754, N. S.
45.   V.   Heman, 28th Jan. 1756.
46.   VI.   Sarah, 24th Dec. 1757.
47.   VII.   Abigail, 11th March, 1761.
48.   VIII.   Rebecca, 9th May, 1763, died April 29, 1854.

31 Jabez Linnel, married Sarah Bacon, 3d, Nov. 11, 1736, 2d, Wid. Sa. Sturgis Sept. 26, '51, died Jan. 31, '68.

49.   I.   Mary, 20th Feb. 1737.
50.   II.   Deborah, 8th April, '39.
51.   III.   Elisha, 20th Oct. '40.
52.   IV.   Joseph, 6th Nov. '43.
53.   V.   Jean, 16th March, '44.
54.   VI.   John, 28th Jan. '48.
55.   VII.   Susanna, baptized 12th Nov. '52.
56.   VIII.   Elizabeth, baptized Nov. 17, '54.

Deborah married Nath'l Allen Nov. 6, 1759.

Joseph married Susan Cobb, Jr., 11th March, 1765.

33 Jona. Linnel, Esq., of Orleans, married Experience Mayo. 2d, Wid. Rachel Smith Aug. 28, 1730.

57.   Experience, married ——— Hickman.
58.   Thomas.
59.   Ruth, married Joshua Hopkins.
60.   Zerviah.
61.   Uriah, removed.
62.   Samuel, died aged 94.

45, Heman Linnel of Y. married Elizabeth ——— .

63.   I.   Betty, Feb. 27, 1793.
64.   II.   Abigail, Sept. 27, 1790.

51, Elisha Linnel, married Mehitable.

65.   I.   Moses, 1st June, 1770.
66.   II.   Jabez, 12th Aug. 1773.
67.   III.   John, 25th Dec. 1775.

Mr. Robert Linnel, the ancestor of this family, came over in 1638, settled in Scituate that year, and removed to Barnstable on the following. The prefix of honor to his name indicates that he was a man of some wealth and consideration in his native land. He brought a letter, certifying that he and his wife had been members in good standing in the Congregational Church in London, and recommending them to the church in Scituate, of which they became members Sept. 16, 1638. Mr. Lothrop, in making his record, calls him "My Brother Robert Linnel," subsequently, "My Brother Linnel;" and in the record of his son Thomas's marriage "Brother Larnett." The use of the pronoun clearly indicates that they were relatives by marriage, and were brothers-in-law. The Probate Records also show that several of the first settlers in Barnstable were also his relatives.

Mr. Linnel took the oath of allegiance to the King and of fidelity to the Colony Feb. 1, 1638-9, and was admitted a freeman on the 3d of December following. He was one of the grantees of the lands at Sippican January 1638-9, and a grand juror at the June term of the Court. His early admission to the privileges and to the duties of a citizen, shows that he was a man of good character, and that he had previously been well known by many of the leading men of the colony. What his occupation was before he came over, does not appear; but it may safely be assumed that a resident of the city of London was not a farmer, the business to which necessity compelled him to resort in his old age.

Mr. Linnel was nearly sixty years of age when he came to Barnstable. His daughter Sarah born, if the Custom House record is reliable, in 1607, married in England Thomas Ewer, and came over in 1635. Her husband died in 1638, and she married Dec. 11, 1639, Thomas Lothrop of Barnstable.* Mr. Savage calls Sarah the daughter of William Larnet or Larned, of Charleston. The spelling of the name in Mr. Lothrop's record of his son's marriage favors that supposition; but that is not reliable, for no Barnstable name is found spelled in so many different forms. Whether Linnel or Linnet is the better spelling, it is difficult to determine. The latter is the old and common pronunciation.

If Sarah was his daughter, he was born as early as 1584, and was too old when he came over to enter vigorously into the business of pioneer life, and his age accounts for the quiet, secluded manner in which he afterwards lived. He died 27th Feb. 1662-3, an aged man, leaving a small estate to his widow and children.

Though the expense of transporting his large family to New England absorbed a large portion of his estate, yet in the assignment of the lands in Barnstable, he ranked among those who were called wealthy. His houselot containing ten acres was bounded northerly by the harbor, easterly by the lot of Thomas Lumbard, southerly by the highway, and westerly by the home-lots of William and John Casely. He also owned three acres of planting land in the Common Field, three acres of meadow at Sandy Neck, nine at Scorton, a great lot containing sixty acres, and rights to commonage.

His wife that came over with him I think died early, and his

---

*That a boy of eighteen should have married a widow aged 32, having several children, seems improbable; but such is the record. Though I have what under ordinary circumstances I should call the best of authority, yet I state the whole matter doubtfully. A link in the chain is wanting. Mr. Linnel in his will names four children, David, Hannah, Abigail and Bethia, and his wife Jennimah.

widow Jemimah was probably a second wife. This is the opinion
of Mr. Savage. There is no recorded evidence that Mr. Linnel
married twice ; but a variety of little circumstances make it quite
certain. He had six children that lived to mature age, and a
daughter Bethia baptized in Barnstable Feb. 7, 1640-1. His
daughter was probably by his last wife. There was also a Shubael Linnel that I name as his son, and probably born in this
country, though there is no record of his birth either in Scituate
or Barnstable.

Mr. Linnel died a poor man. His sons had been nursed in
the lap of ease, and wanted that energy of character which is in-
dispensable for success in life. Wealth has its laws which operate as invariably and as inexorably as the laws which govern the
natural world. The idle, the lazy, and the improvident never can
be rich. The parent may bestow wealth, it is soon dissipated—
little will be inherited by the grandchildren. The tax lists exhibit the folly of bequeathing wealth to thriftless children, to
those who have not been educated to be temperate, honest, industrious and frugal. Of the 24 families who ranked as wealthy and
paid the highest rate of tax in Barnstable in 1703, only 16, or
less than one-half of the families had maintained their relative position in society in 1737, and only three in 1787. Of the fifteen
solid men of Barnstable in 1787, the grandchildren of only one
possesses the property of the grandfather unimpaired. The general rule for the descent of property is this : one-third of the children maintain the position of the father, one-sixth of the grand-
children, and one-ninth of the great-grandchildren. Examine any
tax-list, you will find that only a small minority of those who pay
the highest taxes, inherited their estates—it is the industrious,
the frugal and the energetic, that keep the wheels of business
prosperity in motion, and the parent who so educates his child
confers a greater blessing on him than he will to devise him great
wealth. However, life has higher aims, higher aspirations, than
money making. That is an art that, like making shoes, may be
learned. The wealthiest man is not the happiest, nor the best
member of society. He is often racked by care, and forgets the
duties he owes to his God, his neighbor and his family.

Mr. Robert Linnel in his will dated 23d January, 1662-3,
gives to his wife Jemimah Linnel the use and improvement of his
house and homelot so long as she remains a widow, and his furniture, a plow, a cart, and two cows and a calf forever. Thomas
Lothrop deposed to the will before Mr. Thomas Hinckley, Justice of the Peace, March 12, 1662-3, and in his testimony he
swears that the words "*and a calf*" were put into the will after
the decease of Mr. Linnel on the 27th of Feb. 1662-3. To his
son David he gives his lot on the south side of the road containing four acres adjoining John Caseley's land, three acres of

marsh at Sandy Neck, and his house and homelot, including the swamp he bought of Thomas Lewes after the death or marriage of his wife. To his daughter Abigail three acres of upland and meadow in the common-field, on the north-westerly side of Mattakeese pond. To John Davis (who married his daughter Hannah) his two oxen, on condition that he provided his wife with wood, plowed her grounds, and mowed her meadow two years, if she remained a widow so long, if not, then to be free. To his daughter Bethia one cow, "to have it when my wife will."

Oct. 20, 1669, "Penniah Linnet" complained to the Court that David Linnit had possessed himself of the house and land given her by her deceased husband, Mr. Robert Linnitt, and had given her no satisfaction for the same. The Court ordered that he give her satisfaction for the same before the next March Court, otherwise the Court order that he shall be disposed of the same. As no subsequent action was taken the presumption is, that David did make the required satisfaction.

Mr. Deane in his history of Scituate, page 305, mis-quotes this record. He substitutes "son Robert" for David, and Mr. Savage copies the error. The unusual name Peninah in the Court orders is probably a mistake of the Clerk.

The Home Lot, dwelling-house, and some articles of personal estate, were apprised by Thomas Lothrop and Thos. Lewis at £55,4,6. He owed Mr. Thomas Clark £1,10 shillings, and some other small debts, and the Court ordered March 3, 1662-3, that Joseph Lothrop and Nathaniel Bacon "bee helpful to the Widdow Linnel in seeing the debts payed either out of the whole or pte of the estate."

In the will (evidently drawn up by one not accustomed to framing legal instruments) Mr. Linnel only names three of his children, David, Abigail and Bethia. He names John Davis who married his daughter Hannah then living, but does not call her by name. He does not name his daughter Mary who married Richard Childs. He names neither Shubael nor Samuel Linnel, both of whom were then living if the names are not confounded, and supposed to be his sons.

Mr. Linnel had sold his meadow at Scorton and his great lot containing "three score acres," or perhaps he had given the same to his other children by deed as their portion, a common practice in those times, and therefore not named in his will. The apprisement of his homestead, &c., at £55, may seem a low price. Eight years before Thomas Lumbard sold his homestead adjoining the Linnels, and fully as valuable for £20. Very few persons at their time were worth £100 sterling, or £500 in silver money.

The writer of fiction could hardly select a more interesting subject on which to employ his pen than the history of the Linnel family. He need not plume the wings of his imagination and soar into the regions of romance for incidents—the sober records of history, and the traditionary lore preserved in the archives of memory, would furnish him with ample materials. The story of the courtship and marriage of David Linnel and Hannah Shelly had a romantic interest, and if we could divest it of some of the homely phrases, which Puritan clerks have entwined around it, it would embody quite as much poetic feeling as that of John Alden and Priscilla Mullins, whose loves are immortalized in the poem of Longfellow. Most fortunately for the genius and reputation of the poet, paper and ink were not so abundant when Priscilla courted John, as at that later period when David and Hannah loved and married. John had no fear of incurring the penalty of the old law respecting the "enveagleing of men's daughters and maids under guardians," because Priscilla "made the motion of marriage" against which no law has been made to this day. The Pilgrim fathers enacted, "That if any shall make any motion of marriage to any man's daughter, or mayde servant, not haveing first obtayned leave and consent of the parents or master so to doe, shall be punished either by fine or corporall punishment or both at the discretions of the bench." Under this law David and Hannah were censured by the church, and condemned by the magistrates to suffer its penalties.

That most eccentric personage, Rebecca Blush, was also one of the Linnel family. The Curiosity Shop created by the inventive genius of Dickens was an inattractive collection when compared with "Aunt Beck's Museum." This has already been described, and the story need not be repeated.

Elisha Linnel of Yarmouth, a second edition of Sir John Fallstaff, was of this family. His eccentricities and witty sayings are remembered. In most of the Barnstable families the characteristic peculiarities of the ancestor have been transmitted down to the present generation. This remark will not apply to the Linnel family.

David Linnell, son of Robert, was able to bear arms in 1643, consequently was born as early as 1627. He was married March 9, 1652-3, by Thomas Hinckley, Esq., to Hannah Shelley, a daughter of Robert Shelley, and then in the sixteenth year of her age. Our ancestors encouraged early marriages. He who married at eighteen was admitted to all the privileges, and required to perform all the duties of a citizen ; while, he that remained single, had to tarry till he was twenty-four to be enrolled as a townsman. At the present time the public policy on which such laws were based, is not very apparent. Our fathers, however, did not act from blind impulse—they had reasons for acting,—reasons that were cogent, strong, and in their judgments conclusive for thus discriminating ; some were founded on the circumstances and necessities of the times—some on natural laws, which never change—never cease to operate. They believed that on the man who was the head of a family, more powerful incentives operate to induce him to be temperate, industrious, honest and frugal, than on the man who lives in celibacy. The married man, if there be a spark of energy in his character, that spark will soon kindle into a flame, and he will toil early and late, he will save what he earns that he may have a house of his own—a place that he can call home—a freehold estate of which he is both landlord and tenant. Thus impelled, toil is no burden—he forms habits of industry and thrift, and like other habits they become a second nature. Home and its associations have, especially after a day spent in toil, more attractions for him, than the haunts of vice and dissipation—where evil communications would corrupt his manners, uproot and destroy those germs of virtue early implanted in the mind by parental teachings, and subsequently confirmed by the harmonizing influences of the domestic circle. The young man was bound to his wife, to his children, to his parents, to his native town, to the colony. He had no inducements to wander. Land was wealth—it cost little save the labor of rescuing it from the wilderness—building materials were scattered over the whole land, and industry soon converted them into comfortable dwellings. Families were wanted to build up towns, and to give strength to the colony. Immigration had nearly ceased in 1640; few came over during the next century, and for that reason the population of New England at the commencement of the Revolutionary War was as homogenius a race, as that of any country in the world.

In early times a large family was considered a blessing, which the early tax lists confirm and prove. As a class, those who paid the highest taxes had the largest families. It is also a noticeable fact that the men of standing, influence and respectability, had numerous children. The reverse, at the present time, is perhaps a nearer approximation to the truth.*

Generally our fathers were unable to give large dowers to their daughters. They had land, and herds and flocks; but no money. By common consent or usage, the sons inherited the lands. Sometimes an unmarried daughter was provided with a home at the old homestead. A goodly custom prevailed, and in the families of many farmers has come down to the present time, each girl of the family was allowed to take for her own, a certain proportion of the annual product of wool and flax. This she spun and wove with her own hands into cloth, out of which she made

---

*In one of the small states or circles of Germany, pauperism had increased to such an alarming extent as to make it probable that if some check could not be devised, the whole population would be involved in a common ruin. A law was enacted that no man should have a certificate to marry granted to him until he had first proved to the satisfaction of the magistrate that he had the means of supporting a family. The law was rigidly enforced, and after the lapse of one generation not a beggar was to be found in the State.

bedding and other articles of comfort or convenience, that she would need at her marriage. The girl who could exhibit the greatest number of articles so made was considered the likeliest, if not the prettiest Miss in the neighborhood, and could have her choice among the beaux. This custom partially compensated for the unequal mode in which estates were divided in those days, and it had one good effect, it put the daughters of the poor and the rich on one common level.

David Linnel and Hannah Shelley were "children of the Barnstable Church." In consequence of some miscarriages between them, the particulars whereof are stated in the church records, they were cut off from the privileges of that relation May 30, 1652, and for the same offence, by order of the Court at Plymouth, both were "punished with scourges here in Barnstable June 8, 1652." The town had then been settled thirteen years, and this was only the fourth* case that had required the interposition of the authority of the magistrates. All of them were offences against good morals. but no magistrate at the present day would feel called upon to interpose his authority in similar cases. To judge rightly we must bear in mind that our ancestors allowed nothing that had the appearance of evil to pass unnoticed and unrebuked. In justice to the memory of David Linnel and Hannah Shelley I will relate the circumstances, though I had intended not to give the particulars.

Mr. Robert Linnel was aged and had taken a second wife that "knew not David," and cared little for his well-being. Robert Shelley was an easy, good-natured man, and cared little how the world moved. He was however an honest man, a good neighbor, and a sincere christian. His wife Judith Garnet was, before her marriage, a Boston woman—a member of the church there, proud, tenacious of her own opinions, and had very little control over her tongue, which ran like a whip-saw, cutting everything it came in contact with.

In 1648 some of the sisters of the church held a private meeting. Mrs. Judith was not called—she took umbrage, and vented her spite in slandering the members of the church. She said

---

*The entries on the town records do not confirm the allegations on the colony and church records. These discrepancies, I am aware, can be explained perhaps satisfactorily. Though the proceedings were in accordance with the spirit of the times, I think they were hasty and ill advised, and subsequent events go far to prove that the actors were so satisfied. It is unpleasant, however, to refer to these cases, but the historian is not authorized to manufacture his facts. He has no right to skip over matters of record. That they were small offences, the details on the records show. The complaints were against persons who had no friends to take an active interest in their welfare. Six years afterward, according to family tradition, a similar complaint was made against Hon. Barnabas Lothrop and Susanna Clarke, afterwards his wife. Mr. Lothrop had influential friends and was able to defend himself. The compliant was dismissed and no record made. The case of David Linnel and Hannah Shelly was of the same character. Hannah's mother was a bad woman, and her father an easy good natured man; but the daughter was not to be blamed for the faults of her parents. She was rather entitled to sympathy.

"Mrs. Dimmock was proud, and went about telling lies;" that Mrs. Wells had done the same, that Mr. Lothrop and Elder Cobb "did talk of her" on a day when they went to visit Mr. Huckins, who was then sick at Mrs. Well's house. She continued to affirm these things "as confidently as if she had a spirit of Revelation." Mr. Lothrop in his record adds, "Wee had long patience towards her, and used all courteous intreatyes and persuations; but the longer wee waited, the worse she was."

Nothing like it had before happened in the settlement. The story was soon known to the old and the young—it was discussed in every circle—it was the standing topic of conversation for six months. The messengers of the church waited on Mrs. Judith—they could not persuade her to acknowledge her fault—she denounced Mr. Lothrop and all who were sent to her, in the most severe terms of abuse. She could find no one to sustain her—never could prove anything, and Mr. Lothrop adds, "was wondrous perremtorye in all her carriages." She was excommunicated June 4, 1649.

Hannah was then only twelve years of age, a time of life when the sayings of the mother make a deep impression on the mind. She had heard her mother in a loud and peremptory tone of voice slander the best men and women in the settlement. The father was a good natured, easy man, and did not reprove his wife for speaking ill of her neighbors. Brought up under such influences, is it surprising that the daughter should sometimes speak inconsiderately, loosely, lasciviously? I think not. I think the mother more blameworthy, better meriting the scourges than the daughter.

David and Hannah were summoned to appear at a meeting of the church. They attended May 30, 1652, and there in the presence of the whole congregation confessed their fault. "They were both, by the sentence and joint consent of the church, pronounced to be cutt off from that relation which they hadd formerlye to the church by virtue of their parents covenaunt." The action of the church was not objectionable; but mark the date, May 30, 1652.

The Court was held in Plymouth June 3, 1652, only four days afterwards. Mr. Thomas Dexter, Sen'r, and John Chipman, were the grand jurors from Barnstable, and it was their duty to complain of every violation of law or of good morals that came to their knowledge. The facts were notorious for it is called "a publique fame" on the church records. They were probably present when the confession was made. There were also several others beside the jurors who knew the facts. Thus far the proceedings were in accordance with the customs of the times.

In the list of presentments made by the "Grand Enquest" dated June 2, 1652, neither David Linnel nor Hannah Shelley are indicted ; yet, on the next day, June 3, 1652, the Court condemn "both of them to be publicly whipt at Barnstable, where they live," and the sentence was executed at Barnstable five days afterwards, that is on the 8th day of June, 1652.

These proceedings were in violation of the form of law ; the accused were not indicted by the grand jury—they were not heard in their defence, do not appear to have been at Court, and were condemned and punished for a crime of which they had not confessed themselves guilty.

The conduct of John Alden and Priscilla Mullins technically was not in violation of the law ; but it was a violation of its spirit and meaning. That they should be glorified and their praises sung by the poet, and that David and Hannah should be whipped at the post, seems not to be meting out equal and even handed justice to all. If the Court had ordered Mrs. Judith to have been scourged in public she would have enlisted but little sympathy in her behalf.

David Linnel inherited, as already stated, the homestead of his father. That portion of it that adjoined the public highway he does not appear to have owned in 1686. He may have owned the north part of it, and the description of it in his will favors that presumption, and there he built his two story single house, with a leanto. He was not a prominent man, and little is known of him. He delayed joining the church till July 1, 1688, the year before his death. His wife did not join. His will is dated Nov. 14, 1688, and was proved March 9th following. To his sons Samuel and Elisha, and his daughters Hannah Davis, Mary, Experience, Susanna and Abigail, he gives one shilling each. To his sons Jonathan and John his dwelling-house and housing and all his lands, both upland and marsh, the upland to be divided lengthwise, and his son Jonathan to have his house and to pay his brother John one-half as much as said house shall be judged to be worth by indifferent men ; and both upland and marsh to be equally divided for quantity and quality between them, and to be unto them, and their heirs forever." He gave to his wife Hannah the improvement of one-third of his lands and the leanto room of his house during her widowhood, and appoints her sole executrix. His personal estate was apprised at £28,6,6. In the apprisement corn and barley are rated at 1 shilling 6 pence, or 25 cents per bushel.

The will of Wid. Hannah Linnel is dated Feb. 2, 1708-9, and was proved on the 5th of April following. She names her daughters Abigail Linnel, Mary Sergeant, wife of John, Experience, wife of Jabez Davis, Susanna, wife of Eben. Phinney, and her grand-daughter Hannah Davis, daughter of Dollar. She signs with her mark, and appoints John Phinney, Jr., her executor.

Respecting Shubael Linnel little is known. He is named in

1667 as a guardian of the children of the second Thomas Ewer. A Samuel Linnel of Barnstable was killed at the battle of Rehobeth, and as the only Samuel Linnel of Barnstable in 1776 was Samuel, son of David, and as he is named as living in 1688 he could not have been the man killed in 1676. To reconcile these conflicting statements I have supposed that there is an error in the records, that Shubael, the guardian, is the same person who is called Samuel in the returns of the killed at Rehobeth March 26, 1676.

Jonathan Linnel, son of David, removed to Eastham about the year 1695, and is the ancestor of the Linnels of that town and Orleans. He was a respectable man and accumulated a good estate, though he signs his will, proved Sept. 19, 1726, with his mark. He names his wife Rebecca. To his son Elisha he gave land in Harwich bought of Sarah and Elizabeth Rogers, meadow near Hog Island, &c. To his son Jonathan the remainder of his estate in Harwich and Eastham. He names his daughter Abigail King. To his daughter Hannah Mayo he gave lands in Bridgewater and Middleboro', purchased of Elisha Mayo. He also names his grand-children Elizabeth Mayo and Elizabeth King. His estate was apprised at £1,465,15,9, but it should be borne in mind that a pound was then only about a dollar in silver money. A pair of oxen was apprised at £15, or fifteen silver dollars. This branch of the family has occupied a respectable position in society. The late Jonathan Linnel, Esq., was noted for his business capacity and his ready wit, which sparkled on all occasions.

John Linnel, son of David, is the ancestor of the Barnstable and Yarmouth families of the name. He married Ruth, daughter of John Davis. He was a prudent, industrious and respectable man. He resided a part of his life on his farm in the easterly part of Chequaquet, now called Hyannis Port, and a part, on the John Davis estate. At his death he owned and occupied the house that stood opposite the residence of Dea. John Munroe, now owned by Capt. Foster. He was one of the earliest who removed to South Sea, as the south part of the town was then called. He died Feb. 9, (7th town record) 1747-8, in the 78th year of his age, and his wife Ruth May 8, 1748, in the 75th year of her age. Both have monuments to their memory in the old grave-yard.

In his will dated Oct. 1, 1737, proved 7th July, 1748, he names his wife Ruth and his daughters Thankful Bearse, Bethia Bearse and Hannah Linnel. In a codicil dated July 5, 1748, he says his daughter Bethia is dead. To his daughter Hannah he gave his great chamber and privileges in the house so long as she remained single. To his son Samuel the southwest part of his farm or homestead at South Sea, containing twenty-one acres of upland and seven of meadow; to his son John the middle portion containing nineteen acres of upland and three acres of marsh; to his son Joseph the remaining or easterly part, containing eleven acres of upland and three of marsh; and to his son Jabez, "All his homestead farm lands, meadows, and house wherein he then dwelt." His wife Ruth owned real estate in her own right. Her will, proved July 5, 1748, is witnessed by Solomon Otis, David Crocker and Robert Davis. She refers to her sister Mercy Davis, deceased, and to her unmarried daughter Hannah. She owned land on the east side of the Hyannis road, adjoining Nathaniel Baker's, formerly the property of her father.

All of the name in Barnstable and Yarmouth are descendants of John, son of David. Samuel, the eldest son, married in 1725 the widow Hannah Scudder, and had six children. John, the second son, married Mary Phinney Oct. 24, 1734. I find no record of his family; I think, however, he was the father of the John Jr., who married the eccentric Rebecca Linnel, afterwards the wife of Elisha Blush, and of whose museum I have given a full account in a former article. Joseph, the third son, married Nov. 26, 1747, Dorcas Smith. He removed to Yarmouth in 1755. He had eight children. Heman, his fifth child, died at the Alms House in Yarmouth Feb. 10, 1848, aged 92. His youngest child, Rebecca, died April 29, 1854, aged 91 years.

Mr. Jabez Linnel, the youngest son of John, was a respectable man. He inherited his father's dwelling-house on the Davis estate, afterward the property of the late Hezekiah Doane. Mr. Jabez Linnel married Nov. 11, 1736, Sarah Bacon, 3d, and Sept. 26, 1751, Mrs. Sarah Sturgis. She died Jan. 31, 1768, aged 54. The eight children of this family did not maintain the respectable position in society of the parents. Elisha, one of the sons, born Oct. 20, 1740, was the laziest among the lazy, and he took no offence when reproved for his slothful and vagrant habits. If such notoriety be an honor, Elisha would have undisputed claim to be called the champion of the lazy. He was courteous in his address, had a ready command of language, and there was always a spice of humor in his conversation. He was not a mean beggar, he would not receive a mean gift, or one that involved any effort on his part. He assumed that he had a right to beg, and that it was the duty of the more wealthy to give. As illustrations of his character and manner I select the following from many amusing stories told of him:

Nearly sixty years ago, when I was a child, Elisha called at my father's house. Addressing my father, he said, "I have no corn in my house, I pray that, out of your great abundance, you will give me only half a bushel." My father, knowing Elisha's character and habits, said, "I am busy to-day, if you will go to the crib and shell it yourself you may take 'only half a bushel.'" Quoth Elisha, "I will go a *leetle* further, and if I do not get it ready shelled I will call on my return and shell it." He did not call on his return.

This anecdote is often told, and illustrates his indolent habits. The following shows his independent manner of soliciting charity :

He asked the late Capt. Nathan Hallet to give him some codfish. Capt. Hallet had just bought a quintal for his own use, that were sunburnt in curing, and though they would break easy, and therefore unfit to send to market, were nice and good. He gave Elisha several. He knew that Capt. Hallet was using the same in his family, and he could not refuse to receive them. However, before leaving the yard he dropped them beside the fence. Capt. Hallett told the story. A little time after some one asked Elisha if it was true. "Yes," said Elisha, "it is true. Do you think I will eat broken fish for Capt. Hallet? I want the best. I have poor fish enough at home."

The physiological history of this family is full of interest to the student.* None of the Linnels were vicious men. The Linnel and the Shelly blood, however, did not amalgamate. The history of the family develops two distinct races in all its generations. The pure blooded Linnel is an honest man, a good neighbor, and usually a sincere christian. The Shellys are easy and good natured ; usually indolent and wanting in energy of character, and very rarely accumulate wealth. These views may seem out of place. I think not, for the habits and character of the men suggested them, and I have simply followed the lead. Many of the remarks are general, however, and will apply to other families.

---

*The English aristocracy furnishes a good illustration. If none were elevated from the commonalty to the peerage the old families would soon run out. It is notorious that the most gifted among the nobility were not born of noble blood. The gentle and the plebian blood that has been infused, is all that gives vitality to the aristocracy. Hereditary scrofula and insanity has nearly dstroyed the royal family.

LOTHROP.

REV. JOHN LOTHROP.

This distinguished man was the 12th child of Thomas Lowthropp, first of Cherry Burton, and later of Ellen, Yorkshire, England. Thomas was the son of John, of Lowthropp, a parish in the East Riding of York.

I. Mr. John Lothrop died 8th Nov. 1653. Married, first —— ——; she died 1633. Second, Wid. Ann Hammond, Feb. 17, 1636-7.

Children born in England.

1. Jane, bap. Sept. 29, 1614, at Edgerby, Kent.
2. Ann, b. Mar. 12, 1616, died 1619.
3. John, b. Feb. 22, 1617-18.
4. Barbara, b. Oct. 1, 1619.
5. Thomas, b. 1621.
6. Samuel, —— died 19th Feb. 1701.
7. Joseph, b. 1624, died 1702.
8. Benjamin.

Born in Scituate.

9. Barnabas, bap. 6th June, 1636, 26th Oct. 1715.
10. A daughter, 1638, 30th July, 1638.

Born in Barnstable.

11. Abigail, bap. 2d Nov. 1639.
12. Bathshua, 27th Feb. 1641, died Jan. 8, 1723.
13. John, 9th Feb. 1644, died 18th Sept. 1727.
14. A son, 1649, born 25th Jan. 1649.
    Jane married Samuel Fuller 8th April, 1635.
    Barbara married John Emerson 19th July, 1638.
    Abigail married James Clark 7th Oct. 1657.
    Bathshua married Alex. Marsh.

II. Thomas Lothrop married Wid. Sarah Ewer 11th Dec. 1639.

Children born in Barnstable

14. Mary, 4th Oct. 1640.
15. Hannah, 18th Oct. '42.
16. Thomas, 7th July, '44.
17. Melatiah, 2d Nov. '46, died 6th Feb. 1711-12.
18. Bethia, 23d July, '49, died 10th July 1697.
   Mary married 1st John Stearns 20th Nov. '56. 2d, Wm. French 6th May, 1659. 3d, Isaac Mixer 1684.
   Bethia married John Hinckley July, 1668.
   III. Samuel Lothrop married 1st Eliz. Scudder 28th Nov. 1644. 2d, Abigail ———, 1640, died aged over 100.

Born in Barnstable.

19. John, bap. Boston 7th Dec. 1645.

In New London.

20. Elizabeth.
21. Samuel, 1652.
22. Israel, 1659.
23. Joseph, 1661.
24. Ann, died 19th Nov. 1745, and three other daughters.
   Elizabeth married Isaac Royce 15th Dec. 1669.
   Ann married Wm. Heugh.
   IV. Hon. Joseph Lothrop married Mary Ansel 11th Dec. 1650.

Born in Barnstable.

25. A daughter, 19th Nov. 1651, bur'd 20th.
26. Joseph, 5th Dec. 1652, died Oct. 1676.
27. Mary, 22d March, 1654.
28. Benjamin, 25th July, '57.
29. Elizabeth, 18th Sept. '59.
30. John, 28th Nov. '61, died 30th Dec. '63.
31. Samuel, 17th March, '63-4.
32. John, 7th Aug. '66.
33. Barnabas, 24th Feb. 1668.
34. Hope, 15th July, '71, died 29th Oct. 1734.
35. Thomas, 6th Jan. '73, died 3d July, 1757.
36. Hannah, 23d Jan. '75, died 1st Feb. 1680.
   Mary married ——— Denes.
   Eliz. married Thomas Fuller 29th Dec. 1680.

V. Benjamin Lothrop married Martha ———. Removed to Charleston.
37. Martha, born 3d Nov. 1652.
38. Hannah, 15th Sept. '55.
39. Benjamin, bap. 5th Aug. '60.
40. Mary, 9th June, '61.
41. Sarah, born 10th April, '64, died young.
42. Elizabeth, bap. 21st May, '65.
43. Rebecca, born 14th Nov. '66.
44. Mercy, 17th Dec. '70.
45. John, 15th July, '72, died young.
   Martha married John Goodwin 2d Dec. 1669.
   Mary married Wm. Brown 21st May, 1679.
   Hannah married Henry Swain 21st Aug. 1679.
   VIII. Hon. Barnabas Lothrop married 1st Susan Clark 1st Dec. 1658, died 28th Sept. '97. 2d, Wid. Abigail Dudson, died 21st Dec. 1715.

Children born in Barnstable.

46. John, 7th Oct. 1659, died April 1666.
47. Abigail, 18th Dec. '60.
48. Barnabas, 22d March, '62-3, died 11th Oct. 1732.
49. Susanna, 28th Feb. 64-5.
50. John, 1667, died 23d Oct. '95.
51. Nathaniel, 23d Nov. '69, died 1700.
52. Bathshua, 25th June, '71.
53. Anna, 10th Aug. '73.
54. Thomas, 7th March, 74-5, died 13th Oct. '75.
55. Mercy, 27th June, '76, died 3d July, '77.
56. Sarah.
57. Thankful, 26th May, '79, 2d June, 1752.
58. James, bap. 30th March, '84, died young.
59. Samuel, bap. 14th June, '85, died young.
   Abigail married Thomas Sturgis, 1680.
   Susanna married Capt. Wm. Shurtleff.
   Bathshua married ——— Freeman.
   Anna married Eben. Lewes April 1691.
   Sarah married ——— Skeff.
   Thankful married John Hedge 25th Jan. 1699-10.
   XII. Capt. John Lothrop married 1st Mary Cole, Jr., 3d Jan. 1671-2. 2d Wid. Hannah Fuller 9th Dec. 1698.

Children born in Barnstable.

60. John, 5th Aug. 1673, died 1716.
61. Mary, 27th Oct. '75.
62. Martha, 11th Nov. '77.

63. Elizabeth, 16th Sept. '79.
64. James, 3d July, '81, died young.
65. Hannah, 13th March, '82-3.
66. Jonathan, 14th Nov. '84, died young.
67. Barnabas, 22d Oct. '86.
68. Abigail, 23d April, '89.
69. Experience, 7th Jan. 91-2.
70. Bathshua, 19th Dec. '96.
71. Phebe, Sept. 1701, by 2d wife.
72. Benjamin, 8th April, 1704, by 2d wife.
    Mary married James Howland 8th Sept. 1697.
    Elizabeth married James Lewes Nov. 1698.
    Hannah married John Cobb 25th Dec. 1707.
    Phebe married Elisha Thacher.
    XVI. Thomas Lothrop, Jr., was living in 1697.
    XVII. Melatiah Lothrop married Sarah Farrah 20th May, 1667, died 23d May, 1712.

Children born in Barnstable.

73. Thomas, 22d Aug. 1668.
74. Tabitha, 3d April, '71.
75. Isaac, 23d June, '73.
76. Joseph, 15th Dec. '75, died Feb. 11, 1747-8.
77. Elizabeth, 23d Nov. '77, died Feb. 21, 1763.
78. Ichabod, 20th June, '80.
79. Shubael, 20th April, '82.
80. Sarah, 5th March, '83-4.
    Tabitha married Shubael Dimmock 4th May, 1699.
    Eliza. married Hope Lothrop 17th Dec. 1696.
    Sarah married 1st, Jos. Huckins 18th Sept. 1702. 2d, John Troop 14th Oct. 1708.
    XIX to XXIV. Connecticut families.
    XXIII. Jos. Lothrop, son of Sam'l, had
    Joseph.
    Barnabas.
    Solomon, and four daughters.

Solomon had one son Joseph, D. D., of West Springfield. Dr. Joseph had sons Solomon, Seth, Joseph, Hon. Samuel, and Dwight. The late Rev. John Lothrop, D. D., of Boston, was also descendant of Samuel. [Deane.]

XXVIII. Benj. Lothrop townsman 1683, find no more respecting him.

XXXI. Samuel Lothrop married Hannah Crocker 1st July, 1686.

Children born in Barnstable.

81. Mary, 19th Oct. 1688.
82. Hannah, 11th Nov. 1690, died 1751.
83. Abigail, 10th Aug. '93.
84. Benjamin, 16th April, '96.
85. Joseph, 10th Nov. '98.
86. Samuel, 28th April, 1700.
    Mary married Daniel Davis.
    Hannah died unmarried 1751.
    Abigail, single.
    XXXIV.   Hope Lothrop married Eliza. Lothrop 17th Dec. 1696.

Children born in Barnstable, Falmouth, and Sharon, Ct.

87. Benjamin, 18th Oct. 1697, died 16th June, 1758.
88. John, 3d Oct. '99, died Oct. 1752.
89. Rebecca, 25th Nov. 1701.
90. Sarah, 31st Dec. '03, died 1731.
91. Ebenezer, 1st May, '06, died Sept. 1752.
92. Ichabod, 20th June, '08, died Oct. 1752.
93. Solomon, 10th Sept. '10, died 5th March, 1758.
94. Elizabeth, 20th Jan. '12.
95. Maltiah, 20th Feb. '14, died 1787.
96. Mary, 29th June, '16.
97. Joseph, 12th Sept. '20.
98. Hannah, 19th Nov. '22.
    XXXV.   Thomas Lothrop married Experience Gorham 23d April, 1697, died 23d Dec. 1733.   2d, Deborah Loring 3d June, 1736.

Children born in Barnstable.

99. A son, 10th Jan. 1697-8, died 3d Feb. next.
100. Deborah, 21st April, '99.
101. Mary, 4th April, 1701.
102. James, 9th Aug. '03, died April 1748.
103. Thomas, 8th July, '05.
104. Ansel, July, '07.
105. Joseph, 8th Dec. '09, died 1761.
106. Seth, March, '12.
107. John, bap. 27th June, '25.
108. Lydia, bap. 27th June, '25.
109. Elizabeth, bap. 27th June, '25.
110. Mehitabel, bap. 27th June, '25, died Nov. 1764.
111. Rebecca, bap. 27th June, '25.
112. Ansel, born 25th July, 1725.
    Lydia married Eben. Bacon 17th Jan. 1734.

Eliza. married Thos. Witherel of S., 14th Aug. 1738.
Rebecca married Jos. Hatch of Tollend 16th May, '34.
XXXVI to XLV. Charlestown families.
XLVIII. Barnabas Lothrop, Jr., married Eliza. Hedge
14th Nov. 1687, died 18th Sept. 1747.

Children born in Barnstable.

113. Mercy, 1st March 1689, died 30th July, 1741.
114. Elizabeth, 15th Sept. '90, died 14th Feb. 1768.
115. Barnabas, 10th Nov. '92, died 6th April, 1693.
116. Nath'l, 28th Feb. '93-4.
117. Lemuel, 26th Dec. '95.
118. Barnabas, 8th Feb. '97-8.
119. Susannah, 8th Oct. '99.
120. Thankful, 24th Sept. 1701.
121. Sarah, 22d April, '3.
122. Mary, 15th July, '5.
123. Kembel, 21st June, '8, died March 29, 1734.
Elizabeth married Henry March 14th Dec. 1711.
Susannah married Mr. John Sturgis 12th Nov. 1730.
Sarah married Jeremiah Howes.
L. "John Lothrop, ye son of Esq." Barnabas Lothrop,
married Elizabeth Green of Charlestown. She marrried 2d
Thomas Crocker 23d Dec. 1701. She died Aug. 1, 1752,
aged 89.

Children born in Barnstable.

124. Elizabeth, 3d Sept. 1692, died 11th Nov. 1694.
125. Barnabas, 23d Nov. 1694, died 11th Dec. 1714.
LI. Nathaniel Lothrop, son of Esq. Barnabas, married Bethia ———. She married 2d Robert Claghorn 6th Nov.
1701, died Oct. 1731, aged about 60.

Children born in Barnstable.

126. John, 28th Oct. 1696.
127. Hannah, bap. 21st April, 1700.
LX. John Lothrop, (son of Capt. John) married Esther
———.

Children born in Boston.

128. Joseph.
LXVII. Barna. Lothrop, son Mr. John, married 1, Be-
thia Fuller 20th Feb. 1706, died 26th Oct. '14. 2, Hannah
Chipman 25th Dec. 1718, died 11th June, '48. 3, Thankful
Gorham 3d Feb. 1743-4.

Children born in Barnstable.

129.   John, 25th Aug. 1709.
130.   Hannah, 6th July, '12.
131.   Jonathan, 28th Sept. '19, died 9th Dec. 1784.
132.   Barnabas, 29th June, '21.
133.   Samuel, 5th Oct. '28.
134.   Mary, 12th Mar. '47.
LXXII.   Benj. Lothrop, son of Mr. John, married 1, Ex. Howland of P. 22d Dec. 1727.   2, Experience Bursley 30th April, 1730.

Children born in Barnstable.

135.   Mary, 22d April, 1731.
136.   Joseph, no date, died unmarried.
137.   Benjamin, 1st July, 1741, insane.
Mary married Nathan Foster 21st May, 1753.
LXXIII.   Thomas Lothrop, son of Melatiah, was living in 1711, aged 43.
LXXV.   Isaac Lothrop, son of Melatiah, married ———— ————, had :
138.   Melatiah, and probably others.
LXXVI.   Hon. Joseph Lothrop married Abigail Childs 14th Jan. 1695.

Only child born in Barnstable.

139.   Mehitabel, 22d Oct. 1701, died 17th March, married Dr. John Russel 12th April, 1722.
LXXIX.   Shubael Lothrop.   I find no record of his family.
LXXXIV.   Benjamin Lothrop married Mercy Baker 26th May, 1720.

Children born in Barnstable.

140.   Nathaniel, 8th April, 1723, died young.
141.   Elijah, 18th Nov. 1724.
142.   Elizabeth, bap. 3d Dec. 1727, died young.
143.   Moley, bap. 31st Aug. 1729.
144.   Elizabeth, bap. 9th May, 1731.
LXXXV.   Joseph Lothrop married Rebecca Parker 1725.
145.   Rebecca, bap. 20th July, 1729, died young.
146.   Joseph, bap. 12th May, 1732.
The latter born after the death of the father.
LXXXVI.   Samuel Lothrop married Experience ————.
I find no family on record.
CII.   James Lothrop married Patience Coleman 20th Jan. 1732, died Feb. 1788.

Children born in Barnstable.

147. Deborah, 15th April, 1733.
148. Mary, 6th April, '35.
149. James, 15th March, '37.
150. Martha, bap. 21st June, '41.
151. Eben'r, bap. 15th May, '43.
152. David, bap. 7th Oct. '44.
   Deborah married ———— Turner of Plymouth.
   Mary married Joseph Thomas 5th Dec. 1750.
   Martha married Sam'l Baker 20th April, 1761.
   James, the father, drowned at sea April 1748.
   CIII. Thomas Lothrop married Deborah Loring of Hingham, 3d June, 1736.
153. Thomas, born 1738.
   The father died early. His son, the late Col. Thomas Lothrop of Cohasset, had sons John, Peter and Anson. [Deane.] I think, however, that Thomas CIII married Mary Parker Sept. 16, 1736, and remained in Barnstable.
   CV. Joseph Lothrop married Deborah Perkins of Plympton, 1758.
154. Rebecca, Dec. 20, 1758.
155. Deborah, 1760.
156. Temperance, June 17, '61.
   The latter after the death of the father.
   CVI. Seth Lothrop married Mary Fuller of B. 11thAug.1737, died Jan. 16, '63. 2d, Mary Fuller of S., 8th Aug. 1763.

Children born in Barnstable.

157. Nathaniel, 27th Dec. 1737.
158. Joseph, 1st May, 1740.
159. John, 5th April, '45.
160. Thankful, 18th Feb. '46-7.
161. Mary, 24th March, '48-9.
162. Benjamin, bap. 1st July, '53.
163. Seth, 5th Dec. '56.
164. Thomas, 4th July, '62.
165. Thankful, 2d Aug. '41.
   Mary married Edward Childs.
   CXXVI. John Lothrop married 1, Hannah Hadaway, died Aug. 2, 1741. 2, Thankful Landers of Wareham, to which town she removed in 1752.

Children born in Barnstable.

166. Hannah, April 18, 1728,
167. Mary, June 20, '30.
168. Nathaniel, Sept. 22, '32.

169.   Joseph, July 10, '35.
170.   Lot, Nov. 17, '37.
171.   Barnabas, Oct. 17, '40.
172.   Bethia, bap. Oct. 6, '45.
173.   Abigail, bap. April 12, '52.
       CXXXI. Jonathan Lothrop married 1, Mary Thacher,
       Dec. 12, 1751, died May 11, '61.   2d, Eunice Cobb, June
       27, 1762.

Children born in Barnstable.

174.   Joseph, (O. S.) 9th Oct. 1752.
175.   Rebecca, (N. S.) 29th Oct. '55.
176.   Mercy, 10th July, '58.
177.   Thomas, 9th April, '63.
178.   Jonathan, 13th Feb. '66.
179.   David, 20th June, '70.
       CXXXII. Gen. Barnabas Lothrop married Mrs. Thankful,
       Gorham Feb. 3, 1743, N. S.

Children born in Barnstable.

180.   Hannah, 4th March, 1745, Monday.
181.   Mary, 12th March, '47, Thursday.
182.   Barnabas, 27th Jan. '49, Friday.
183.   Abigail, 8th April, '52, Sunday.
184.   Isaac, (N. S.) 8th Feb. '54, Thursday.
185.   John, 23d Nov. '55.
186.   Isaac, 6th Sept. '57.
187.   Deborah, bap. 30th Dec. '59.
188.   Benjamin, 4th April, '62.
189.   Rachel, 5th May, '65.

I omitted to write the history of Gov. Thomas Hinckley, because I did not feel competent to do justice to his memory.   For
the same reason I should have omitted a memoir of Rev. John
Lothrop, had not a friend on whose judgment I rely, urged me to
print the facts I have collected.

Of the early life of Mr. Lothrop little is known.   I have
been unable to ascertain the year of his birth, the place of his na-
tivity, or the school at which he was educated.   The Rev. Dr.
John Lothrop, late of Boston, in a memoir published in the first
volume of the second series of the Mass. Historical Society's publications, says that there is "no doubt that Oxford was the place
of Mr. Lothrop's public education."   He refers to Wood's
Athenæ et Fasti Oxonienses, published in 1691, as his authority.
Wood professes to record the names of those "who have been admitted to one or two academical degree or degrees, in the ancient
and most famous university of *Oxford*."   He names "Mr. John

Lothrop," not however in the list if those educated at that university. Mr. Savage, who has given much attention to the subject, and has personally examined the records of several of the colleges, says *tradition* is the authority for the statement that Mr. Lothrop was educated at Oxford. Deane, in his history of Scituate, states that Mr. Lothrop was educated at Oxford. He relied on Dr. Lothrop as his authority, who evidently mistakes the meaning of the passage in Wood's Fasti.*

The ancestor of the family wrote his name John Lothropp. All his sons omitted the final p. His son Samuel sometimes wrote his name Lathrop, and many of his descendants in Connecticut and Western Massachusetts so spell the name. In the records we find the name written Lathropp, Lothrop, Lathrop, Laythrope, and Lawthrop. In Wood's *Fasti* the name is written Lathrop and Lowthrope.† Calamy, Neal, Crosley, Winthrop and Prince, write the name Lathrop. The name indicates that the family belong to an old English stock. *La* is Saxon, *Lo* is English, and both have the same meaning; that is, look. see, behold, observe. Shakespeare and other old writers use the word in both forms. In the Bible it is written *lo*, thus : "Lo, here is Christ," Matthew xxiv ; "Lo, we turn to the Gentiles," Acts, xiii ; and by Pope, "Lo, the poor Indian." Throp or thrope is the Saxon word for village or town, and the compound word Lothrop means see the village. Surnames were originally discriptive terms. The first who took the name of Lothrop probably resided at a place from whence some town or village could be seen.

After Mr. Lothrop had graduated from his College he took holy orders, and was settled in the ministry at Egerton, in the County of Kent, about fifteen miles from the city of London. He was married as early as 1620, and it is probable that he had been ordained at least five years when he renounced holy orders, and separated himself from the church of England.

In 1624 Mr. Lothrop removed to London, and was chosen the successor of the Rev. Henry Jacob, the first pastor of the first Independent or Congregationalist Society in London. Wood, speaking of Mr. Jacob, says he "was a Kentish man, born in 1563, entered a commoner in Saint Maries Hall 1579, aged 16 ; took the degree in arts and holy orders, and became beneficied in his own country. He was a person most excellently well read in theological authors, but withal a most zealous puritan ; or, as his son Henry used to say, the first Independent in England." The historian adds, "*Henry Jacob*, educated in the low countries under *Thomas Erpenius*, the famous critick, was actually created

---

*I feel confident, after a careful examination of the authorities on which Dr. Lothrop and Rev. Mr. Deane relied, that the Rev. John Lothrop, of Barnstable, was not educated at Oxford. Christ's College, Cambridge was probably his alma mater.

†Dr. Lothrop says Lathrop. I find the name also written by Wood, Laythrope.

Bachelor of Arts by virtue of the letters of the chancellors of the university, written in his behalf. He was soon after elected probationer fellow of Merton College, and is hereafter most deservedly to be inserted among the writers in the 2d volume of this work." [*Athenæ et Fasti Oaxen.*]

He was one of the puritans who fled from the persecution of Bishop Bancroft. At Leyden Mr. Jacob conferred with Mr. Robinson, and embraced his peculiar sentiments of church discipline, since known by the name of Independency. In 1616 he returned to England, and Mr. Neal in his history of the Puritans infers that he imparted his design of setting up a separate congregation, like those in Holland, to the most learned puritans of those times, it was not condemned as unlawful, considering that there was no prospect of a national reformation Mr. Jacob having summoned several of his friends together, and obtained their consent to unite in church fellowship for enjoying the ordinances of Christ in the purest manner, they laid the foundation of the first *Independent* or *Congregational* church in England."

This statement of Mr. Neal is perhaps not historically exact. There were Independents in England as early as the time of Wickliffe. The first Independent Church organized in England was that at Scrooby, by Bradford, Brewster, Robinson and others, in 1606. As this church consisted only of a few members, and in a few years after its organization removed to Leyden, perhaps it is not entitled to the honor of being called the first in England; certainly not if permanency is considered an element in arriving at a right conclusion. Mr. Neal knew the history of the Scrooby church, yet did not consider it entitled to the honor of being called *the first*. This is an interesting fact, because many of the members of the Barnstable church had been members of the church in Southwalk, London. Mr. Jacob had resided some at Leyden prior to the year 1616, and was familiar with the discipline and government of Mr. Robinson's church, and adopted its forms and its covenant in the organization of the church in London.

When in 1620 a part of the church at Leyden removed to Plymouth, they carried with them the old Scrooby covenant, and recognized the form of church government adopted by the Independents in Holland and England. The famous compact drawn up and signed on board of the Mayflower, called by eminent legislators the *first written constitution*, was borrowed from this church organization with some slight variations to adapt it to their wants as a civil community. The first church in Salem, in Charlestown, the second in Boston, the Scituate and Barnstable churches, had essentially the same covenant. Very few of the first settlers of the Massachusetts Colony had belonged to Independent churches in England or Holland. The large majority were Separatists or

Puritans, as nick-named by their opponents. There was, however, little difference between them in matters of faith and practice. The Plymouth people were more Catholic, more tolerant to those who differed from them in opinion.

Neal thus describes the manner in which the first Independent Church was formed in London. "Having observed a day of solemn fasting and prayer for a blessing upon their undertaking towards the close of the solemnity, each of them made open confession of his faith in our Lord Jesus Christ; then standing together they joined hands, and solemnly covenanted with each other in the presence of Almighty God, to walk together in all God's ways and ordinances, according as he had already revealed, or *should further make* known to them."

"Mr. Jacob was then chosen pastor by the suffrage of the brotherhood, and others were appointed to the office of deacons, with fasting and prayer, and imposition of hands." Mr. Jacob continued with his people about eight years; but in the year 1624, being desirous to enlarge his usefulness, he went with their consent to Virginia, where he soon after died.

Upon the departure of Mr. Jacob the church chose Mr. Lothrop pastor. Mr. Jacob was the *first* pastor of the first Independent Church in England, Mr. Lothrop the *second*. The early writers do not furnish an account of the exercises at the installation of Mr. Lothrop; but the presumption is that he was inducted into office as Mr. Jacob was, and as he subsequently was at Scituate, by the election of the brethren, by fasting, by prayer, and by the imposition of hands.

In the few simple details, already given, we have the history of a movement which has already produced most remarkable results,—the leaven which is leavening the whole lump of the christian and the political world. The essential principle of Independency is, it asserts the manhood of the race, that the power is in the church and congregation, not in ministers nor in bishops, or popes, not in kings or parliaments, but in the people. It is essentially democratic, and a man cannot long be an Independent in his religious faith and not be a republican in politics, an asserter of the rights of the people, in opposition to the power of lords spiritual and lords temporal.

I am aware that it may be said that the offices of the church at Southwalk, London, were from necessity installed by the members thereof, because no churches or ministers could be invited to assist, there were none to invite. It is a sufficient answer to this to say that in 1635, when Mr. Lothrop was ordained pastor of the Scituate church, there were churches and ministers that might have been invited, but none were. The members of the church elected, ordained and installed its own officers, and this fundamental principle of Independency or Congregationalism is acknowledged and acted upon to this day. Ministers and churches by their delegates are invited to *assist* at ordinations, not to *ordain*, though some careless writers speak of councils as the *ordaining power*. Though Independents differ among themselves in matters of faith and practice, especially the Baptists and Unitarians, yet they all subscribe to these fundamental principles, namely :

That a church should consist of as many members as can conveniently meet together for worship.

That when so met they have power to elect the officers of the church and install them.

Mr. Lothrop was pastor of the London church eight years. He was a man of learning, of a meek and quiet spirit, tolerant in his opinions, ever treating those who differed from him with kindness and respect. The subject of baptism was the cause of uneasiness in England and after he came to New England. While the pastor of the Barnstable Church he published a tract in London, in which he states his own views with clearness, and supports them with much vigor of thought and sound reason. In England a member of his church carried his child to be baptized* by the parish minister. Some of Mr. Lothrop's congregation insisted that the child should be re-baptized because the other administration was not valid. This opened the question, whether or not the parish churches of England were true churches. Mr. Lothrop and the leading members of the church acted discretely, and resolved not to make any declaration on the question at issue, because if they were to declare by their vote that the parish churches were not true churches of Christ, it would be inviting the persecution of the Bishops who were waiting to find an excuse for breaking up and dispersing this little congregation.

"Upon this some of the more rigid, and others who were dissatisfied about the lawfulness of infant baptism, desired their dismission, which was granted to them ; these set up by themselves, and chose Mr. Jessey their minister, who laid the foundation of the first Baptist congregation that I have met in England. But the rest renewed their covenant to walk together in the ways of God, so far as He had made them known, *or should make them known to them*, and to forsake all false ways. And so steady were they to their vows that hardly an instance can be produced of one that deserted to the church of England by the severest persecutions." (Neal).

April 29, 1632, Mr. Neal states that Mr. Lothrop's congregation was discovered by Tomlinson, the Bishop's pursuevant, at the house of Mr. Humphrey Barnet, a Brewer's clerk in Black Fryers, where forty-two of them were apprehended, and only

---

*I have not a copy of Neal to which I can turn to verify the accuracy of this statement. Dr. Lathrop uses the word re-baptize, which is not consistent with subsequent statements.

eighteen escaped. Of those taken some were confined in the clink, others in New Prison and the Gate House, where they continued about two years, and were then released on bail, except Mr. Lothrop, for whom no favor could be obtained; he therefore petitioned the King (Charles I, Archbishop Laud, having refused every favor,) for liberty to depart from the Kingdom, which was granted." Mr. Nathaniel Morton, author of New England's Memorial, was personally acquainted with Mr. Lothrop, and had a better opportunity to be accurately informed than Mr. Neal. Several of those confined with Mr. Lothrop were afterwards his neighbors and friends, and it would be surprising if he did not know the exact facts. He says, "Mr. Lothrop was some time preacher of God's word at Egerton, in Kent, from whence he went to London and was chosen pastor of a church of Christ there. He was greatly troubled and imprisoned for witnessing against the errors of the times. During the time of his imprisonment his wife fell sick, of which sickness she died. He procured liberty of the Bishop to visit his wife before her death, and commended her to God in prayer, who soon after gave up the ghost. At his return to prison his poor children, being many, repaired to the Bishop to Lambeth, and made known unto him their miserable condition by reason of their good father, his being confined in close durance; who commiserated their condition so far as to grant him liberty, who soon after came over into New England and settled some time at the town of Scituate, and was chosen pastor of their church, and faithfully dispensed the word of God amongst them. And afterwards, the church dividing, a part whereof removed to Barnstable, he removed with them, and there remained until his death. He was a man of a humble and broken heart and spirit, lively in dispensation of the word of God, studious of peace, furnished with godly contentment, willing to spend and to be spent for the cause of Christ. He fell asleep in the Lord November 8, 1653 "

Mr. Neal, who is usually accurate and reliable, says Mr. Lothrop petitioned King Charles for his release and liberty to depart the Kingdom. Mr. Morton states that after the death of Mrs. Lothrop his poor children, being many, repaired to the Bishop at Lambeth, who commiserated their condition and granted liberty to their father. It may be that Mr. Lothrop petitioned King Charles, and that his children went to the Bishop at Lambeth, but it is not probable that King Charles ordered the release of Mr. Lothrop on the condition that he would depart the Kingdom.

This was in 1634. The exact date is not given, but a near approximation may be made to it. Mr. Lothrop and forty-two of the members of his church and congregation were arrested April 29, 1632, and refusing to take the oath "*exofficio*" were cast into prison, where they remained about two years. The forty-two were then released on bail ; but that privilege was denied to Mr. Lothrop, and he remained in prison "two full years," that is till April 29, 1634, probably till May. About the time the forty-two were released his wife fell sick, and the Bishop permitted him to visit her. Very soon after this visit she died, either in April or May, 1634, leaving six children to be taken care of and supported by Mr. Lothrop's friends. Thomas, the eldest son, was then thirteen years of age, and Benjamin perhaps not over two. Jane was older than Thomas, and perhaps Barbara was also. Their friends had willing hearts, but were oppressed and poor, and utterly unable to help the families of all who had been imprisoned by the tryanny of Archbishop Laud. According to tradition, the children for some little time had no home, and were obliged to beg bread in the streets of London. Their friends being unable to protect them and to provide for their wants, sent them to the Bishop of Lambeth, who had charge of Mr. Lothrop. He could not resist this touching appeal to his mercy, granted their request, and ordered the release of the father. This was in May or the beginning of June, 1634. Immediately after his enlargement he made arrangements to come to New England. The Griffin and another ship arrived at Boston Sept. 18, 1634, with about two hundred passengers, among whom were Rev. John Lothrop and thirty of his followers, Rev. Zachariah Symms, and the famous Mrs. Ann Hutchinson. Six weeks was an average passage in those times, consequently Mr. Lothrop left London about Aug. 1, 1634. In the same ship there came over a copy of the commission granted to the two Archbishops and ten others of the council, to regulate all plantations.

The object of this commission was to embarras puritan ministers desirous of coming to New England. All passengers were required to obtain a certificate from the minister or the magistrates of the town in which they resided, of their good character and conformity to the order and discipline of the church of England, and that they had taken the oath of allegiance and supremacy and were no subsidy men.

I am aware that King Charles the first made duplicity a study, and practiced it when and wherever he thought it would subserve his interests, but his object in 1634 in passing the order in council was to prevent puritan ministers from leaving England, and it is very improbable that he should at the very same time order the release of Mr. Lothrop on the condition that he leave the Kingdom. I give the statement of Mr. Neal, and that of Mr. Morton. The latter is undoubtedly accurate. It is in conformity with tradition, and records preserved by one of his grandchildren. It is in conformity with a statement made by Mr. Lothrop himself, as recorded by Gov. Winthrop. In October, 1634, before his settlement in Scituate, he was in "Boston upon a sacrament day, after the sermon, &c., desired leave of the congregation to be present at the administration, &c.; but said he durst not desire to partake in it, because he was not then in order, (being dismissed from his former congregation,) and he thought it not fit to be suddenly admitted into any other, for example sake, and because of the deceiptfulness of man's heart."

In order to take the required oaths, Mr. Lothrop had to renounce his orders as a minister of Christ, and came to New England as a private individual. Mr. Anthony Thacher, who had been rector at Old Sarum, entered his name on the lists April 6, 1635, as a tailor, and many distinguished men who came over about that time had to resort to similar subterfuges or take passage in the ships without having their names entered on the list of passengers. Mr. Lothrop probably did not enter his name because he could not take the oath of conformity. The Rev. Hiram Carleton labored to show that the West Barnstable church was a continuation of the first church in London,—that it removed first to Scituate, then to Barnstable. In proof of that position he quoted from Neal, Crossley, and other early writers, passages which seemed to favor that supposition; but the above quotation from Winthrop sets that theory at rest. Mr. Lothrop himself states that he was dismissed from the church in London, consequently his church did not remove, though thirty of his followers came over with him, and some had come previously, and many came subsequently and were afterwards members of his church in Scituate and in Barnstable, The church in London was not broken up when Mr. Lothrop left, for he states in his records that in 1638 his brother Robert Linnel and wife brought over to him a letter of dismission from the church in London.

I should be pleased to endorse the beautiful theory of Mr. Carleton, but the above facts prove conclusively that the Barnstable church is an offshoot of the London, not the church itself.

No list of the passengers that came in the Griffin or the other ship has been preserved. The names of the thirty followers who came with Mr. Lothrop, and settled with him at Scituate, some of whom followed him to Barnstable, it would be pleasant to record. Many of the thirty were women and children. Of Mr. Lothrop's six children three probably came with him : Jane, his oldest child, Thomas and Barbara. Jane must have been a woman grown at the time, for she was married to Samuel Fuller April 8, 1635, about six months after her arrival. Barbara was perhaps the next older child, and Thomas was then thirteen years of age. The three other children, Joseph, Samuel and Benjamin, probably remained in England. The younger children were often left behind till a home was provided in New England.

Mr. Lothrop was a learned man ; but he could not have had

leisure to attend to the systematic education of so numerous a family, and there are circumstances that indicate that a portion of his children were educated in England. Thomas, the elder, was a good mathematician and a skilful surveyor of lands. Joseph had a good English education, had read the laws, was a good conveyancer, and a superior clerk. Samuel associated with the best men in Connecticut, and appears to have been a man of learning and good parts. Of Benjamin I have no information. Mr. L.'s children born in New England were well instructed, but their education does not appear to have been so thorough. Barnabas wrote an old English hand. Some of the best executed manuscripts I have seen were executed by him. Every letter drawn in the most approved style, carefully executed, and as easily read as a printed page. Like all who so write, he executed very slowly, and when compelled by circumstances to write rapidly, he wrote a hand difficult to decipher. John was only nine at the death of his father, he was then in England probably at school. As he was afterwards a sea captain, he left little from which an opinion can be safely drawn respecting the thoroughness of his education.

Mr. Timothy Hatherly, one of the merchant adventurers, in prosperity and in adversity, was a staunch friend of Mr. Lothrop. He was honest, frank and truthful; and his too confiding spirit led him to believe that others were like himself, till he found by a bitter experience that the wicked sometimes assume the cloak of piety. He was one of the Forefathers, came to Plymouth in the Ann, had his house burned at the fire in 1623, and returned to England that year. He came over again in 1631 in the ship Friendship as the agent of his associates, and arrived in Boston July 14. After finishing his business he returned, and the next year took passage in the ship Charles of Barnstable, sailing April 10, 1632. There is no record that he was a member of Mr. Lothrop's church in London, but the probability is that he was, and that by leaving London early in April he escaped imprisonment. The Scituate church was a reunion of "many who had been in covenant before." The church was organized Jan. 8. 1634. Mr. Hatherly and his wife joined on the next Sabbath, Jan. 11.

He was connected with all the great financial transactions of the Colony. The purchase of the ships Friendship and White Angel was attended with great loss. Mr. Isaac Allerton was then the agent of the Colony, and Mr. Hatherly and his associates presumed that he was acting in his official capacity; but he had no authority, and the loss falling on Mr. Allerton individually he was unable to respond for his proportion of the loss, and for other losses on transactions in which he was individually engaged. Mr. Hatherly's claim against him amounted to 2000 pounds sterling, nearly all of which was lost by himself and the other partners.

Notwithstanding his severe losses in his efforts to promote the common interests of the colonists, Mr. Hatherly was ever ready to assist the poor and the distressed, particularly the members of the church at Scituate and his beloved pastor. Adversity binds men by stronger ties than prosperity. It awakens a sympathy not satisfied with the commonplace words of consolation—it opens the purse as well as the heart.

In 1634 Independency had seen its darkest days in England. It had then numerous adherents among the lowly and many powerful friends in high places. King Charles, instigated by the infamous Laud, Archbishop of Canterbury, had adopted extreme measures to crush non-conformity; but like all extreme measures, their tendency was to strengthen what they were intended to destroy. The mass of the people held that the King had usurped power, in violation of their reserved rights and those of parliament, and felt justified in opposing, by all constitutional means, his arbitrary acts.

John Lothrop and his followers were held by the people to be martyrs in the cause of Independency. No persecutions—no severity that their enemies could inflict, caused him, or a solitary one of his followers to waver—they submitted without a murmur to loss of property, to imprisonment in loathsome jails, and to be separated for two long years from their families and friends, rather than to subscribe to the forms of worship that Charles and his bigoted prelates vainly endeavored to force on their consciences, and compel them to adopt. No power could thus compel, they considered it far more glorious to suffer for the cause of Christ and his visible church than to submit to arbitrary power, though with submission came worldly wealth and temporal distinction.

From these men three-fourths of the present inhabitants of Barnstable descend. Ought they to be ashamed of their ancestry? Is there one of them so vile as to wish that he could trace his descent from the chivalry, the cavaliers, or some sprigg of nobility whose blood ''Has coursed thro' scoundrels ever since the flood.'' If there be such a one, he had better take the poet's advice and

"Go and confess his family is young,
Nor own his fathers have been fools so long."

But there is another standpoint from which Mr. Lothrop and his followers appear more honorable as men—more lovely as christian brethren. They denounced Popery as the great harlot of Babylon; but they never denounced the doctrines of the church of England as anti-christian, or asserted that the parish churches were not true churches, and that the members thereof were not true christians—they warred against the forms and ceremonies that the English church had borrowed from Rome, against its Bishops and Archbishops, its prelatical rule, and claim to bind men's consciences. They contended that the gospel should be preached in its purity, as it was in the apostolitic times, before councils and synods and forged creeds by which to bind men's consciences; that the Bible was the only creed, and that christians should "covenant with each other in the presence of Almighty God, to walk together in all God's ways and ordinances, according as He had already revealed, or should further make known unto them, and to forsake all false ways;" that man was not responsible to his fellow man in matters of conscience, but to God alone, and that the life is the evidence of faith, as the fruit is of the goodness of the tree.

The first Baptist church, as already stated, was an offshoot from Mr. Lothrop's church. They were then known as ana baptists, and in England were persecuted, tortured, imprisoned, and put to death. In Massachusetts they were also imprisoned, put in the stocks, whipped, and banished from the colony. Mr. Lothrop, though he did not sanction immersion, never in London, or Scituate, or Barnstable, refused them christian fellowship, neither did any member of his church. The mode of baptism they considered as non-essential, respecting which no christian had the right to judge his brother.

When that hydra-headed monster, Quaker persecution, stalked through New England Mr. Lothrop had gone to his final rest. Had he been living, he would have stood side by side with the ancient members of his church, Hatherly, Cudworth, Isaac Robinson, John Smith,* and many others who had listened to his teaching, and learned toleration in the school of persecution.

The beauty of the system of christian faith and practice taught by Mr. Lothrop, commends itself to the common sense of mankind. He was a Calvinist, but he followed John Calvin no farther than Calvin followed the oracles of God. He maintained not only the independence of the churches, but of the individual members, asserting the manhood and equality of the race, and laying the foundation of the christian church on its broadest basts, the individual heart.

Mr. John Lothrop, though he received the doctrines of the reformed churches, and adopted the forms of church government of the blessed John Robinson, was an independent thinker. He received no doctrine on the faith of others, he examined for himself, decided for himself. Though bold and decided in his denunciations of the arbitrary acts of the bishops, he was as meek as

---

*I regret that I cannot add the name of Gov. Thomas Hinckley; but no man more seriously regretted his own course in after life than he did. He was not the severe man that his opponents represented him to be. See "Hinckley" and "Cudworth."

the lamb in reproving the faults of his brethren, and the children of his church.

Creeds and confessions of faith he rejected. The Bible was his creed. All others he considered traps or snares, to catch men, bind their consciences, make them nominal, not true members of the church of Christ. The Athanasian creed received by the reformed churches as the foundation of the doctrines taught in the scripture, he did not hold to be binding on his conscience. That creed, approved and sanctioned by synods and councils of learned divines, was the handiwork of a fallible man, and as such was not to be received as a binding authority.

Justification by faith was the foundation on which he built his religious system. Being an independent thinker, and a plain, practicable man, he took a common sense view of religious truth, and adapted his system to the nature and wants of men. The doctrine of salvation by faith and election as taught, and as illustrated by him in his discipline, few will condemn as heretical. Faith he considered the germ which produced the spiritual man, the christian. It had a higher mission than the salvation of the individual, its influence saved others. In his essay on Baptism he teaches that by the faith of the men who brought the sick of the palsy to Christ, "the man sick of the palsy was healed." In his argument in favor of infant baptism, his main reliance is on the efficacy of faith. He says, "The faith of the parents induce them to carry their infants to Christ's ordinance, confessing original sin, believing God is their God, and the God of their seed, showing the need their infants have of Christ, and so leading the infant in the house of God to grow up in his courts, at the soles of Christ's feet." At the commencement of his essay he also teaches that baptism by water is only symbolic, that "they only put on Christ who are baptized by spirit," the infant being incapable of acting for itself, and incapable of being baptized into the Holy Spirit, yet by the baptism by water, becomes a participant in the faith of the parent, the promise being, "to them and their seed," and that infants are of the Kingdom, thro' the good pleasure of the father.

The practice in Mr. Lothrop's church was to baptize the children on the Sabbath next following their birth. I have noted instances that children born on the morning of the Sabbath were carried two miles the same day, and at the most inclement season of the year, to be baptized. In recording the deaths of children it was also his practice to note the fact, if they died unbaptized. I infer from these facts that he had not entirely discarded the popular theology of his times. He certainly believed and taught that infants that had received the ordinance of baptism were saved; but it is not certain that he held that the unbaptized infant in all cases was saved. The logical inference to be drawn from his essay and his practice is, that the baptized infant was saved, the unbaptized was not.*

Whatever exceptions we may take to Mr. Lothrop's theological opinions, all must admit that he was a good and true man, an independent thinker, and a man who held opinions in advance of his times. Even in Massachusetts a half century has not elapsed since his opinions on religious toleration have been adopted by the legislature, accepted by the people, and incorporated into the organic law of the State. Respecting faith "the world will disagree." It is spiritual in its essence, seen only by God, and He alone is its judge, and in His hands we may safely commit its keeping. Legislation never did, never can restrain errors of opinion. Truth and free discussion are the only weapons that will avail, in banishing error from the world.

Mr. Lothrop fearlessly proclaimed in Old and in New England, the great truth that man is not responsible to his fellow-man in matters of faith and conscience, a truth that lies at the foundation of religious and political liberty. Differences of opinion he tolerated, he kindly reproved the wayward, and gently led the lambs of his flocks. During the fourteen years that he was pastor of the Barnstable church, such was his influence over the people that the power of the civil magistrate was not needed to restrain crime. No pastor was ever more beloved by his people, none ever had a greater influence for good.

The line to which the power of the magistrate and of the church extends, is clearly defined in his records of church discipline. It is the acts of the individual which makes him responsible. Business men never rely on professions, why should magistrates or pastors? The greatest sinner will assume to be the greatest of saints, in order to compass his ends. The only safe rule for all is, "by their fruits ye shall know them."

To become a member of Mr. Lothrop's church no applicant was compelled to sign a creed or confession of faith; he retained his freedom; he professed his faith in God; and promised that it should be his constant endeavor to keep His commandments, to live a pure life, and to walk in love with the brethren.

On minor points of doctrine much freedom of opinion was permitted. The subject of baptism, as already stated, was from the first a cause of uneasiness in the church. About the year 1644 Mr. Lothrop, or some of his friends, published a tract of seven pages, written by him. I have not seen the original. It was written in catechetical form. Hanbury, in his work, furnishes the following synopsis. I should much prefer an exact copy.

*This I believe to be a true statement of the line of argument adopted by Mr. Lothrop. Of its soundness I express no opinion. The facts in the case I feel confident are these. The kindly spirit of Mr. Lothrop rejected the horrid doctrine of infant damnation, and to avoid it he maintained that the infant was saved by the faith of the parent, and through the good leasure of the Father.

The head line of the work is "Queries concerning Baptism." In his address to the reader Mr. Lothrop says : "What I have received by hearing and seeing, I desire to manifest in defence of the Baptism and Form we have received ; not being easily moved, but as Christ shall more manifest himself ; which I cannot conceive to be in the dipping the head, the creature going in and out of the water. The form of Baptism doth more or less hold forth Christ. Baptism declares Infants to be Virgins ; the Supper declares Believers to be Sponses."

Mr. Lothrop assumes that Infants are of the Kingdom, through the father's good pleasure ; that they are ingredients of the "many nations whom the Saviour shall sprinkle ; that they are of the spouse, or church, washed in Christ's blood, as were those of old, or the vines of Egypt, even of those who were all baptized in the cloud and in the sea."

"Baptism, under the Gospel, is the church's office ; done in the name of the Three, by the power or authority of Christ : They only put on Christ who are baptized into or unto Christ, by the spirit, not all that are baptized by water. No one is fully baptized without pouring, sprinkling and washing ; not dipping of the head, any more than whole wafers in the supper ; bread there is, but no *breaking*, showing forth Christ's sufferings ; so whole rivers show not forth Christ's sufferings, *pouring* him out like water, *besprinkling* all his raiment. As by their faith who brought him to Christ, the man sick of the palsy was healed ; so the faith of the parents induceth them to carry their Infants to Christ's ordinance, confessing original sin ; believing God is their God, and the God of their seed ; showing the need their Infants have of Christ ; so leading the infant in the house of God, to grow up in his courts at the soles of Christ's feet. To dip an infant, there is a dim light of Christ. For a creature to go in and out of the water ; the dipper to dip down the head ; is no showing of Christ at all. Sweating water and blood, then was Christ buried by baptism ! Being under the wrath of the Father, all his waves were over him ; there were the elect buried with him, having communion with him in his death ; when many came aforehand to anoint his body ; it being manifest to believers, when they are baptized by the spirit, dying unto sin and rising again unto newness of life ; but, when Christ was buried by Nicodemus in the dust, there was no need of showing forth that burial, nor his resurrection ; seeing he was seen after his resurrection. Christ died for sin, and rose again for our justification ; so believers die to sin, and rise to newness of life ; justifying themselves to others, that they are risen with Christ."

"The two seals under the Gospel are of one nature ; but washing makes *us* capable of eating ; so circumcision made *them* capable of eating the passover. There, say such as be called

Anabaptists, why do not children eat the supper? Children were not capable of eating the passover before they were capable of instruction; asking the parents what it meant; so the children of the church are not capable of the supper, before they can examine themselves: Wherefore let such as deny Infant Baptism, and go into the water, and dip down the head, and come out, to show death and burial, take heed that they take not the name of the Lord in vain; more especially such as have received baptism in their infancy."

The above is not a specimen of Mr. Lothrop's style of writing. It is disconnected passages, extracted by Mr. Hanbury from the tract to show the manner in which Mr. Lothrop treated the subject. Isolated passages are brought together, and there is a want of connection and a want of clearness.

Mr. Henry Jessey was the successor of Mr. Lothrop. In 1635 Mr. Neal says he was invited to be pastor of the congregation, this his modesty led him to decline for some time, but after many prayers and much consideration he accepted the invitation and continued in this post until his death. Soon after, the controversy respecting baptism arose. After much deliberation he changed his sentiments. Palmer says "his first conviction was about the *mode* of baptism. Tho' he continued two or three years to baptize children, he did it by immersion. About 1644 the controversy about the *subjects* of baptism was revived in his church, when several of them gave up infant baptism, as did Mr. J. himself." "He was in June, 1645, baptized by Mr. Hansard Knollys."

It would seem a matter of fair inference that this little tract of Mr. Lothrop's was printed by some of those members of the church who were opposed to Mr. Jessey's tendencies, and those of a portion of the church towards the Baptists. The expression "To dip an infant there is a dim light of Christ," shows clearly that it was written after Mr. Jessey had adopted the practice of baptizing infants by immersion.

Antiquarians have not recorded the list of the members of Mr. Lothrop's church and congregation in London, nor of the forty-one who were imprisoned with him in 1632, nor of the "thirty followers" who came over with him in 1634. As this is a subject in which antiquarians feel a deep interest, I propose to examine it. I do not expect to arrive at a very satisfactory result. My object is to clear off irrelavant matter, and endeavor to lay a foundation on which future inquirers may safely build.

Respecting the forty-one, we may from the known facts safely infer that they were adult male members, and that the eighteen who escaped were also adult male members. There is nothing in the accounts that we have, or in the circumstances involved, that militates against this theory. We know that the members of Mr.

Lothrop's family were not imprisoned. He was the leader, the man against whom the bishops had the strongest enmity, and if they allowed his family to go free, it is not probable that the families of other members were incarcerated. As a question of policy it was inexpedient; it would have been in violation even of the spirit of the arbitrary orders in council, and even of the customs prevalent in those intolerant times. This point, I think, may be set down as certain, that on the 29th day of April, 1632, Mr. Lothrop's church and congregation consisted of at least sixty male adult members.

Of the eighteen that escaped from the pursuevants of the Bishop, it is probable that they all came to New England. It is certain that most of them did. Some came to Plymouth, some to Salem, and others settled in Boston and the adjacent towns. As no list of their names has been preserved, we cannot trace them with certainty, yet we are in possession of records from which safe inferences may be drawn.

Mr. Lothrop arrived in Boston Sept. 18, 1634, O. S., and soon after he and most, if not all those who came over with him went to Scituate, where there was a small settlement of his old friends, who welcomed him and invited him to become their pastor. No permanent settlement appears to have been made in Scituate before 1633 or 4. There is a deed on record by which it appears that lands had been enclosed there as early as 1628. Mr. Lothrop furnishes a list of the houses, and gives the dates when built. This is an authentic and reliable document. He says that when he came to Scituate "about the end of Sept. 1634," only nine houses had been erected, "all small plaine pallizadoe Houses."* Below I give the list. The dates immediately following each name is the date of admission to the Scituate Church.

In the preceding genealogy it is stated on the authority of his deposition, dated April 4, 1701, that Thomas Lothrop was born in 1621. In that paper he states that he is "about 80 years of age," and that he is a son of Mr. Lothrop. The latter in his will calls Thomas his "eldest son," and from the general expression in the will I inferred that he was his first born, and that 1621 was the true date of birth. From these I inferred that Mr. Lothrop was married in 1620, and settled in the ministry at Edgerton in Kent, as early as 1619.

That deposition is seemingly good authority, though it involves some conclusions hard to be believed, one of which I have named in this and former papers, namely, that on the 11th of Dec. 1639, Thomas Lothrop, a boy of eighteen summers, married Sarah Ewer,

---

*The pallisade house was not the building known as a log house. Two parallel rows of holes, about four inches apart, were bored into the sills, and corresponding ones into the plates of the building. Into these small poles were inserted, and the space between filled with stones and clay. It thus appears that no framed houses had then been put up.

a widow aged 32, and having at least four children then living, and that his sister Jane married Samuel Fuller at the tender age of 12 or 13 years.

A careful re-examination of the direct and collateral testimony leads to the following conclusions : That Mr. Lothrop was an older man than I had supposed him to be, born as early as 1590, probably settled at Edgerton in 1615, and married as early as 1616. This view explains some matters otherwise involved in doubt, and undermines the foundation on which rests the evidence of the early marriages of some of his children.

Mr. Deane states that the leading men among the first settlers of Scituate came from the city of London, and the adjoining county of Kent; that the principal street in the town on which they built their dwellings was called Kent street, and that the men themselves were called "the men of Kent" to distinguish them from the settlers who came from other parts of England. These facts are well established by tradition and by records, and are confirmed by subsequent investigations of the individual histories of the men. A few were farmers, or planters, as they were called after their arrival; but the majority were mechanics and tradesmen. Nearly all of them were well informed, intelligent men. A few only were rich in this world's goods; but all had laid up treasures where "neither moth nor rust doth consume."

It does not appear that Mr. Lothrop immediately after he had "renounced holy orders in the church," went to London. He appears to have been known to the Independents scattered through the county of Kent, and it is probable that he had preached occasionally to little congregations in most of the towns. His church and congregation in London were not probably all residents in that city, but in the neighboring towns and villages. In those early times men, and even delicate women, thought it no cross, but a "blessed privilege" to walk ten or fifteen miles in the morning to attend meeting on the Sabbath, and return in the evening. In the mild season of the year they took their stockings and shoes in their hands, to be put on when they arrived near the meeting house, and removed again on their return. This custom they brought with them to New England, and in many of the country towns it was continued to a period within the memory of many now living.

Some of them came over soon after Mr. Lothrop went to London in 1624, and settled in Plymouth and Massachusetts. Mr. Lothrop went to Scituate, where nine families of his friends had settled. Many of those who had settled in other parts of the Colony sold out soon after and removed to Scituate, to enjoy the preaching of their old pastor. Many came over from Sandwich in 1635 and settled at Scituate. We here see the cause of the rapid growth of the town in 1635 and 6, and the reason why the place soon became "too straite for their accommodation."

The towns in New Plymouth were settled by churches. The pastor was the master-spirit to whom all looked for direction in temporal, as well as in spiritual affairs. Our fathers were hopeful in regard to the future. They hoped to build up a State in which religion would be the hand-maid of science, of virtue and free government. Their theory of church discipline, that all power originates in the consent of the individual, they designed to engraft into their political institutions. They hoped that all would be church members, all freeman, and all have equal political rights. To reduce this theory to practice, the leading minds in the Colony labored incessantly. They seemed to forget that men have to deal with the actual, with what is, not with what they would have. Men cannot control the circumstances by which they are surrounded. If religious liberty had been the only motive that induced men to come to New England, and if only such men as Lothrop, Brewster, and Hatherly, had come over, there would have been less difficulty in realizing the fondly cherished hopes of our ancestors. The fisheries annually attracted thousands of men to the coast, and many deserted from the vessels and sought refuge in the Colonies. Trading vessels annually visited the Colonies, bringing passengers who had led scandalous lives at home. Though not wanted, an asylum could not be denied to deserters or passengers, and they found employment at first as servants and afterwards became townsmen and freeholders, and to these the freeman were soon obliged to yield a share of political power.

Mr. Lothrop found nine families at Scituate, friends that he had known in England. They had, Sept. 30, 1634, built nine "*pallizado houses*," as temporary residences, to be replaced by more substantial ones when they had the time and means. From the time Mr. Lothrop came to October, a period of two years, there were thirty-one houses built, and in 1637 nine, making the whole number of dwelling houses fifty-six. The Meeting House was finished and dedicated Nov. 10 and 11, 1636.

To Mr. Lothrop's list of the houses I add the dates, if known, when the builders came over, and the dates of their joining his church. The serial numbers indicate the order in which the houses were built, the date next following each name, the time when the party came over, and the last, the time when he joined Mr. Lothrop's church. In order to compress as much information as I can into each line, the following abbreviations are used: K, signifies Kent, or County of Kent; L, London; S, Scituate; B, Barnstable; Gd. Goodman; an interrogation point means *doubtful*.

"The Houses in ye plantation of Scituate att my Comeing hither, onely these wch was aboute the end of Sept. 1634,—all wch small plaine pallizadoe Houses."

1, Mr. Hatherlyes, 1623 & 1632, L., Jan. 11, 1634-5, S.

2, Mr. Cudworthes, a 1632, L., Jan. 18, 1634-5, B. S. Sold (1636) to Gd. Ensigne, — — — S.

3, Mr. Gillsons, a 1632, K.? Jan. 8, 1634-5, S.

4, Gd. Anniballs, 1623,— Jan. 8, 1634-5, B.

5, Gd. Rowlyes, 1632, K.? Jan. 8, 1634-5, B. (See No. 23. No record of sale.)

6, Gd. Turners, 1628, K.? Jan. 8, 1634-5, S. Sold (1636) to Gd. Jackson, a 1634, K.? Feb. 25, 1637-8, B.

7, Gd. Cobbes, (see 32), 1632, K. Jan. 8, 1634-5, B. Sold, 1st, Gd. Rowlye, 2d, Wid. Vinal.

8, Gd. Hewes, 1632, Wales, — — S. Sold (1636) Gd. Cooper, a 1632 K.? — — B.

9, Edward Fosters, 1632, L.? Jan. 8, 1634-5, S. "Since my comeing to Octo. 1636." — —

10, My House, Sept. 18, 1634, L., Jan. 8, 1634-5, B.

11, Gd. Foxwells, (see 50) 1630, — Jan. 8, 1634-5, B. Sold (1636) to Henry Bourne, a 1634, — Jan. 25, 1634-5, B.

12, Samuel House, Sept. 18, 1334, L., Jan. 8, 1634-5, B. & S.

13, Gd. Chittenden's, 1635, K. Feb. 12, 1636-7, S.

14, Gd. Lumber's, (see 27) 1630, L.? Ap. 19, 1635, B. Sold (1636) to Gd. Winter, a 1634, L. Ap. 9, 1637, S.

15, My Sonns, son-in-law Sam'l Fuller, 1620, Leyden Nov. 7, 1636, B.

16, Gd. Haites, 1635, K. Ap. 19, 1635, S. Sold (1636), to *Mr. Bower.*

17, Gd. Hatches, 1635, K. — — — S.

18, Gd. Lewice, Senior, a 1634, — B. Sold to Gd. Dorkins? a 1634, — probably Thos. Dimick, B.

19, *Goody* Hinckley, 1635, K. B.

20, Mr. Tilden, a 1628, K. — — S.

21, * * * The Smiths, Gd. Hoit's brother, — — — — — — S.

22, Gd. Lewice, Junior, a 1635, K. — — S.

23, Gd. Rowleyes new house, on his lot, — See No. 5, —

24, Mr. Vassels, 1630, L. Nov. 28, 1636, S.

25, Gd. Stockbridge, ye wheeler, 1635, L. S.

26, Gd. Stedmans, 1635, L. July 17, 1636, S.

27, Gd. Lumber's, uppon his lot, 1630, see No. 14, —

28, Meeting House, — — — see above —

29, Isaac Robinson's, 1629, Leyden Nov. 7, 1636, B. Sold (1637) to Gd. Twisden.

30, Mr. Cudworth's house on his lott, 1632, L.? see No. 2, —

31, Brother Turners, on his lott, 1628, — see No. 6, —

32, Brother Cobb's, on his lott 1632, — see No. 7, —

33, Gd. Hewes, on his lott, 1634, — see No. 8, —

34, Gd. Lewice, on his lott, 1632, — see No. 18, — Sold to Gd. Williams—1632, K.? — — S.

35, Gd. Lewice, Junior, his new house, 1635, see No. 18, —

36, Gd. Kenrick's, a 1634, K. Ap. 9. 1637, S.

37, Mr. Besbetch, 1635, K. Ap. 30. 1637, S.

38, The young master, Edward Fitsrandolphs, a 1634, K.? May 14, 1737, B. Sold to Gd. Syllice, a 1634, K.? Dec. 24, 1637, S.

39, Robert Shelleyes, 1632, K.? May 14, 1637, B.

40, John Hanmers, — -- — — — — S. Sold to Gid. H. — — — — — — —

41, Henry Ewells, 1635, K. Ap. 3, 1636, B. Sold to Gd. Merritt, a 1628, S.

42, Mr. Hatches new House, — — — —

43, George Suttens, — — — — — —

44, Brother Crocker, Jr., a 1634, L. Dec. 25, 1636, B.

45, John Emmersons, a 1634, L.? S.

46, Gd. Holmes, — — — --- — S.

47, John Hamners on the cliffe, — — — —

48, Gd. Bird, 1628, — — — S., 1637.

49, Isaac Robinson's new house, 1629, Leyden, see No. 29, —

50, Gd. Foxwell's, on his lot, 1630, — see No. 11, —

51, My house on the lott, erected Sept. 27, — see No. 10, ---

52, Thomas Lapphams, — — K.? Ap. 24, 1636, S.

53, Gd. Edenton's, — — — — — S.

54, Gd. Hylands, — --- K. S.

55, Gd. Rawlings, 1630, — S.

56, William Parkers, S.

57, Gd. Lewice, Senior, —

To these I add church members.

Robert Linnel, 1638, L. Sept. 16, 1538, B.

William Betts, Oct. 25, 1635, B.

Thomas Lothrop, Sept. 8, 1634, May 14, 1637, B.

Christopher Winter, Dec. 24, 1637, S.

Thos. King, L. 1635. Feb. 25, 1637-8, S.

Thos. Boiden, Ipswitch, 1634, May 17, 1635, S.

Whole number that joined Mr. Lothrop's church in Scituate,	63
Of these, 26 were females,	26
Males, or heads of families,	37
Removed to Barnstable in 1639,	20
Leaving,	17

Of this number several had removed to other towns, some had deceased, and only eleven, namely, Syllice, Hatherly, Foster, Turner, Vassel, King, Lapham, Chittenden, John and Christopher Winter, and Steadman, of the male members, were left in church state, when Mr. Lothrop removed, that is, it does not appear by Mr. Lothrop's records that either of these eleven had deceased or removed from Scituate in Oct. 1639, though it does not appear by subsequent records that more than half of the number were left in church state. Of these eleven Vassal was of London, but probably not a member of Mr. Lothrop's church in that city. He was the son of John Vassal, alderman of London and one of the original patentees of the Massachusetts Colony, and an assistant of the Governor. Hatherly was for a time a merchant in London and probably a member of Mr. Lothrop's church; but it is probable that Devon was his native County, and Barnstaple in that shire was the port where he fitted his ships and where he was principally engaged in business. It is very doubtful whether any of those who came over in the Charles and White Angel were Kentish men. Why should they travel two hundred miles across the country to Barnstaple when they could take passage from London or some of the adjacent ports.

It is evident that one page of Mr. Lothrop's records is missing, that is the list of admission to the church from 1638 to 1643, for many of the names of members of the church in Barnstable are not on the list of admissions. To the twenty above named who removed from Scituate to Barnstable the following six must be added: William and John Casely, John Crocker, Thomas Lumbert, Isaac Wells, and Thomas Hinckley, making 26 families from Scituate.

Barnstable was incorporated June 14, 1639, N. S. Thirteen families had then settled in the town, namely: Rev. Joseph Hull, his son Trustram, and his son-in-law John Bursley, making one family, Thomas Shaw, Austin Bearse, Henry Coggin, James Hamlin, William Tilly, Thomas Allyn, Lawrence Litchfield, Thomas Huckins, John Smith, Roger Goodspeed, John Scudder and Nathaniel Bacon, Mr. John Mayo and his son Samuel, were early inhabitants, Mr. Mayo having a house when Mr. Lothrop came. Smith, Bacon, Bursley, T. Hull, and S. Mayo, were not householders June 1639. If to the above he added Abram Blush, Dolar Davis, Thos. Hatch and John Hall, who came in afterwards, it completes the list of townsmen as recorded Jan. 1643-4.

There were at least fifteen dwelling-houses in Barnstable in June, 1639. Some who belonged to Mr. Lothrop's church came before October. Mr. Dimmock had built in June; and Thomas Lumbert and Isaac Wells probably had. Nearly all of Mr. Hull's company appear to have been from the west of England, mostly from Devonshire and Somersetshire, perhaps a few came from Wales, on the opposite coast of the Bristol Channel. Barnstaple was the most convenient port for these men, and our Barnstable derived its name from its Devonshire namesake, probably because that was the town from which the first settlers sailed.

Yarmouth obtained its name in the same manner. The leading men among the first settlers were from Norfolk County, of which Yarmouth was the principal seaport, hence the name.

Some particulars respecting Mr. Lothrop's residence in Scituate already given, I shall repeat, in order to give a connected narrative of events. He arrived in Boston Sept. 18, 1634, and stopped nine days in that town to confer with friends and decide respecting his future movements. He met with many who had known him in his native land; all had heard of his labors, and his sacrifices for the cause of Independency, and all most cordially welcomed him to the shores of New England. Gov. Winthrop notes his arrival, and commends the modesty and the reserve of one who had so prominently, so ably, and so fearlessly, upheld the Puritan faith.

Many who had heard him proclaim the truths of eternal life in Kent, and in London, had previously come to New England, and were like sheep without a shepherd, scattered in divers places in the Massachusetts and in the Plymouth Colonies. Several had set down in Scituate, and they invited Mr. Lothrop to visit them. On the 27th of September he went down to that place, and was most enthusiastically welcomed by former brethren and urged to again become their pastor. The kindly reception which was extended to him, and the cordial welcomes with which he was greeted, were most gratifying to his feelings, and he resolved that Scituate should be his future home----the fold into which he would gather together the estrays of his scattered flock. His grateful heart believed that the hand of God had opened this door for him,----had at last given him a resting place from his toils. Here, protected by law, he could build up church institutions, and here he and his family could dwell together in peace, surrounded by the loving friends of his youth. Willing hands quickly built a house for his family, of "meane" proportions, and of "meaner" architecture, yet it was a shelter from the storm---- a place that he could call his own---- a blessing from "Him who had not where to lay His head." Mr. Lothrop had probably passed four years of his life a student at Christ's College, Cambridge. To this day the magnificent proportions, the gorgeous splendors, and the architectural beauties of its ancient edifices command the admiration of every beholder. Until his imprisonment he had been accustomed to reside in well built and well furnished dwellings. He could most truly say his house in Scituate was "*meane.*" The walls were made of poles filled between with stones and clay, the roof thatched, the chimney to the mantle of rough stone, and above of cob-work, the windows of oiled paper, and the floors of hand sawed planks. Mr. Lothrop elsewhere calls such structures *booths*, and says they were open and cold, and in winter a high piled fire had constantly to be kept burning. All the houses in the village were alike----there was no opening for pride to claim supremacy. Mr. Lothrop believed that every event of life is ordained of God for good,----he was therefore content, and the two years that he dwelt under a thatched roof was perhaps the happiest period of a well spent life. With better built and better furnished houses came strifes and contentions, rendering his abode in Scituate unpleasant, and from which, in his letter to Gov. Prence, he states, "I desire greatly to be released."

Nov. 6, Dec. 25, and Jan. 8, 1634, O. S., were set apart as "days of humiliation." No meeting house had been built, and the meetings were held at Mr. Cudworth's house. To organize a church was the object of those meetings. Jan. 8, as the preceding fast days had been, was spent in humbling themselves before God in prayer, and at night thirteen who "had been in covenaunt before, joyned in covenaunt together."

Monday, Jan. 19, 1634, O. S., January 29, 1635, N. S., was also set apart as a day of humiliation at Mr. Lothrop's house. Seventeen had then joined in church covenant----eleven male and six female members. Eight of the eleven were householders when Mr. Lothrop came to Scituate, and the other three were himself, Samuel House, who probably came over with him, and Richard Foxwell, who came to Massachusetts in 1630. At this meeting John Lothrop "was chosen pastor by the votes of the brethren, and by them invested into office." The mode in which he was inducted is not particularly stated ; but it is evident that the same forms were adopted as at the installation of Mr. Jacob in London. The neighboring churches were not invited to be present and assist. They held that the neighboring churches were true churches of Christ, and they had a high respect for the talents and piety of the ministers ; but they wished by their example to vindicate the great principle of Independency, that all power in the churches originates on the consent of the individual members. The day was spent in fasting, in humiliation, and in prayer. Mr. Lothrop was elected pastor by the brethren of the church, and he was invested in office, with prayer, and by the imposition of the hands of those who had elected him. This is pure Independency. It is now merged into Congregationalism, a system of church government essentially the same, and differing originally only in one, perhaps non-essential particular : Congregationalists then held that churches had the right to give, and the right to extend to, or to withhold from neighboring churches the right hand of fellowship, and consequently to withdraw it from one that did not walk orderly.

Of the thirty followers who came over with Mr. Lothrop it does not appear that many were heads of families. Samuel House, or Howes, was a ship carpenter. Thomas Prior, who came over, says Deane, in the same ship with Mr. Lothrop, brought a part of his family with him, the remainder came in the Hopewell in 1635. He died in June, 1639, and does not appear to have been a member of the church. Henry Bourne probably came with Mr. Lothrop, but having no list it is unprofitable to conjecture. During the winter of 1634-5, few additions were made to the population. In the summer of 1635 several families from Tenterden and other places in Kent came over in the Hercules from Sandwich and settled in Scituate, and a number came in from neighboring towns ; but the population did not increase that year sufficiently to warrant the building of a meeting house. Mr. Hatherly and Mr. Gibson had good estates ; but most of the other settlers were poor men, and relied on their own strong arms for success in life.

The church had increased in members and strength. Aug. 13, 1635, after a "day of humiliation," Henry Cobb was elected the first deacon of the church, and on the 15th of December following "was invested into the office,"----that is, ordained, as all officers were, with prayer, and by the imposition of the hands of the elders and brethren.

In 1636 the town rapidly increased in population. Mr. Lothrop's old friends scattered in various towns, sold out their estates and removed to Scituate. The increase gave strength to the plantation ; but it brought with it much privation and suffering. The people were also anxious to procure "helpes in the ministry," their first and their last care ; and they feared that the Indians on their borders would prove treacherous. To avert these threatening calamities Friday, April 7, 1636, was observed as a day of humiliation.

The congregation had at this time so largely increased that there was no building in the town sufficiently spacious for its accommodation. Notwithstanding their poverty, and the scarcity that prevailed, they resolved to build a meeting house. On the 2d and 3d days of August the frame was raised, and it was completed and dedicated Thursday, Nov. 10, 1636. The following day a fast was held at the meeting house "for a blessing upon their consultation aboute the Lawes for settling the State of this Patent."

Connected with the last record there is a statement that some difference of opinion existed among the members, which were by the mercy of God reconciled April 27, 1637. On what subject the members differed is not stated. We may however infer what caused the difficulty by the text from which Mr. Lothrop taught on that day : "And Abram said unto Lot, let there be no strife, I pray thee, between me and thee, and between my herdsmen and thy herdsmen, for we are brethren." Gen. 13 :8. This text furnishes the key that unlocks the door.

The raising of stock was then the most profitable business pursued in the Colony. Many in England had sent over cattle, and put them out for half the increase. It was a business that required no capital, and the poor could successfully compete with the rich. The quantity of meadow land was limited, and the capacity of the country for keeping cattle and horses depended on the amount of fodder that could be laid up for winter. As each claimed an equal right in the meadows, dissentions naturally arose "between my herdsmen and thy herdsmen." We find them complaining at this early period that the "place was too straite for them." The meaning of this is, there was but little cleared land in Scituate adapted to the raising of grain, and though there was sufficient pasturage in the woods for their cattle during the mild season of the year, they were in winter *straightened* for fodder. This was the prudential reason that induced Mr. Lothrop and a majority of his people to remove to Barnstable. In his letters to Gov. Prence, which will presently appear, he states the matter with much clearness, and it is unnecessary for me to recapitulate his reasons.

There was another cause of uneasiness and "difference in judgment." About this time Mr. William Vassall removed to Scituate. He was a son of John Vassall, an aldermen of London, and the brother of Samuel, a wealthy merchant of that city. He was dissatisfied with the policy of the leading men of Massachusetts. He was a latitudinarian in his opinions and had strong radical tendencies. He had known Mr. Lothrop, in London, and sympathized with him in his views. There was however, a wide difference in the characters of the two men. Mr. Lothrop was firm, yet gentle, discreet, cautious, and though always open to conviction, and a constant seeker for new light, he formed no opinions hastily. Mr. Vassall, though brought up under aristocratic and conservative influences, was most radical in his views and opinions. He was firm, often over-bearing and in all his undertakings exhibited a strong disposition to lead, never to follow. He often acted from impulse, and though a man of noble and generous feelings, a man of learning, a ready writer, and a man of wealth, his impulsive nature unfitted him to act prudently in the hour of trial and difficulty.

A mutilated passage in Mr. Lothrop's records, unfortunately mixed up with another record, by one of the transcribers, however shows the standing of Mr. Vassall at this time. Dec. 28, 1636, (probably this is the true date) the records say "Divers of the people having some *dissatisfaction* to Mr. Vassall, and he with them," but it does not clearly appear that they were reconciled and that they settled their differences and renewed their covenant till Nov. 20, 1637.

Mr. Deane gives a full account of Mr. Vassall, and copies his numerous letters, written after Mr. Lothrop left Scituate. In those letters the wayward character of the man is clearly exhibited. He soon removed to Barbadoes, where he died before 1655.

I have made many quotations from the church records. The passages to which I shall hereafter refer are of a similar tenor. The careful examination of these and other records has satisfied me that Neale, Crosley, Deane, and other writers on ecclesiastical history, are mistaken in saying that the subject of baptism caused uneasiness in Mr. Lothrop's church in London, in Scituate, and in Barnstable; and that the first Baptist church in England separated itself from Mr. Lothrop's congregation in London. If not in this article, I have in other papers made similar statements.

I was misled by the authority of great names, and if this is my only mistake I am thankful.

I regret that I was unable, at the commencement of this article, to make the following statement:

The subject of baptism was not the chief cause of uneasiness in Mr. Lothrop's church in London, in Scituate, or in Barnstable. Every cause of trouble or inquietude that occurred, he seems to have named and made a special subject for prayer at the frequent fasts which he observed. If the mode of baptism was a subject of such deep dissention as to rend his church, it is most surprising that a man who noted the most trivial events should not have recorded one of so vital importance as this. Mr. Lothrop could not record events that did not occur, and that is the true solution of the question.

The difficulties in the London church occurred ten years after Mr. Lothrop left; that is, during the time that his successor, Mr. Jessey, was the pastor. Mr. Jessey, as already stated, became a baptist, and his church was the first baptist church in England. Mr. Lothrop's "Queries respecting baptism" were written in Barnstable about the year 1644, and published by some of his old friends remaining in London very soon afterwards. Mr. Lothrop sent some of his children to England to be educated, and had maintained a correspondence with old and new friends in London. They would naturally write to him for his opinions on a subject in which they felt a deep interest. This is not only a legitimate inference from known facts, but the dates show beyond controversy that the division, or rather the transformation of the First Independent church in London to the First Baptist, occurred not during the ministry of Mr. Lothrop, but ten years after he left. This view enables us to explain satisfactorily the apparently contradictory statements in Neale, Crosby, and other writers on the ecclesiastical history of the times.

Respecting Mr. Lothrop's church in Scituate, I cannot endorse all the statements of Mr. Deane, for it is evident that the mode of baptism was not the chief nor one of the causes of dissension among his people. I regret to be obliged to differ from so respectable and generally so reliable an authority. Mr. Lothrop names many minor causes of dissension and trouble, but does not directly nor indirectly refer to baptism as one of the causes. Contemporaneous authorities do not name it,—do not furnish any collateral evidence in its support, and it therefore seems to be folly to attempt to perpetuate the error that "the mode of baptism was the chief cause of dissensions in Mr. Lothrop's church."

In Barnstable, the mode of baptism caused no dissension. The subject is referred to only once on Mr. Lothrop's records. "John Allen and Elizabeth Bacon married, alsoe by him (Thomas Hinckley) Oct. 10, 1650, both Anabaptists." At that time the doctrines of the Anabaptists were not tolerated in the Massachusetts Colony. The most bitter words of denunciation were applied to members of that sect, and many suffered imprisonment and stripes. In the sister Colony a magistrate could not have been persuaded to officiate at the marriage of Anabaptists, yet Gov. Hinckley, who has been stigmatized as an intolerant man, did officiate, and Mr. Lothrop records the event without comment.*

It is unnecessary to pursue this in giving farther. Mr. Lothrop believed that sprinkling was the mode of baptism taught in the Word ; but he did not condemn the brother who believed in immersion.

THE FIRST THANKSGIVING DAY.

Dec. 22, 1636, the first Thanksgiving day was celebrated. The exercises at the Meeting House, and subsequently at the homes of his people, are thus noted in the church records :

"Beginning some halfe an hour before nine, and continued until after twelve a clocke, ye day being very cold, beginning with a short prayer,—then a psalm sang,—then more large in prayer,—after that another psalm, and the Word taught,—after that prayer,—and then a psalm. Then making merry to the creatures, the poorer sort being invited by the virtue."

The quaint expressions of this synopsis of the doings on their first day of thanksgiving are suggestive of the habits, condition, and feelings of the people. It has been fashionable to call our Pilgrim ancestors a gloomy, austere race, who held that any and all indulgence in "creature" comforts was sinful. It is pleasant to note that Mr. Lothrop thought it no sin "to make merry." "To everything there is a season, and a time to every purpose under Heaven." "A time to mourn, and a time to dance." The God of nature has ordained that the young shall indulge in innocent sports,—they are necessary to develop their physical powers to make them healthy and strong, and to fit them for usefulness in life. Thus christianity gives a cheerful tone to the character, and fits a man to enjoy temporal as well as spiritual blessings. The bigot can draw no line of distinction between the use and the abuse of a thing,—he cannot see that the one is virtue, the other vice. Our ancestors were not bigots. They thought it no sin to match their skill in athletic sports, or test their strength in wrestling. Their children played at games which had come down from a remote English ancestry, and which continue to delight the young of the present generation.

Some of the second and third generations were bigoted and

---

*There is an old saying, "contraries meet," and it is founded on a deep knowledge of the laws of the human mind. If the Baptist denomination be viewed from the stand point of baptism, we call its members narrow, exclusive, intolerant; yet from other standpoints the denomination holds to the broad and enlightened views of its mother church.

intolerant. The lamp of the fathers which had burned so brilliantly enlightening all their paths, now burned with an uncertain and flickering blaze. The forms of religious truth remained, but the spirit which animated the fathers had fled.

Mr. Lothrop taught that christianity was a system adapted to man's nature and state, and because it was so adapted, its tendency was to make a man better, to make him happier here and happier hereafter. He did not teach that the christian must hate all that he loved before his conversion, that all amusements or "making merry to the creature" were in and of themselves sinful; only when they lead direct and inevitably to sinful habits, or when they inflicted a wrong on the neighbor.

Oct. 26, 1637, another day of thanksgiving was held. The exercises at the Meeting House were the same as on the previous year. Thanks were given for "two particulars: 1, For the victory over the Pequets. Ye 2, For Reconciliation betwixt Mr. Cotton and the other ministers." After the service the poorer were invited to dine with the richer, and make themselves merry.

Fast days continued to be held from time to time. June 22, 1637, for success in the war against the Pequots, for composing differences among the brethren in the Bay, and for help in the ministry at Scituate. Feb. 22, 1637-8. At a fast held on that day Edward and Foster and Thomas Besbetch were chosen deacons and invested into office.

REMOVAL TO MATTAKEESE.

At five days of fasting, and at other meetings of the church, the subject of removal was discussed. At first they intended to remove to Sippican, now Rochester, but June 13, 1639, it had been decided to remove to Mattakeese, now Barnstable.

As I have already in the Dimmock and other articles extracted from the colony and church records the notices given respecting the settlement of Barnstable, I shall not again copy the papers in full, excepting Mr. Lothrop's letters, of which I have printed only short extracts.

In 1638 the Colony Court granted the lands at Sipican, now Rochester, to several members of Mr. Lothrop's church, where he and a majority of his people proposed to remove, and form a town. Feb. 22 of that year was a fast day appointed by the church, the especial object being to take measures respecting the removal to Sipican. The matter is not named again in the church records till January 23, 1638-9, where after a season of humiliation and prayer it was agreed, that those who had resolved to remove to Sipican be divided into three companies "in this service, for preventing of exceptions." They elected their town committees to have the care and direction of the settlement, to make orders to be observed in beginning of the settlement, and for the after management of its affairs. They also sought the guidance of God to procure more spiritual help for those who were about to remove, and also for their brethren who were to remain in Scituate.

The summer of the year 1639 was very dry, and partly on that account a day of humiliation was observed June 13, O. S. They prayed that God would direct and provide for them, being "in the point of remoueall." The place to which they were about to remove is not named, but Mattakeese was undoubtedly intended ; for on the 26th of the same month a fast was held "For the presence of God to goe with us to Mattakeese."

In the latter part of 1637, or beginning of 1638, the date is not given on the colony records, the lands at Mattakeese were granted to Mr. Richard Collicut, and a company, mostly from the town of Dorchester. Mr. Collicut was engaged in the service of the Massachusetts Colony, and was prevented from giving his personal attention to the settlement of the town. The Plymouth Colony Court became impatient at the long delay, voted that if Mr. Collicut and his associates did not organize a town before the June Court, 1639, the lands would be granted to other associates. At the assembling of the June Court no town had been organized, and June 4, O. S., 14th new, Mattakeese was incorporated as a town and named Barnstable, and the lands granted to Rev. Joseph Hull and Elder Thomas Dimmock, as a committee of their associates. At that time there were about fifteen families settled in the town. The fact that the Plymouth Court was impatient on account of the delay of Mr. Collicut was well known to Mr. Lothrop in the spring of 1639, in fact a number of families from Scituate had then removed to Mattakeese, and as the extensive salt meadows at the latter place made it a more desirable residence than Sippican, Mr. Lothrop and his people changed their purpose very soon after the meeting held Jan. 23, 1638-9.

The following letters of Mr. Lothrop to Gov. Prence were preserved among Mr. Winslow's papers. No especial care appears to have been taken in their preparation. They are interesting documents relative to the early history of Barnstable, and the best specimens preserved of Mr. Lothrop's style of writing :

FIRST LETTER.

"*To the right worthy and much-honoured Mr. Prince, our endearoured governor of Plimouth,—Grace, mercy, and peace, be multiplyed.*

My dear and pretious,

Esteemed with the highest esteeme and respect, above every other particular in these territoryes : being now in the roome of God, and by him that is the God of gods, deputed as a god on earth unto us, in respect of princely function and calling. Unto whom wee ingenuously confesse all condigne and humble service from us to bee most due. And if we knowe our hearts, you have our hearts, and our best wishes for you. As Peter said in another case, doe wee in this particular say, It is good for us to be heere: (wee mean under this septer and government) under which wee can bee best content to live and dye. And if it bee possible we would have nothing for to separate us from you, unlesse it be death. Our souls (I speak in regard of many of us) are firmely lincked unto your worthy selfe, and unto many, the Lord's worthyes with you. Wee shall ever account your advancement ours. And I hope through grace, both by prayer and practice, wee shall endeavour to our best abilitye, to advance both the throne of civill dignitye, and the kingly throne of Christ, in the severall administrations thereof in the midst of you. Hereunto (the truth is) we can have no firmer obligation, than the straite and stronge tyes of the gospell. If we have no more, this would alwayes be enough to binde us close in discharge of all willing and faithfull duetye both unto you and likewise unto all the Lord's anointed ones with you. But seeing over and above, out of your gratious dispositions (thro' the grace and mercy of the Highest) you are pleased to sett your faces of favour more towards us, (though a poor and contemptable people) than towards any other particular people whatsoever, that is a people distinct from yourselves. As wee have had good and cleare experience hereof before, and that from tyme to tyme; so wee now againe in the renewed commiseration towards us, as most affectionate nurseing, fathers being exceeding willing and readye to gratifye us, even to our best content, in the pointe of removeall; Wee being incapacitated thereunto, and that in divers weighty considerations, some, if not all of which, are well known bothe to yourselfe, and to others with you. Now your love being to us transcendent, passing the love you have shewn to any without you, wee can soe much the more, as indebted unto our good God in praises, soe unto yourselves in services. We will ever sett downe in humble thankfullness in the perpetual memory of your exceeding kindnesse. Now we stand stedfast in our resolution to remove our tents and pitch elsewhere, if wee cann see Jehovah going before us. And in very deed, in our removeing, wee would have our principal ende God's own glorye, our Sion's better peace and prosperitye, and the sweet and happie regiment of the Prince of our Salvation more jointly imbraced, and more fully exalted. And if externall comfortable conveniences as an overplus, shall bee cast in, according to the free promise of the Lord, wee trust then, as wee shall receive more compleate comfort from him, so he shall receive more compleate honour by us: for which purpose we humbly crave, as the fervencye of your devotions, soe the constancye of your wonted christian endeavours. And being fully perswaded of your best assistance herein, as well in the one as in the other, wee will labour to wait at the throne of grace, expecting that issue that the Lord shall deeme best.

In the intrim, with abundance of humble an unfeigned thankes on every hand on our parts remembered, wee take our leave, remaining, obliged forever unto you, in all duety and service.

JOHN LOTHROPP.

From *Scituate*, the 28 of this 7th month, [*September*] 1638. (Oct. 8, 1638, N. S.)

N. B.—Three names are subscribed beneath the name of Mr. Lothropp: Anthony Aniball, Henry Cobb, Isaac Robinson; to which are added the words, "In behalf of the church." [Superscribed thus:]

To the right worthy and much-reverenced Mr. Prince, Governor at Plimouth.

SECOND LETTER.

"To the right worthy and much-reverenced, Mr. Prince, governor—Grace, mercy and peace beforever multiplied.

Sundry circumstances of importance concurring touching the present state of myself and the people in covenant with me, presse me yett againe to sett pen to paper, to the end that the busyness in hand might with greater expedition be pressed forward, if it may be: not willing to leave any lawful means unattempted, that we are able to judge, to be the means of God, that soe we might have the more comfort to rest in the issue that God himself shall give in the use of his own means. Yett I would be loth to be too much pressing herein, least the more haste on our part should occasion the less speed, or, over-spurring, when by reason of abundance of freeness, there needs none at all. I should dishearten, and so procure some unwillingness. But considering your godly wisdome in discerning our condition, and presuming of your love unfeigned to us-ward, which cannot but effect a readiness on your part, in passing by and covering of our infirmitye, I am much emboldened, with all due reverence and respect, both to your place and person, to re-salute you.

The truth is, many grievances attend mee. from the which I would be freed, or att least have them mittigated, if the Lord see it good. Yett would I raither with patience leave them, than to grieve or sadd any heart, whose heart ought not to be grieved by me, much lesse yours; whom I honour and regard with my soule, as I do that worthy instrument of God's honour, together with yourselfe, Mr. Bradford, because I am confident you make the advanceing of God's honour your chiefest honour. And the raither I would not bee any meanes to grieve you, inasmuch as I conceive you want not meanes otherwise of grief enough. But that I be not too tedious, and consequently too grievous. The principal occasion of my present writing is this; Your worthy selfe, together with the rest joyned and assisting in government with you, much reverenced and esteemed of us, having gratiously and freely uppon our earnest and humble suits, granted and conferred a place for the transplanting of us. to the end God might have the more glorye and wee more comfort : both which wee have solidd grounds to induce us to believe, will be effected : For the which free and most loveing grant, we both are and ever remain to bee, by the grace of the highest, abundantly thankful. Now here lyes the stone that some of the breathren here stumbel att ; which happely is but imaginarye, and not real, and then there will be no need of removeall. And that is this, some of them have certaine jelousies and fears, that there is some privie and undermineing and secrett plotting by some there, with some here, to hinder the seasonable successe of the work in hand, to witt of our re-moveall, by procuring a procrastination. in some kinde of project, to have the tyme deferred, that the conveniencye of the tyme of removeing beeing wore out before we can have free and cleare passage to remove, that so wee might not remove att all. But what some one particular happely with you, with some amongst us here, may attempt in this kinde for private and personal ends, I neither know, nor care, nor fear, forasmuch as I am fully perswaded that your endeared selfe, and Mr. Bradford, with the rest in general, to whom power in this behalfe belongeth, are sincerelye and firmelye for us, to expeditt and compleate the busyness as soon as may be, so that our travells and paines, our costs and charge, shall not be lost and in vaine herein, nor our hopes frustrated. Now the trueth is, I have been the more willing to endite and present these feew lines, partly to wipe away any rumour that might bee any wayes raised upp of distrustfullness on our partes especially, to clear my owne innocencye of having any suspition herein; as alsoe to signifye since the place hath been granted and confirmed unto us; some of the breathren have sold their houses and lands here, and have put themselves out of all. And others have put out their improved grounds to the half increase thereof, upon their undoubted expectation forthwith as it were to begin to build and plant in the new plantation. Wherein if they should be disappointed, it would be a means to cast them into some great extremitye. Wherefore let me intreate and beseech you in the bowells of the Lord, without any offence, both in this respect, as also for other reasons of greater importance, which I will forbear to specifye: To do this further great curtesey for us, to make composition with the Indians for the place, and priviledges thereof in our behalf, with that speed you cann: and wee will freely give satisfaction to them, and strive to bee the more enlarged in thankefulnesse to you. I verily thinke wee shall never have any rest in our spiritts, to rest or stay here; and I suppose you thinke little * * otherwise, and am therefore the more confident that you will not neglect any opportunitye, that might make for our expedition herein. I and some of the breathren have intreated our brother John Coake, who is with you, and of you, a member of your congregation, to bee the best furtherance in such occasions, as either doe or may concerne us, as possibly he may or cann, who hath alsoe promised unto us his best service herein. Thus wishing and praying for your greatest prosperitye every wayes, I humbly take my leave.

Remaining to be at your command and service in the Lord.

JOHN LOTHROPP.

From *Scituate*, Feb. 18, 1638. (Feb. 28, 1639, N. S.) [Superscribed thus:]

To the right worthy and much-honored Governor Prince, att his house in Plimouth. Give these I pray.

REV. JOHN LOTHROP REMOVED TO BARNSTABLE.

On the 29th of June, 1639, O. S., (July 9, new), the pioneer company left Scituate for Mattakeset. Their purpose in removing thus early was to secure a winter's supply of provender for their cattle, and to build houses for themselves, and for the larger company, who were to remain in Scituate till the annual crop had been secured. Mattakeeset was incorporated as a town June 14, 1639, new style, and called Barnstable or Bastable, as the name was commonly pronounced, and frequently written. It received its name from Barn*staple* in Devonshire in England, the port from whence many of the first settlers took their departure from their native land. The English town is still called Barn*staple*. Capt. John Smith and many old writers uniformly spell the name Bastable, a circumstance that indicates that both names were originally the same. The usage of more than two centuries has established a different orthography; which, if it were desirable, cannot now be changed.

A church had been established, but does not appear to have

been legally organized, of which the Rev. Joseph Hull, who had removed the preceding May from Weymouth, was the pastor, and Rev. John Mayo the teaching elder. No meeting house had been built, and tradition points to the large rock near the dwelling-house of Mr. Edward Scudder as the place where he and his followers held their first meetings for public worship. That rock formerly stood on the bluff on the south side of the road. It was gradually undermined by the washings of the rains, and finally rolled down to its present position on the opposite side of the road. It is not stated, in any ancient record, that the first settlers assembled around that rock for public worship, yet the tradition seems to be reliable. The first Meeting House was built in 1646, and prior to that date the meetings were either held in private dwelling-houses or in the open air. Mr. Lothrop states in his records that the meeting on Sunday, May 26, 1644, was held in the open air. It is probable that all the meetings of the congregation prior to May 10, 1646, were so held when the weather was mild and pleasant, because there was no building in the plantation sufficiently spacious to accommodate all, for none of the people, who were physically able, absented themselves from public worship. A stern necessity thus comes to our aid in establishing the truth of the tradition. A large part of the rock was split off and used for the foundation of the Jail, yet a large mass remains, and like Plymouth Rock, should be preserved as a memento of the fathers.

If the truth of this tradition be admitted, it indicates that Barnstable Rock was not far from the centre of the settlement made in the spring of 1639. Mr. Hull probably pitched his first tent on the land adjoining Coggin's Pond, that he afterwards sold to Samuel Hinckley. This was about a quarter of a mile east of the Rock.

The early settlers selected their houselots in places convenient to water, wood, and the salt meadows, and usually set their dwellings in locations sheltered from the north and northwest winds. They built in two neighborhoods—one in the vicinity of Goodspeed's, now Meeting House Hill, and the other near Coggin's Pond. The houselots were laid out in parallelograms, and contained from eight to twelve acres each. I have before remarked that the lots that were longest east and west were probably laid under the authority of Mr. Collicut; but on a careful examination of the land I find that the nature of the country required that they should be so laid out, and hence the supposition that they were laid by Mr. Collicut does not appear to be warranted by the facts in the case, or by the subsequent acts of the first settlers in the spring of 1640.

A portion of the first settlers built, in 1639, substantial frame houses, one of which yet remains, the Goodspeed House, and Mr. Lothrop's also, built a few years after the settlement. Mr. Hull, Mr. Mayo, Thomas Lumbert, Mr. Dimmock, Elder Cobb, and a few others, put up frame houses, the others temporary buildings, such as have been described as first built in Scituate. No log houses were built, because the timber was not adapted to such use. Saw mills had then been erected, and hand sawed lumber was not expensive. Houses of one story about 20 feet square, with boarded walls, and a thatched roof, were put up for £5, equal to $20 in silver money.*

As the better class of substantial frame houses cost only 20 or £25, the industrious and the prudent were in a few years provided with comfortable residences, fully as comfortable as many of the more elegant structures of the present day. They were all built, except the fortification houses, in one style, two stories high, about 20 by 26 feet square on the ground, with very sharp roofs, because a flat roof covered with straw or thatch could not shed water. The posts were twelve or fourteen feet long, the lower story finished about seven feet in the clear, and the upper about six. They all fronted due south, and the great room or parlor occupied the southeast corner. This room was usually about 16 feet square, and was occupied for a kitchen, dining room, and parlor. A bed often occupied the northeast corner, and the looms the southeast. The sills were hewn from the largest trees of the forest, and projected into the room forming a seat on the south and east side. The floor was laid on sleepers that rested on the ground, and it came up even with the lower part of the sill, so that on entering the front door, which was at the southwest corner, you stepped down about a foot. The fireplace was on the west side, and occupied the whole space from the doorway to within about a foot of the north side of the room, and was usually four feet deep. The fire was kindled in the center, leaving ample chimney corners (a luxury now unknown) where the younger members of the family had comfortable seats in cold weather, and could gaze at the stars through the ample flue. The oven opened into the back part of the fireplace on the left hand side. The place of the mistress of the house was on the right hand side, near the low suttle in the corner. The master's place was a large armed chair or round-a-bout placed directly in front of the fire. The fashionable now discuss the merits of furnaces and patent stoves; but if you have a plenty of wood, and want to enjoy good health, and take comfort in cold winter weather, build an old-fashioned fireplace—there is no stove equal to it.

The rear of the lower floor contained a small room at the northwest corner having a small fireplace, and was sometimes called the kitchen, but rarely occupied for that purpose. A small room, sometimes occupied as a bedroom and sometimes for other purposes, was on the east, and at the northeast corner a narrow pantry or closet, in which was a trap-door opening into the cellar.

The second story was divided nearly in the same manner as the

---

*This was the price paid William Chase for building the old Hallet house which has been described.

lower. A large square chamber occupied the space directly over the parlor, with lodging rooms on the rear. The garret, which was spacious, was occupied by the servants, and as a general place of deposit. Some of the early settlers kept their bee-hives in the garret, placing them on a shelf on the outside in the summer, and removing them inside in winter.

Very little was expended to please the eye. Paint was unknown, and excepting the seams between the boards, few rooms were ever plastered. White sand from the beach supplied the place of carpets, and the furniture was of rude domestic manufacture.

Mr. Lothrop and the large company arrived in Barnstable Oct. 11, 1639, O. S., Oct. 21, new, bringing with them the crops which they had raised in Scituate.

Though they had much to do to prepare for the winter, yet they did not forget their duty to God. Oct. 31, 1639, O. S., was set apart as a day of fasting, humiliation and prayer. It was the first fast day observed in Barnstable, the special object whereof was, "For the grace of our God to settle us here in church estate, and to unite us together in holy walking, and make us faithful in keeping Covenaunt w'th God and one to another."

The Rev. Joseph Hull and the Rev. John Mayo were both residents in Barnstable when Mr. Lothrop came, but there is no record that a church had been organized. Mr. Hull was the leading man in the plantation—the lands had been granted to him and Mr. Dimmock as a committee in behalf of themselves and their associates; he had procured an act of incorporation, had established a civil community, and had exercised his gifts as a preacher before any of Mr. Lothrop's church came. Very soon after we find him an exile, a wanderer, a persecuted man. In my account of Mr. Hull the details are given. However great may be our veneration for Mr. Lothrop and his followers, our sympathies are irresistably enlisted on the side of poor Mr. Hull. The historian finds it a difficult matter to explain; he cannot "make bricks without straw."

On the 11th day of Dec. 1639, O. S. the first day of Thanksgiving was observed in Barnstable. The public service was at poor Mr. Hull's house. The special object of the meeting was to give thanks to God for his exceeding mercy in bringing them safe to Barnstable, preserving their health in the weak beginnings, "of their plantation and in their church estate." The day was very cold, and after the close of public service they divided into "three companies to feast together, some at Mr. Hull's, some at Mr. Mayo's, and some at Brother Lumberd Senior's."

During the first winter they had no lack of food. Fish were abundant in the waters, wild game visited the coast in immense flocks, and the woods were filled with deer and other animals that tested the sportman's skill. Of the forty-five families then in Barnstable not more than ten, probably not more than eight, had comfortable two story frame houses. Three-fourths of the families occupied tenements that poorly sheltered them from the storms.

Mr. Lothrop was no better provided for than the mass of his followers. He built a small house where Eldridge's hotel now stands. It was two stories high and a frame house, was occupied many years. During the first winter it was open and cold, and not so comfortable a residence as an ordinary barn at the present time. Hills protected him from the cold northwest wind; but the northeasters buffeted, in all their fury against his frail tenement.

1640. During the winter of 1639-40, there was little sickness in the plantation and no death occurred. The bills of mortality kept by Mr. Lothrop show that Barnstable was one of the most healthy towns in the Colony. During the year 1639 there was no deaths; in 1640, 3; '41, 10; '42, 2; '43, 1; '44, 4; '45, 1; '46, 4; '47, 0; '48, 3; '49, 5; '50, 3; '51, 1; '52, 1; and to Nov. 1653, 1, making 38 in all. Of these 8 were still-born, 23 children, and 7 of mature age. Two of the latter were drowned at Nauset. In the spring of 1640 there were 45 families, and taking the usual average of 5, it gives 225 as the number of inhabitants. In 1653 the number of families had increased, and three hundred is not a high estimate of the number of inhabitants. If the average number of inhabitants be called only 250 during the whole period, it shows that the average annual mortality was only one in each one hundred. For so long a period it is doubtful whether a parallel case can be found.

The greatest mortality was in 1641. The spring was unusually cold and wet, the whooping cough prevailed, and several children died of that disease. In 1647 there was sickness in every family, scarce an individual escaped, yet no death occurred in the plantation that year. In 1649 the chin cough and the whooping cough prevailed among children and there were some cases of small pox. Though the deaths amounted to five that year, most of them appear to have died of other diseases. Mr. Lothrop was confined to his house, and unable to attend to the duties of the ministry for seven weeks by a cough and "a stitch in his side."

The statistics show that the first settlers of Barnstable had an abundance of nutritious food, were comfortably clothed, and lodged, during the first period of fifteen years.

Of the cereals, they had rye, barley, and some wheat, and an abundance of Indian corn; all the vegetables now generally cultivated, excepting the potato; pork, poultry, and venison; and of fish and grain they had a great abundance. They were not able to add much to the stock of clothing which they brought over. They raised flax, and manufactured some linen cloth. * * * *
It was many years before wool was raised in sufficient quantities to supply the domestic demand. Deer and other skins, which the natives understood the art of dressing in a superior manner, they sub-

stituted for woollen cloths in making their outside garments. Many of the first settlers were tanners and shoemakers, and none suffered for want of covering for the feet.

In the course of three years all had comfortable, though not elegant houses. The poorer kinds were one story, and the walls and floors were of hand-sawed boards. The favorite locality was the southeastern declivity of a hill, near to wood and water. They dug into the hill-side, and the bank was a support to the stone chimney and oven. The seams between the boards were "daubed" with mortar or clay, and the walls were banked up as high as the windows in winter, with drift from the sea-shore which kept out the cold winds. Many of the better class of houses were built on side-hills. The Nathaniel Bacon house was so built, the timber of which was as sound after two centuries as on the day it was hewn. Not being covered, it became thoroughly seasoned, and impervious to rot.

The first settlers of Barnstable had little whereof to complain. None but the idle and improvident lacked the conveniences of life. They were happy and contented—a law unto themselves—vice did not obtain a foothold in their little community.

Mr. Lothrop was as distinguished for his worldly wisdom as for his piety. He was a good business man and so were all his sons. Whenever one of the family pitched his tent, that spot soon became a center of business, and land in its vicinity appreciated in value. It is the men that make a place, and to Mr. Lothrop's in early times Barnstable was more indebted than to any other family.

The division of the common lands was the subject that mainly engrossed attention in the winter of 1639-40. April 25 was set apart as a day of fasting to invoke the divine blessing on their efforts to divide the lands quietly and justly. In many settlements the division of the lands had been the cause of much angry discussion and ill feeling. Mr. Lothrop and the other leading men were prudent and discreet, and the following rule adopted 26th of March, 1640, O. S., April 5, 1640, N. S., "by the general consent of the inhabitants," was satisfactory to all interested.

"One third part to every houselot equally ; one third to the names that are unmovable ; and the other third according to men's estates." *

This rule was adhered to in all the subsequent divisions of the common lands. Its meaning at the present time may not be apparent ; but it was well understood at the time. The division was not

*The houselots were afterwards called "tenement rights"—that is a lot of land of six or more acres set off to an individual, with an agreement that a house should be built thereon. If a man owned a houselot and neglected to build thereon, he had no right to the common lands by virtue of his ownership; but the right being worth more than it would cost to put up a tenement, few forfeited their rights. If a man put up a house on the common land, such house did not give him a tenement right. By names immovable is to be understood accepted townsmen, those who intended to reside permanently in the town. By mens estate was intended personal estate.

made till June, 1641, after the whole Indian title in the East Parish had been purchased, except a small reservation.*

At the fast, April 25, Mr. John Mayo was ordained a teaching elder of the church, otherwise an assistant or associate pastor. The forms adopted were those of pure independency. The church elected Mr. Mayo and invested him into the office. The neighboring pastors and churches were not formerly invited by their delegates to be present and assist, because such invitations would be a concession that each church had not the sole right to ordain its own officers. Mr. Lothrop, Mr. Hull, and Elder Cobb, in the presence of the congregation, laid their hands on Mr. Mayo and publicly announced that they thereby, in the name and behalf of themselves and their brethren, invested him into the office of Teaching Elder.

Beside the ordination of Mr. Mayo, and the division of the common lands, another subject was a special matter for consideration at the April fast : the providing of a place to hold meetings. The settlers were neither prepared or able to put up a meeting house. The Indian title to only a small portion of the territory, less than one-half of the East Parish, had then been extinguished. The settlement would necessarily have to extend west and south, and a point that would then be central would, in a few years, be far on one side. Several were intending to remove to the farm or "great lots" as soon as the division was made, and among these were some of the most substantial men, namely: Anthony Annable, Samuel Hinckley, William Crocker, John Bursley, Edward Fitzrandolphe, John Smith, Thomas Shaw, Roger Goodspeed, and others.

Under the circumstances a temporary arrangement had to be made. In cold and stormy weather the meetings were held at private houses, and none were of sufficient size comfortably to accomodate a congregation of one hundred and fifty, the average attendance.

The lands in the vicinity of Mr. Lothrop's house were low and damp, and had not been drained or cleared of bushes, and the people desired a drier and more central location. Mr. Lothrop had a large family, and the meetings frequently held at his house were inconvenient, and the people desired that their pastor should have a larger and better residence. It was, therefore, proposed that Mr. Lothrop

---

*There were many changes in the ownership of the houselots between 1640 and 1654. This is particularly true of the lots between Calves Pasture Lane and Jail Hill, in fact as far east as the Hyannis road. Joseph Lothrop was a young man in 1639, and was not a townsman till after 1644, and consequently was not an original proprietor, and was not entitled to a houselot. That called his in 1654 was originally laid out to one of the first comers. James Neighbors was not an original proprietor. He purchased his lots also. These three lots I think were originally laid out to John Hall, Henry Rowley, and John Smith, or perhaps on the eastern to Barnard Lumbard. Mr. Lothrop probably bought the western lot for his son Joseph, and therefore it was called his. Mr. Lothrop's will was not signed or executed by him, yet it was admitted to probate, no objections being made, the understanding probably being that after the death of Mr. Lothrop the land should be Joseph's, and there is some evidence that he built his first house where Judge Day's now stands. His house in 1686 was on the eastern declivity of Jail Hill, where the Berry house now stands. Mrs. Lothrop lived till Feb. 25, 1687-8, and during the 25 years she was a widow appears to have resided in Mr. Lothrop's "new house."

should build a larger house in a pleasant location, and nearer the then center of the settlement, with a room sufficiently large to accommodate the members of the church at their meetings, and with the other rooms so arranged that all the lower floor could be occupied on the Sabbath.

Mr. Lothrop's new house was 21 feet on the front or south side, and 29 feet on the east side. The chimney was on the west side, the oven projecting outside of the wall. The front posts were eleven feet high,* and the rear five and one-half feet, between the sill and the plate. As the floors were laid even with the lower side of the sills, which were a foot square, the lower rooms were about 6 feet 6 inches in the clear, between the summer beam and the floor. The framing of the front room corresponded with the height of the rear posts, consequently the front posts extended about three and one-half feet above the chamber floor, making a half story in front.

The first alteration was made by adding a room on the west; the second, by lengthening the front posts, making the building two full stories on the front; the third was made by the late Isaac Chipman, who raised the rear up to two stories; and the fourth or last by converting the west part of the house into a public library room. The original part of the house remains, excepting the finish, as it was when occupied by Mr. Lothrop.

Mr. Lothrop's Great Lot was sold to John Scudder. The dwelling-house of the Widow Sally Otis stands on its northwest corner bound, and it extended from the bound "twelve score poles into the woods." It was bounded on the west by the lot owned by Jabez Lumbard, and on the east by Mr. Dimmock's great lot, the boundary on the east being the land now owned by Mr. Joshua Thayer.

His grant in the common field was on the east of the Indian reservation, adjoining the Reed Swamp, and is frequently referred to as Mrs. Lothrop's land. His "Great Marsh" is not described, but it may be safely inferred that it was the meadow near the outlet of Rendezvous Creek afterwards owned by his sons Joseph and Thomas.

In 1661 his son Joseph entered on the town records the boundaries of the land on which Mr. Lothrop built his second house. Why the meadow "on the east adjoining to Rendevous Creek," and the grant in the commonfield, are called Mr. Lothrop's, and the houselot Joseph's, I am unable to explain with certainty. As Mr. Lothrop's new dwelling-house, built about the year 1644, is now standing, and has recently been fitted up as a dwelling-house and a public library, and is now one of the most elegant buildings in the village its history at the present time is one of especial interest.

---

*In some instances the rafters indicate that the low leantoe on the rear was a part of the original house; but this is not certain evidence, new rafters may have been put in when the addition was made. This is certain in regard to the William Allen house, where both sets now remain. The style of the house of 1680 is outward by the same, as the remodled house of the first settlers; but the two may readily be distinguished. In the old house the front posts are spliced, while in the later built houses they are not.

The description given in Mr. Lothrop's will of the situation of
the house in which he then dwelt and "the ground belonging thereunto," applies to the lot recorded in 1661 as the property of his son
Joseph.   Between Rendevous Lane and Mr. Lothrop's first lot there
were three houselots, the western is called Joseph Lothrop's, and the
other two, in 1654, were the property of James Neighbors.   Up to
the year 1703 no house had been built on either of the two last
named lots near the present County road.   The Russell house, now
owned by Mr. Frederic Lewis, built about the year 1723, was the
first erected on the road between the two houses named in Mr. Lothrop's will.   July 21, 1656, James Neighbors sold these two lots to
Thomas Lothrop, and describes them as bounded westerly by the
land of Joseph Lothrop and easterly by the ancient highway to Rendevous Landing.   The western boundary was the range of fence
running north and south between the dwelling house and estate of
Mr. Walter Chipman and the Sturgis estate.   He conveys three
acres of meadow adjoining on the north, bounded easterly by Barnard Lumbard's meadow, and westerly by Joseph Lothrop's.   The
northern boundary is not named in the deed; but in the record of
Joseph Lothrop's meadow he states that he is bounded on the south
by the meadow that was Goodman Neighbors and north by Mrs.
Lothrop's, and easterly by Rendevous Creek.   This is an indirect
mode of arriving at a conclusion, yet it is perfectly conclusive, for
no other lot of land but that called in the records of 1654 and 1661
Joseph Lothrop's had a lot of meadow on its east side, extending to
Rendevous Creek, as stated by Mr. Lothrop in his will.

He did not build his second house on either of the lots owned
by James Neighbors, nor did he build on the lot of his son Thomas
on the west of Rendevous Lane; because the meadow attached to
that lot was not bounded by Rendevous Creek, and was a long distance from the "island" named as a part of the boundary of Mr.
Lothrop's meadow.   It is unnecessary to continue the examination
of the records.   A plan of the lots as originally laid out would make
it apparent that Mr. Lothrop's new house was built on the land described in the records as Joseph Lothrop's.

That the house now known as the Sturgis Library building was
the new house named in Mr. Lothrop's will and built about the year
1644, hardly admits of a doubt.   Its history from year to year cannot be traced by written records; but we have equally good evidence.   It was built in the style in which all the first settlers built,
not in the style of 1680 or of any later period.   It was better built
than any of the old houses which I have examined.   The workman-
ship was better.   It was larger, being about 25 feet in front and
deeper in the rear.   Its large sills, sleepers of the lower floors, originally laid on the ground, thirteen feet posts, with cock tail tenans,
its inch and a quarter matched boarding, sharp roof with legers
across the rafters, are the unmistakable characteristics of the frame

houses of the first settlers. The Goodspeed house, built in 1639, was framed and built in the same style,—so was Mr. Lothrop's house and the Nathaniel Bacon house, built in 1642. The Geo. Allen house in Sandwich, built in 1646, and another in the same neighborhood, said to be older were constructed in the same style. The William Allen house, which has been particularly described in a preceding article, exhibits in its construction evidences that it was built a little later, and so did the John Bursley house at West Barnstable. The style of building in 1680 was a modification of the old, yet in some of the details essentially different.

The person who takes an interest in antiquities, and notes the mode of building, at different periods, cannot be easily deceived in regard to the age of a house. He that counts, the annual layers in the grain of the oak, reads a record of its age which there cannot possibly be a clerical error. The style of building is not so particular a record, but it is almost equally as good evidence. The Lothrop house has now stood 220 years, and every antiquarian will rejoice that it is to be preserved another century.

Mr. Lothrop died on the year that the Colony Court ordered that each man's possessions should be bounded and recorded in the town's books, (1653.) The earliest records, made in pursuance of the Court Order, were in 1654, the year following his decease. In his will he names "the house I first lived in, in Barnstable, with the ground belonging thereunto, and the marsh joyning to the lower end thereof, which butts and bounds upon the creek northward." Also, "the house where I now dwell, and the ground belonging thereto, with the marsh land that lyeth on the east beside Rendevous Creek, and also my grant in the Commonfield." He also orders that his "great lott, and his great marsh, shall be sold to some particular person."

Excepting his second houselot, and his "great marsh," the situation and boundaries of the lots he names in his will are well known.

1. The houselot, originally assigned to him, and on which he built "the house he first lived in, in Barnstable," is now owned by Messrs. Waterman & Eben. H. Eldridge, and Mr. Lothrop's house stood on the spot now occupied by their hotel. The Eldredges own the whole of Mr. Lothrop's lot, and part of the adjoining lots on the east. It was in 1654 bounded south by the present County road, west by the highway to Rendevous Creek Landing, north by said creek, and east partly by the meadow of Capt. John Dickinson, and partly by George Lewes'. It contained about twelve acres, nine of upland and three of salt meadow. The ancient boundaries remain to this day, excepting on the east, the Dickinson and some other meadow now being included in the Eldridge lot. The general course of Rendevous Creek is from north to south, but at the foot of Mr. Lothrop's lot it makes a sharp turn to the east. Why it was

called by this French name I have no certain information, but it was probably so called because it was the place where the first settlers agreed to *rendevuse* or *meet*. Up to about the year 1812 Rendevous Landing was a center of business. There was a landing and wharf on Mr. Lothrop's land on the south and another on the north side, on the land laid out to Elder Henry Cobb. Mr. Josiah Lewis had a shipyard on the north, and after his decease the late Mr. Charles Dimmock continued the business till 1812. One of the last vessels built there was the brig Russell. She was rigged and ready for sea when launched. It is now more than fifty years since any business has been done at Rendevous Landing, and though in the immediate vicinity of the Court House only a few aged persons know where that landing was.

Mr. Lothrop's first house was, a two story frame house, built in the ancient style, and about 22 feet by 26 on the ground. It was taken down in 1824. It had been enlarged and remodeled at least twice, a room had been added on the west, and a leantoe on the rear. The frame was of large timber and covered with inch and a quarter planks; but the walls not being plastered, or mulched, and the roof being covered with thatch, Mr. Lothrop had good reasons for complaining that it was "open and cold."

After he built his new house it was occupied several years by tenants. Henry Rowley appears to have been the occupant immediately after Mr. Lothrop. Hon. Joseph Lothrop was the last owner of the family name. He died in 1748, and divided his large estate to his five grand-children of the name of Russell, and children of his only daughter and child Mehitable, who died in 1747.

When "the ancient house," as it is called in the Probate Records in 1748, was taken down, the memorial brick was found on which was inscribed the date of the building of the house, 1639, but no accurate copy of the inscription can now be obtained. No one took a sufficient interest in that memento of the past, and it was used in the construction of the chimney of the present hotel.

[At this point Mr. OTIS abruptly ceased from writing, in consequence of engrossing cares and anxieties, and never resumed the work for which he had so much enthusiasm and fullness of information. In order that this record of the old families of Barnstable may be complete, the publishers of the PATRIOT will endeavor to procure sketches of those of the first comers not embraced in the foregoing papers—some ten or twelve in number—which will make a full and comprehensive record of the early history of this ancient town,—a municipality which has contributed as much to the patriotism and jurisprudence of the State as any within its borders.—C. F. SWIFT.]

CONTINUATION

OF

GENEALOGICAL NOTES

OF

BARNSTABLE FAMILIES.

PREFATORY REMARKS.

The writer of the succeeding brief sketches approaches the task with sincere misgivings. He does not assume to have had the opportunities for acquiring information respecting the Barnstable families, even if he has the ability and enthusiasm for the work, which Mr. Otis possessed in so remarkable a degree. Yet desiring to see these sketches continued to the end, and no native of the town being found who will undertake the work, he will endeavor to compile some account of the remaining first comers, whose history Mr. Otis has left unwritten, so that the series may be rendered in some degree complete. The genealogical tables, however, will not be usually traced beyond the second, or, at the most, the third generation. The authorities upon which the writer will rely, are the colonial, town and church records, Savage's Genealogical Dictionary, Pierce's Colonial Lists, and the preceding pages of Mr. Otis. C. F. S.

LOTHROP FAMILIES.

[CONTINUED.]

The male descendants of Rev. John Lothrop are not now numerous in Barnstable, though many of them are widely scattered throughout New England. Of his sons, Joseph and Barnabas were men of wide influence and a good deal of ability.

THOMAS, the eldest son was, as before stated, born in England in 1621. He joined his father's church in Scituate 14th May, 1637, being then but 16 years of age; married, according to Savage, 11th Dec. 1639, Sarah, widow of Thomas Ewer, being then about 18 years of age. His posterity are given in Mr. Otis's Notes. He was named in the list of inhabitants of the town in 1640, and again in 1670. In 1661, Nov. 29, he was one of the committee for laying out the land in Sacconnessett. He was a respectable and useful man, but not equal in ability to his brothers, Joseph and Barnabas.

JOSEPH, also born in England, besides being a civilian of distinction was a military officer of merit. He was deputy to the colony court in 1667, and for 18 years afterwards. In 1676, Lieut. Lothrop, as he was then styled, was the Barnstable member of the council of war, consisting of one member from each town in the colony, during King Philip's uprising; and again in 1685. In company with his brother Barnabas, in 1676, he acted as agent for the settlement of Rochester. He was Register of Deeds and Register of Probate in 1702 and succeeding years, Sheriff from 1715 to 1721, and Judge of the Court of Common Pleas 1701 and several years following.

BARNABAS, bap. at Scituate, where he was born, 6th June, 1636, was a civilian of much prominence. He was a deputy to the colonial court in 1675, continuing in that office until 1685, inclusive; in 1675 was also one of the council of war to devise measures for repelling the attacks of hostile Indians; was the Barnstable member of the Select Courts in 1676; an agent for the settlement of the new town of Rochester in the same year; a Justice of the Court of Common Pleas in 1692 and several years following; Judge of Probate Court 1702 to 1714. Besides these local offices, he was an assistant to the governor from 1681 to 1686, inclusive. Upon the union of Plymouth Colony with that of Mass. Bay, he was selected, under the new charter, by the influence of Increase Mather, it is said, in company with his neighbor and friend, Gov. Thomas Hinckley, as one of the Councillors of the Province of Massachusetts Bay, under the administration of Sir William Phipps. There was a good deal of comment upon the make-up of this new Council, and many were inclined to think that Gov. Hinckley and his friends were not disinclined to surrender the Plymouth charter and to become life members in the new and consolidated government. The fact that the governor, Mr. Lothrop and Mr. Walley, recently of Barnstable, were three out of four of the members of the Council from what had been the Plymouth colony, gave some color to this impression. Men were in those days as suspicious and jealous of the acts and motives of public officers as they now are; human nature still remains the same as of yore. But there is no good reason for the imputation that Gov. Hinckley was not true to the interests of the colony. It was, at best a struggling and feeble community. It was unable to raise funds to sustain an agent to guard its interests in England, and it came very near being annexed to New York. Mr. Mather did the best thing in his power for the colony, by securing its union with Massachusetts; and he provided for its prominent men by having them named as members of the new council. It is strong evidence of Mr. Lothrop's standing and influence, that he should have been called to this honorable and responsible position. He died in 1735 in the 79th year of his age.

JOHN, the youngest son of Rev. John, was probably born in Barnstable, about the year 1642. He was not in public life. He married, in 1672, Mary Cole of Plymouth.

LITCHFIELD.

Lawrence Litchfield was one of the company from Scituate who came to Barnstable in the spring of 1639. He settled beside Coggins's (now known as Great) pond, near the estate of Gov. Hinckley. He did not remain here long. In 1646 he was again in Scituate, where he died in 1650. He is thought to be the progenitor of all of that name now in New England, but none of them are now within the limits of Barnstable.

LOMBARD.

——

This name is variously written, and members of the family of the same derivation severally call themselves Lombard, Lumbard, Lambard, Lambert, Lumbert and Lumber. The Barnstable Lombards came from Tenterton, Kent County, England. There were four or five of the name in Barnstable in the early period of its settlement, but there are only a few remaining there at the present time.

THOMAS LOMBARD.

Thomas Lombard was born in Tenterton, Kent, about the year 1610, and was married as early as 1630, to Joyce ————. Early marriages were common in those days, the first settlers not unfrequently becoming heads of families before reaching their majority. He came over in the Mary and John, in 1630, settling in Dorchester. He requested to be made a freeman 19th Oct. of that year, and was admitted 18th of May, 1631. He removed in a few years to Scituate, and was one of the earliest of the company who came to Barnstable. In Mr. Lothrop's diary, in speaking of the arrival of his immediate company in town, it is recorded : "After praises to God in public were ended, as the day was cold, we divided into three companies, to feast together, some at Mr. Hull's, some at Mr. Mayo's and some at brother Lombard, Sr's." These were presumably the three largest and most eligible houses in the settlement, and this passage indicates the standing and means of their possessors. In 1639 the court record states that "Thomas Lumbert* is allowed to keep victualling, or an ordinary, for the entertainment of strangers, and to draw wines in Barnstable."

BERNARD LOMBARD.

Bernard, brother of Thomas, was also born in Tenterton, and probably came to Dorchester, in 1630. He was in Scituate in 1634, and he and his wife joined Mr. Lothrop's church 19th April, 1635. He came to Barnstable in the fall of 1639, and his house-lot was near the site of the old mill, towards the shore. In 1660 he was appointed by the colony court to lay out lands granted to inhabitants of Eastham ; and in 1665 to lay out 100 acres of land in Chatham allowed to Wm. Nickerson. He was one of the seven persons in town in 1664 having the prefix of "Mr.," a title which at that time signified that its possessor was a man of public and social consideration. He was also ensign of the military company in Barnstable in 1652, a place of distinction in those days. In 1667 he was appointed one of the committee to lay out lands in Succanessett. He died about 1667, aged not far from 60 years.

Mr. Savage, in his Biographical Dictionary, asserts that the Thomas Lombard who came to Dorchester in 1630 was father of the Thomas who also came to Barnstable in 1639. They were, most probably one and the same. The genealogy of the family is involved in so many obscurities that I do not feel competent to trace it out, and rather than give it in an imperfect form prefer not to undertake the task.

The Truro family of the name is derived from Thomas. This branch has made its mark in the financial and commercial circles of the country as few names have done. In the Western States hardly a town exists that has not had intimate business relations with the banking firm of Lombards.

---

*The early records show that the name was originally spelt "Lumbert," but the usage has many years since changed.

MARSTON.

JOHN MARSTON.

There was a John Marston in this town as early as 1657, when he married Martha, daughter of Bernard Lombard, having two sons. He removed to Swansey about 1660. There was probably no connection between John and

BENJAMIN MARSTON.

Benjamin, the progenitor of those of the name in this town and county, came from Salem. He was an energetic and enterprising citizen. He received from the town, in 1738, extensive mill privileges, in the village which since that time has been known as "Marston's Mills," and devoted himself to dressing the fabrics of those who brought to his establishment the products of their wheels and looms. By his marriage with Elizabeth Goodspeed, April 26, 1716, he had John, Feb. 25, 1717; Patience, Jan. 1, 1720; Benjamin, Jan. 2, 1725; Nymphas, Feb. 12, 1728; Lydia, March, 1731; Prince, March 24, 1736; and John, Dec. 3, 1740. Nymphas, the third son of Benjamin, was a man of talent, public spirit and distinction. He graduated at Yale, and represented Barnstable in the Legislature in 1765. He sat with the Court of Common Pleas and General Sessions, in 1774, at the time of the suspension of the courts by "the Body of the People," and fully sympathized with the patriots who resorted to that extreme measure, and in the measures of resistance to Great Britain which followed he contributed his full share, both by precept and by monetary accommodations, making large advances from his private means. It is related that on one occasion, the soldiers called out from below for the defence of Falmouth, on their return home called upon him, and after accepting his bountiful hospitalities, gave vent to their patriotism by firing a salute in the house, thereby shattering the plastering in the dining room. He remarked that his guests were quite pardonable, if they would only carry out their zeal in shattering the ranks of the common enemy; and suffered the marks of the explosion to remain during the remainder of his life. He was elected, with Shearjashub Bourne, a delegate to take into consideration the proposed constitution of the United States, and died Feb. 11, 1788, leaving no issue. From Prince, fourth son of Benjamin, 1st, was Nymphas, who graduated at Harvard 1807, and after service as Senator, and Judge of Probate, died May 2, 1864. Few men have enjoyed a greater degree of popularity and influence than Judge Marston, and his success as an advocate was something marvelous. His brother Charles also filled many high and responsible posts—Representative, Senator, Executive Councillor and Sheriff. Charles's son, Hon. George, whose recent lamented decease is fresh in the recollection of this generation, was in his day Representative, Judge of Probate and Attorney General of Massachusetts.

MAYO.

REV. JOHN MAYO.

Although this is an Irish name, the subject of the following sketch was born in England and graduated from an English university. He came over probably about 1638, and in 1639 was in Barnstable, where he was ordained a teaching elder in connection with Rev. John Lothrop. He was a freeman in 1640. In 1646 he removed to Eastham and subsequently took charge of the church in that town, where he continued until 1655, when he was settled over the second, or North, church in Boston. In 1673, in consequence of advanced age and infirmities, he went again to Barnstable, and there and at Eastham and Yarmouth passed the remainder of his life with his children, dying at the latter place in May, 1676. He was a man of prominence as a minister, and in 1658 preached the annual election sermon. His wife was named Tamosin, or Tamsin; she died in Yarmouth in 1682. His children, all of whom were born in England, were: Hannah, Samuel, John, Nathaniel and Elizabeth.

SAMUEL MAYO.

Samuel, son of Rev. John was in Barnstable in 1639. He adopted the profession of mariner, running a packet for some time between the Cape and Boston. He afterwards became connected with some members of the Sandwich church in the purchase of Oyster Bay, Long Island. There was a wide difference among the Sandwich settlers on theological points, but in this instance the minister, Rev. William Leverich, and his sympathizers, were the liberal and tolerant wing, and were in the minority. Mr. Leverich and his associates resolved upon removal, and Mr. Mayo conveyed their goods and effects to the new settlement. The Dutch were then our enemies, and under a warrant from an officer of Rhode Island, in 1654, Mr. Mayo's vessel was seized at Hampstead harbor, for alleged unlawful intercourse with them.— This being regarded as a high-handed offence against the dignity of Plymouth Colony, commissioners were sent to Rhode Island to look after the matter. The act was disclaimed by the government of Rhode Island, and an award of £150 damages made.— Mr. Mayo afterwards removed to Boston, where he died in 1663. He married Thomasine, daughter of Wm. Lumpkin of Yarmouth and his children were: Mary, 1645; Samuel, 1647. These two were baptized together 3 Feb. 1650. The long lapse of time for those days between the births and baptism, and the fact that the mother joined Mr. Lothrop's church Jan. 20 preceding the baptism, indicates that she was in sympathy with the disaffection towards the majority of the Yarmouth church and the minister, which was known to exist at that time. Other children were: Hannah, born Oct. 20, 1650; Elizabeth, May 22, 1653; Nathaniel, Apl. 1, 1658; Sarah, 1660. The last two were born in Boston.

The Cape families of this name are derived from John and Nathaniel, who went with their father to Eastham, where they settled. John married Hannah Reycroft, according to the Colonial Record, and his children were: John, born Dec. 15, 1652; William, Oct. 7, 1654; James, Oct. 3, 1656; Samuel, Aug. 2, 1658; Elisha, Nov. 7, 1661; Daniel, Jan. 24, 1664; Nathaniel, April 2, 1667; Thomas, June 24, 1670, who died soon; Thomas again, July 15, 1672. Nathaniel, married Hannah, daughter of Gov. Thomas Prence, and had Thomas, born Dec. 7, 1651; Nathaniel, Nov. 16, 1652; Samuel, Oct. 12, 1655; Hannah, Oct. 17, 1657; Theophilus, Dec. 17, 1659; Bathsheba, 1662. He was a Representative in 1660, and died in 1662. Those who desire to tıace the descent of any branch of this family can easily do so from the names given above.

Mr. Mayo's daughters married, Hannah in 1642, Nathaniel Bacon of Barnstable, and Elizabeth, Joseph Howes of Yarmouth. It was in the family of the latter that Mr. Mayo died.

OTIS.

The Otis family was not one of the "first families" of the town in point of residence, but certainly one of the very first in the country in respect to conspicuous talent and exalted public service; and its location in town dates as early as 1675, if not earlier. The precise year when John Otis came to this place cannot be determined with certainty from any data now available. But on that year he was fined "40s. for selling cider." This was not a very flagrant offense, for the descendants of the men of that era have decided that cider is one of the beverages containing more or less of alcohol the sale of which, under certain restrictions, has no inherent element of depravity, and therefore its sale is not a penal offence. There were then no political considerations which operated in favor of vending the juice of the apple, and consequently its sale did not then take moral precedence over the traffic in the extract of rye, corn or malt.

The Otis family of this county is derived from Gen. John, who was born in Barnstaple, Devonshire County, England, in 1581, and who came to Hingham in 1635. His son, John, who was born in England in 1620, also came with his father to Hingham and Scituate, and thence to Barnstable, from whence he returned to Scituate, leaving here his son John, whose offence in allaying the thirst of his bibulous fellow-citizens has been re-marked upon. He was the father of "Col. John" who was repre-sented as a gentleman "of distinguished talents, of powerful wit, great affability, sagacity, prudence and piety"—an assemblage of the virtues hard to be matched in these latter days. It would seem natural that a man possessing all these qualities should be sought out by his fellow men, in those days, when high character-istics and not a plethoric pocket-book, were the proper certificate for distinction. Consequently he was representative for 20 years, commander of the militia of the County for 18 years, first judge of probate 13 years, chief justice of the Court of Common Pleas, and of His Majesty's Council 21 years. His children were : Mary, born Dec. 10, 1685 ; John, Jan. 14, 1687 ; Nathaniel, July 18, 1690 ; Mercy, Oct. 15, 1693 ; Solomon, Oct. 13, 1696 ; and James, June 14, 1702.

Of the foregoing children of Col. John, Gen. John was a representative and member of the council for 9 years, and also "King's attorney." He died in 1758. Nathaniel settled in Sand-wich, married the daughter of Rev. Jonathan Russell of Barnsta-ble, was Register of Probate for many years, and died in 1739. His wife was more remarkable in point of talent than he, and had she lived in days when woman had her opportunity for develop-ment, would have made her mark in the world. Solomon, the third son, was Register of Deeds, County Treasurer, etc., and died in 1778.

Col. James, the youngest son of Col. John, was a man of distinguished abilities, whose services have been eclipsed by the genius and eloquence of his distinguished son of the same name. Col. Otis though educated to mechanical pursuits became at length a counsellor of prominence and marked success. Accidental circumstances led to his engaging in the legal profes-sion. Being at court in Barnstable on one occasion, a neighbor who had a case pending and was unprovided with counsel, so-licited his aid. Consenting to act, he managed the case with such ability as to receive the strong encomiums of the court, and appre-ciative friends induced him to study for the profession of the law, in which he soon acquired a commanding position. He was chosen a Colonel of the militia, was a member of the provincial legisla-ture, and two years Speaker of the House, Judge of Probate and Chief Justice of the Court of Common Pleas, in 1764. After be-ing many times negatived by the royal Governors, he was chosen and confirmed as a member of the Council, and from the departure of Gage to the adoption of the State constitution, by virtue of be-ing the senior member of the body, he exercised during that period the functions of chief executive magistrate of Massachusetts. He married Mary Allyne, whose father had removed to Wethersfield,

Conn., and is described as "a woman of superior character." But that sort of women had little opportunity to distinguish themselves in those days. They had ten children, the oldest of whom, James, "the patriot," so styled, was the most distinguished.

This is not the time and place to record the services, and make an analysis of the character or a record of the achievements of James Otis, Jr. His matchless eloquence and legal ability in resisting the "writs of assistance," the stamp act, and the other obnoxious measures which led to the Revolutionary war, are matters of general knowledge and need no elucidation here. John Adams's tribute, however, may be appropriately quoted as a *resume* of his character and services: "I have been young and now am old, and I solemnly say I have never known a man whose love of country was more ardent or sincere,—never one who suffered so much—never one whose services for any ten years of his life were so important and essential to the cause of his country as those of Mr. Otis from 1760 to 1770." Mr. Otis married Miss Ruth Cunningham, and his only son, James, a midshipman in the revolutionary war, died at the age of 21, in 1777, on board a Jersey prison ship. His daughter, Elizabeth, married Capt. Brown of the English army, to the great grief and displeasure of her father. His youngest daughter, Mary, married Benj. Lincoln, son of Gen. Lincoln of revolutionary memory.

Of the other children of Col. Otis, Mercy married Gen. James Warren, brother of Gen. Joseph, who fell in the battle of Bunker Hill. She was a woman of rare talent, a friend and correspondent of John and Samuel Adams and the other Revolutionary characters, and wrote a valuable history of the "times that tried men's souls." Samuel Allyn Otis, James's brother, was for many years clerk of the U. S. Senate.

Gen. Joseph Otis, more popularly known as "Brigadier Otis," was the second son of Col. James, and also a brother to the "patriot." He was an active partizan of the popular cause, and performed valuable and important service during the Revolutionary war. He was afterwards for many years clerk of the court of Common Pleas, and a member of the Legislature. He was appointed Collector of Customs of Barnstable district by Gen. Washington, which position he held until his death, Sept. 23, 1810.

Hon. Harrison Gray Otis, for years the leader of the Federalists of Massachusetts, was derived from the Barnstable family. Mr. Amos Otis, the intelligent and indefatigable historical and antiquarian writer, says Dr. Savage, "is derived from another stock, emigrating at least twenty years later than the Hingham pioneer, and coming from a part of England widely remote from the first."

PHINNEY.

This name is variously written, Phinney, Finney, Fennye, but more generally the former. John Phinney, the first of the name in town, was first in Plymouth, where in 1638 his son John was born, and where in 1649 his wife Christian, died. He was not a very rigid sectarian, for this son was not baptized until 1653, after his removal to Barnstable. In 1650 he married Abigail, the widow of Henry Coggin, a wealthy merchant and adventurer, who was among the first settlers of the town. She, dying in 1653, John Phinney for his third wife married, in 1654, Elizabeth Bayly. His children were:

1. John, born in Plymouth, Dec. 24, 1638.
2. Jonathan, Aug. 14, 1655.
3. Robert, Aug. 13, 1656.
4. Hannah, Sept. 2, 1657; married Ephraim Morton, 2d.
5. Elizabeth, Mar. 15, 1659.
6. Josiah, Jan. 11, 1661.
7. Jeremiah, Aug. 15, 1662.
8. Joshua, Dec., 1665.

Mr. Phinney, with his townsman, Major Walley, became interested in the fertile region about Mount Hope, R. I., where he removed, after holding the office of constable in Barnstable. The importance of this office is not to be estimated by its relative consideration at the present day. A constable, in the time of the fathers, was a most imposing and awe-inspiring personage, and those who saw fit to indulge in any levity at his expense, would find it to be a fatal and costly experiment.

SECOND GENERATION.

John, of Barnstable, married Aug. 10, 1664, Mary Rogers, had John, born May 5, 1665; Melatiah, Oct., 1666, died next year; Joseph, Jan. 28, 1668; Thomas, Jan., 1672; Ebenezer, Feb. 8, 1674; Samuel, Nov. 4, 1676; Mary, Sept. 3, 1678; Mercy, July 10, 1679; Reliance, Aug. 27, 1681; Benjamin, June 18, 1682; Jonathan, July 30, 1684; Hannah, March 28, 1687, died young; Elizabeth, baptized May 10, 1691. Most of the

Barnstable families of this name are supposed to have been descendants of John.

Josiah, of Barnstable, married Jan. 19, 1688, Elizabeth, daughter of Joseph Warren. His descendants, if any, are not on record.

Robert, of Barnstable, third son of John, born 1656, joined the expedition of Wm. Phips, (afterwards Governor of Mass.,) against Quebec. This expedition did not reflect much credit upon the foresight or military skill of the commander, and in it Robert Phinney, like many others, lost his life.

THIRD GENERATION.

John, born 1665, and died Nov. 27, 1746, married Sarah Lombard, and had Elizabeth, 1690 ; Mary, 1692 ; John, 1696 ; Thomas, 1697 ; Hannah, 1700 ; Sarah, 1702 ; Patience, 1704 ; Martha, 1706 ; Jabez, July 16, 1708.

Thomas, born 1672, married widow Sarah Butler, and had Gersham, 1700 ; Thomas, 1703 ; Abigail, 1704 ; James, 1706 ; Mercy, 1708.

Ebenezer, born 1673, married Susannah Linnell, and had Mehitable ; Mercy ; Martha ; Samuel ; Ebenezer ; and David, born June 10, 1710, who married Mary Pope, of Sandwich, Sept. 27, 1733.

Benjamin, married Martha Crocker and had Temperance, 1710 ; Melatiah, 1712 ; Barnabas, 1715 ; Silas, 1718 ; Zaccheus, 1720 ; Seth, 1723.

Jonathan, married Elizabeth ———, had Thankful, 1713 ; Joseph, 1716 ; Jonathan, 1718.

Zaccheus, married Susanna Davis, and had Benjamin, 1744 ; Timothy, 1746 ; Barnabas, 1748.

Capt. John Phinney, born 1696, and son of John and of Sarah Lombard, was the founder of the town of Gorham, in Maine. The second and third generation of our forefathers, began to feel that they were cramped in planting and pasture lands, and that they needed more territory for development. The first emigration from the Cape was in the easterly direction. Maine was a part of Massachusetts, and the undeveloped territory there was at the disposal of our people. The soldiers of the Indian wars felt that they had a claim upon this territory, and in 1727, after many delays and discouragements, the legislature of Massachusetts granted to the officers and soldiers of the Narragansett expedition, during Philip's war, and their heirs, a township six miles square in the Province of Maine, to each 120 persons whose claims should be established within four months of the passage of the act. Seven townships were laid out in pursuance of this act. The 7th town was named Gorham, in honor of Capt. John Gorham of Yarmouth, who commanded the Cape expedition in that war, and the settlers were from Barnstable, Yarmouth, Eastham and Sandwich.   The first man who took up his residence there was Capt. John Phinney of Barnstable.   May 26, 1736, Mr. Phinney and his son, Edmund, who was afterwards a distinguished officer of the Revolutionary war, disembarked from his canoe on the Presumpscot river, with his axe and a small stock of provisions, with a design to make a home for his family in the then wilderness, but now a large and flourishing town.   Edmund felled the first tree for a settlement.   Capt. John Phinney and his wife Martha, both died at the age of 87.   Among the other first settlers in the town we find the names Bacon, Bourne, Bangs, Davis, Gorham, Harding, Higgins, Hinckley, Hamblen, Lewis, Linnell, Lombard, Paine and Sturgis.   A monument standing in the centre of the town bears this inscription :

May 6, 1805
CAPT. JOHN PHINNEY
commenced the
First Settlement in this town.
May, 1736.
Gr. by the General Court 1732 to the
Narragansett Soldiers.
This
assigned to Capt. John Gorham
and 119 others
then called Narragansett No. 7.
Town inc. 1764.

Dea. Timothy, born 1746, was a man of note and distinction in his day.   In some recent writings he is said to have been Sheriff of the County, but this is probably a mistake.   No doubt he was principal deputy for some years, and in 1811 he was Senator from the Cape.   He built the house now owned by the family of the late Ebenezer Bacon, and afterwards removed to Rhode Island, where, it is believed, he died and was buried.   He was the father of Timothy, who died Sept. 1883, at the age of over 99, and of Mrs. Nancy Munroe, wife of Dea. John Munroe, who survived until 1881, dying in her 88th year.   From this branch also sprung our fellow-citizen, Major Sylvanus B. Phinney, whose career is fresh in public knowledge, and whose life and achievements have recently been set forth in a volume to which many of our citizens have access.

Benjamin Phinney, the elder brother of Timothy, above-mentioned, born 1744, and died 1843, was father of Dr. Elias Phinney of Lexington, a distinguished agriculturalist and author, of the last century.   He was, from 1831 to the time of his decease, clerk of the Middlesex County courts.

ROBINSON.

Isaac Robinson, son and third child of John Robinson, the Leyden pastor of blessed memory, was born in that city in 1610. He came to this country in 1631. He was first settled in Plymouth, was in Duxbury in 1634, and went to Scituate in 1636, on which year he was admitted as a freeman. He the same year married Margaret Hanford, daughter of Rev. Thomas Hanford, the first minister at Norwalk, Ct., and a niece of Timothy Hatherly, a London merchant, the founder of Scituate. He took a letter of dismission from the church in Plymouth, and here joined Rev. John Lothrop on the 7th of July, 1639. His first estate in Barnstable was opposite to that of Gov. Hinckley. This he sold and took another of twenty acres further to the west. In 1639 and 1648 he was a member of the Grand Inquest for the colony. In 1641 he was on the jury for trials. In 1645 he was a deputy from Barnstable to the General Court at Plymouth, and in 1646, '47 and '48 was "receiver of excise" for the town. In 1651 he was again a deputy. These positions indicate the confidence and esteem in which he was held, up to this time.

The Quaker persecution showed the moral quality of this man and his sympathy of spirit with his illustrious father, who declared to the departing Pilgrims, in a sermon which was so much in advance of the age, and even of most of his hearers, "The Lord has more truth *yet* to break forth out of his holy word. * * I beseach you, remember it, 'tis an article of your church covenant, that you be ready to receive whatever truth shall be made known to you from the written word of God." In 1659-60, the laws forbidding attendance upon Quaker meetings were so far relaxed as to permit and encourage certain persons, among them Gen. James Cudworth and Isaac Robinson, to attend these meetings and try to convince the Quakers of their errors. The effect was contrary to expectation. Robinson and Cudworth were never Quakers; but they firmly believed these people to be following the dictates of their own consciences; that it was their right and duty to do so ; that as a consequence persecution was unchristian and in opposition to the principles of natural justice. Having made a written appeal to the magistrates in their behalf, March 7, 1659-60, it is recorded : "The court takes notice of sundry scandals and falsehoods in a letter of Isaac Robinson's, tending to the prejudice of this government and encouragement of Quakers ; but forbears censure till inquiry shall be made." What an unprejudiced tribunal and what thoughtful forbearance, to be sure ! In such a frame of mind, it is hardly to be wondered at that on the following June he is declared a "manifest opposer of the government" and is ordered to be disfranchised.

The year following, Isaac Robinson and Jonathan Hatch settled at Succennesset, now Falmouth, and the same year Robinson had a grant of land given him near his house. In 1664 he was licensed to keep an ordinary at Falmouth, on account of the number of travellers to Martha's Vineyard, and in 1670 he had gone. This was the natural restlessness of a man smarting under unjust persecution. 1673 found him "recorder" at Tisbury, and for several years he was one of the selectmen of that town. It was while Robinson was a resident here that Gov. Prence of Plymouth died. He had been one of the firmest and most relentless opposers of the Quakers, and though public sentiment and the commands of the monarch had relaxed the severity of the legislation of the colonies, there is no reason for supposing that the governor ever modified his sentiments or changed his feelings in relation to them. Josias Winslow was chosen his successor. He had formerly been somewhat embittered against the Quakers, in consequence of some of their reproachful speeches directed towards him, and being a young man of spirit had resented the remarks of these sharp-tongued controversialists. Time had greatly modified his views of the best way of dealing with them, and when he assumed the office of governor he determined upon a change of policy. Cudworth was called from his retirement and reinstated in official position in the colony. The court undertook to make amends for the treatment of Robinson, but did it in the most ungracious way, and instead of owning their fault, tried to give the matter the appearance of being simply an error or accident. The record of the court ordering his disfranchisement, is crossed off, and underneath is the following entry : "There being some mistake in this, the said Isaac, at his request, is re-established." This may have looked like a simple matter to the court, but thirteen years of unjust obloquy suffered by Mr. Robinson had intervened ! He was never a Quaker. Had he been one, his liberality would have had but little significance. He remained in full communion with the Barnstable church for 70 years, and there is no evidence that he did not fully retain the sympathy of his townsmen. He sacrificed the favor of the government to a sense of duty, as his noble father had done before him.

In 1700 he had divided his estate equally between his three sons, and in 1701 deeded his homestead and garden in Falmouth to his son Isaac. This was the first house built in town, and stood on the south side of Fresh Pond. The site is easily identified. The next year, probably, he returned to Barnstable, to live with his daughter, Fear, the wife of Rev. Samuel Baker. He doubtless had some landed estate remaining in Barnstable, for the town voted "to give old Mr. Robinson an acre and a half of marsh," which they would hardly have done unless he had been possessed of other real estate.

Chief Justice Sewell, who was making a tour of the colony in 1702, saw Isaac Robinson at Tisbury, where, he must have been on a visit, if the date of his removal to Barnstable has been correctly stated. The judge seems for some special reason to have been very desirous to see him. He writes in his diary : "He saith he is 92 years old, is ye son of Mr. Robinson, pastor of ye ch. of Leyden part of wch came to Plymo. *But, to my disappointment*, he came not to New England till ye year in which Mr. Wilson was returning to England after ye settlement of Boston. I told him I was very desirous to see him for his father's sake and his own. Gave him an Arabian piece of gold to buy a book for some of his grandchildren." The next day the Judge lost his way. He called on Mr. Robinson, who offered him "some good small beer," and one of his sons to bear him company for awhile on his journey. At this time Mr. Robinson was represented as a hale, vigorous person, with hair as white as snow. Prince, in his Annals describes him as "a venerable man whom I have often seen." He died at Barnstable in 1704. "If any humble slate ever marked the spot where they laid him", says Mrs. Dall, "it has crumbled away." But it is fitting that a life of such patient liberality and unambitious steadfastness in the cause of truth, should be fitly commemorated.

ISAAC ROBINSON AND HIS POSTERITY.

Isaac Robinson, born 1610 ; married Margaret Hanford, June 27th, 1636. They had five children :

1. Susannah, baptized Jan. 21, 1638 ; but dead before 1664.

2. John, baptized April 5, 1640 ; married Elizabeth Weeks, May 1, 1667, and went from Falmouth to Connecticut in 1714. He was the first deputy from Falmouth to the Colony Court, in the year 1690 and '91.

3. Isaac, baptized Aug. 7, 1642 ; married Ann ; was drowned at Falmouth, without issue, Oct. 6, 1668.

4. Fear, baptized Jan. 26, 1645 ; married Rev. S. Baker, of Barnstable.

5.   Mercy, baptized July 4, 1647 ; married Wm. Weeks, Mar. 16, 1669.

Margaret Robinson died, and was buried, with a stillborn child, June 13, 1649.   In 1650 Isaac married as his second wife Mary, the sister of famous Elder Faunce, of Plymouth, and by her he had four children :

6.   Israel, baptized Oct. 5, 1651.   After Isaac was drowned, in 1668, Israel seems to have taken his father's name.   *Israel*, afterward *Isaac*, lived at Tisbury until 1728, when he died without issue.

7.   Jacob, baptized May 15, 1653 ; married Experience ; died 1733.

8.   Peter, said to have gone to Norwich, Ct.

9.   Thomas, baptized Mar. 6, 1666, and removed to Guilford, Ct.

The decision of the inquest appointed to view the body of Isaac Robinson, 2d, in 1651, is preserved as a specimen of the style of the times :

"Wee, the jury of inquest appointed to view the corpse of Isaac Robinson, jr., do apprehend according to view and testimony that the means of his death was by going into the pond to fetch two geese, the pond being full of weedy grasse, which we conceive to be the instrumental cause of his death, he being entangled therein."

The reason which makes it apparent that Israel Robinson took the name of Isaac, after the latter's death, is that the name of Israel thereafter disappeared from the family history ; and it was a uniform custom of those times when one bearing a leading family name deceased, to give the name to a younger child.   This usage has caused a great deal of confusion to genealogists.   A recent writer observes that "those people who think that the science of medicine has made no advance in the last century should give one glance at the early records of our churches, where it is a common thing to find the same infant name three or four times repeated, before it is borne safely over the second summer."

THIRD GENERATION.

Children of John and Elizabeth :

1.   John, born March 20, 1668.
2.   Isaac, born Jan. 30, 1670 ; married Hannah Harpur in 1690, and Alice Dexter in 1741.
3.   Timothy, born Oct. 30, 1671 ; married Mehitable Weeks, May 3, 1699.
4.   Abigail, born 1674 ; married Joseph Percival 1699.

5. Joseph, born 1679;   married Bethia Gall, Oct. 22, 1700;
    Bethia Lumbert, Dec. 1704.
6. Mercy.
7. Mary ———— ; married Benj. Davis, 1704.
8. Love, born Dec. 12, 1683, died Dec. 16, same year.
9. Love, born May 1, 1688 ; died Aug. 8, 1688.

Owing to the imperfect state of the Falmouth public records,
it is not possible to fill all the blanks in the foregoing.

By the marriage of Isaac, above mentioned, with Hannah
Harpur, the grandson became identified with the society of
Friends, as his grandfather never had been, except to protect and
defend their liberties and their right of following the dictates of
conscience in spiritual concerns. Very few of the family however, in Falmouth, ever went farther in that direction than its
founder in that town, but to this day have continued their relations to the old Congregational order of their ancestors.

It may not be difficult for those who are of the Robinson
lineage in this County and vicinity, from the foregoing data to
trace their line of descent from the great apostle of liberty of
thought and conscience, John Robinson of Leyden, and his
worthy though less distinguished son.

Mrs. Caroline H. Dall spent some time several years since in
investigation of the subject of Isaac Robinson, his persecution by
his intolerant contemporaries, his changes of residence, and his
descendants ; and to her investigations the writer of these notes,
who feels proud to trace descent from Isaac Robinson and his illustrious father, wishes to express his obligations, for many of
the facts contained in this paper.

SCUDDER.

John Scudder, the common ancestor of those of the name in Barnstable, was born in England, in 1619, came from London to America, in 1635, and located first in Charlestown, where he was admitted a freeman in 1639. The next year he removed to Barnstable, where he was again admitted a freeman, in 1654, and continued to reside there until his death, in 1689. His wife, Hannah, survived him. His sister, Elizabeth, removed from Boston to Barnstable, in 1644, and the same year married Samuel Lothrop, son of the Rev. John, at the father's house. John Scudder's lot and house were near the house of the late Joshua Thayer.

Children of John Scudder.

The children of John Scudder were :
1. Elizabeth, } baptized May 10, 1646.
2. Sarah, }
3. Mary, buried Dec. 3, 1649, probably very young.
4. Hannah, bap. Oct. 5, 1651, who married Joshua Bangs.
5. John, doubtless son of the foregoing, date of birth not known. He married Elizabeth, daughter of James Hamblin, July 31, 1689, and died at Chatham, 1742, "very aged." His wife died in Chatham, in Jan. 1743.

Children of John Scudder, 2d.

1. John, born May 23, 1690.
2. Experience, born April 28, 1692.
3. James, bap. Jan. 13, 1695.
4. Ebenezer, bap. April 26, 1696.
5. Reliance, born Dec. 10, 1700.
6. Hannah, June 7, 1706.

The above, in accordance with our plan of presenting the first two or three generations, gives the births and marriages of the Scudder family up to the eighteenth century. Those of the

Scudder lineage who wish to trace back their ancestry can easily do so from the above data.

The Scudder family has been one of the first and most distinguished in Barnstable, and has produced a number of men conspicuous in the professional and business walks of life.

David Scudder, derived from Eleazer, through Ebenezer, born Jan. 5, 1763, was an eminent citizen, and many years Clerk of the Courts for the County of Barnstable. He married Desire Gage, and had Charles, born June 5, 1789, who settled in Boston, and died Jan. 21, 1861, after a long life of usefulness and distinction as a merchant. Frederick Scudder, for several years County Treasurer and Register of Deeds, was a younger brother of Charles. Frederick Scudder is well remembered by this generation, for his intimate connection with the County offices, his courteous demeanor, his devotion to his public duties, and his upright and useful life.

Hon. Zeno Scudder, who is derived from Josiah, through Ebenezer, grandson of the first John, and his wife Rose (Delap), was born in (Osterville) Barnstable, in 1807. In his boyhood he was inclined to follow the seas, but soon after engaged in mercantile pursuits. Before he had attained his majority a paralysis of the right leg induced lameness, which led to further change of plans for life. Under the direction of Dr. Nourse of Hallowell, Maine, and at Bowdoin college, he prosecuted the study of medicine. Finding his infirmity an impediment to the practice of his profession, he at once applied himself to the study of the law. He took a preparatory course at the Cambridge law school, and being admitted to the bar in 1836, opened a law office in Falmouth; but he shortly changed his location to Barnstable. He soon acquired a lucrative practice, and was regarded as an accurate, learned and diligent lawyer. He was elected to the State Senate from Barnstable County, in 1846, and was twice re-elected. In his third term of service he was chosen President of the Massachusetts Senate, the duties of which office he performed with dignity and ability. He was elected a member of the 32d Congress of the United States, and took a good rank among the new members. His speech, delivered Aug. 12, 1852, on the American Fisheries, evinced great research and an intimate knowledge of the subject. The other interests of his constituents were guarded by him with jealous care. His career as a representative of the peculiar interests of the Cape promised to be one of commanding success and influence. He was re-elected to the 33d Congress, but a fall, which caused the fracture of a limb, proved so inconvenient that he was obliged to resign his seat, and he was succeeded by Hon. Thomas D. Eliot of New Bedford. His death followed, June 26, 1857. He was never married.

His younger brother, Henry A. Scudder, was also born in

the village of Osterville, Nov. 25, 1819.   He graduated at Yale College in 1842, and studied law at Cambridge.   He was admitted to the Suffolk bar in 1844, and entered upon the practice of his profession in Boston, where his abilities were soon recognized. He was a member of the Massachusetts Legislature of 1861-2-3 ; was a member of the National Convention which nominated Abraham Lincoln for re-election, and supported him with characteristic ardor.   In 1869 he was appointed by Gov. Claflin, a Justice of the Superior Court of Massachusetts, in which position he soon acquired a high reputation, which bid fair to lead to early advancement in the judiciary.   But ill health, in 1872, compelled his resignation, and a prolonged absence in Europe followed.   In 1882 the office of Judge of Probate and Insolvency was tendered to him, by Gov. Long, which, owing to the same cause, he felt obliged to decline.   Judge Scudder married, June 30, 1857, Nancy B., daughter of Charles B. Tobey of Nantucket.   His summer home is in Marston's Mills, near the scenes of his earlier days.

The brothers of the foregoing, were Josiah, merchant, born Dec. 3, 1800, died Dec. 29, 1877 ; Freeman S., merchant, born March 16, 1805, died Dec. 3, 1852 ; Edwin, merchant, born Sept. 23, 1815, died May 25, 1872.   A sister, Persis, born Aug. 14, 1810, married Joseph W. Crocker, and died April 24, 1844.

SMITH.

JOHN SMITH.

Although this name is somewhat numerous, there is no occasion for making it, in consequence, the subject of levity. The *first* of the name in New England, has, most certainly, stamped his individuality upon the topography and history of the country. He added to the fame of an adventurer, that of a scholar and an observer of current events. And he also seems to have been a gentleman and a man of affairs. It is easy enough to see that the name was derived from the occupation. A smith was a valiant worker on metals, and was thus in the social scale, superior to the villeins, or other adherents of the lords of the soil. In time the number increased and became influential.

The John Smith of Barnstable, was here in 1640; it would have been strange if there had been no John Smith at hand at that date. He was a member of the first families of Barnstable, having, in 1640, joined the church, and was a brother-in-law of Gov. Thomas Hinckley, having married his sister Susannah. His children were:

1. Samuel, born April, 1644.
2. Sarah, bap. 1645.
3. Ebenezer, b. Nov. 22, 1646, and died next month.
4. Mary, b. Nov. 1647.
5. Dorcas, b. Aug. 18, 1650.
6. John, b. Feb. 22, 1652, buried in two days.
7. Shubael, b. March 13, 1653.
8. John, Sept. 1656.
9. Benjamin, b. Jan. 1659.
10. Ichabod, Jan. 1661.
11. Elizabeth, Feb. 1663.
12. Thomas, Feb. 1665.
13. Joseph, Dec. 6, 1667.

Large families being the rule in those days, the Smith posterity does not seem to be disproportionate to the times. In 1659, John Smith of Barnstable was, with Isaac Robinson and others, permitted to visit the Quaker meetings and report his observations thereon. Like Robinson, he was of the opinion that the best way to deal with the Quakers was to let them alone ; not persecute, not antagonize them. He did not receive such harsh treatment as Cudworth and Robinson, but was for a time under the cloud of the government influence.

In consulting the records of the towns and the genealogical dictionaries, the writer finds the genealogies of the Smiths, and especially the John Smiths, beyond his power to unravel, and leaving this matter here, at the first generation of the Barnstable Smiths, declines the task of further untangling the highly respectable but somewhat confused genealogical pedigrees. He may, in conclusion, be permitted to say, that the Barnstable Smiths have ever proved themselves good citizens, and have very seldom been convicted of offences against the laws of the country of which so many of them are citizens.

There seemed to be an undue tendency among our ancestors, which their descendants have not yet outgrown, to name their sons JOHN ; no doubt out of a feeling of admiration for the first great Smith of American history. This commendable phase of hero worship has been the great perplexity and embarrassment of genealogists in all future times. When we try to untangle the mystery of the Smith family the Johns are so numerous that it is difficult—yea, impossible—to decide which Smith is involved in the investigation.

AMOS OTIS.

In closing this series of papers, it seems fitting that the author of the greater portion of them—AMOS OTIS—should receive the degree of recognition to which his character and services to the cause of historical research seem to entitle him. In the Historical and Genealogical Journal of January,1876, there appeared a paper prepared by the writer of these continued sketches, and read at the preceding meeting of the New England Historical and Genealogical Society, and by vote of the members was printed among its transactions. As he cannot much add to what he there said, he reprints that paper as a suitable close of the volume now completed :

AMOS OTIS, Esq., departed this life, at his home in Yarmouth Port, on the morning of October 19, 1875. He was born in Barnstable, August 17, 1801, making his age 74 years, 2 months and 2 days. His health had been failing for nearly a year, but until two or three weeks past, he attended in some measure to his usual duties.

Mr. Otis came from that historic Cape Cod stock which has given so many illustrious and useful men to the service of their native county and the state. He was himself one of the most remarkable and useful men of his generation, and in some respects it will be difficult, if not impossible, to fill his place.

Mr. Otis's early life was spent on the farm of his father, Amos Otis. Being of a studious turn of mind, he early devoted his leisure to books. He fitted for college under the instruction of the late Dr. Danforth P. Wight, but the condition of his father's fortune and other causes compelled him to forego his desire for a liberal education.

For more than fifteen years he was engaged in teaching, and was a very successful instructor of youth.

In May, 1836, he became cashier of the then "Barnstable

Bank," at Yarmouth Port, and continued in that position, as cashier of that institution and its successor, the "First National Bank of Yarmouth," for nearly forty years.

He was also the first secretary and treasurer of the Barnstable County Mutual Fire Insurance Co , incorporated in March, 1833, in which office he continued to the time of his last sickness.

Mr. Otis never held political office, the duties of his business professions engrossing the greater part of his active life. He, however, served for several years on the school committee of Yarmouth, and was frequently appointed on committees of the town, where familiarity with the ancient records and usages were required.

He was also for several years one of the directors of the Cape Cod Branch Railroad, and a trustee of the Yarmouth Public Library at the time of his decease. His fidelity and industry in these positions were remarkable. He investigated carefully every question presented, and was never satisfied unless he had given to them his personal attention and weighed their merits for himself.

He was a remarkably prolific writer as well as a diligent student. He contributed hundreds of columns to the Cape Cod newspapers, upon a great variety of subjects, the preponderance being upon practical matters. Our local history he has made his study for the last fifty years, and in that department his labors have been invaluable. No man living or dead has done so much to elucidate the character, motives and acts of the men who settled on Cape Cod, and of their heroic successors ; and no one ever had a more just appreciation of their character and achievements. He believed in them thoroughly, although not insensible to their faults. His facts were largely drawn from original sources, and his studies were pursued with a zeal and enthusiasm which were prompted by a thorough love of his subject. He has left a vast accumulation of material, which will be invaluable to future investigators in this field of study. It had long been his desire to leave a complete history of his native town, but other cares and the infirmities of age prevented his accomplishing his purpose, beyond a series of sketches of the families of the town, published some 15 years ago—articles so full of information and clothed in such an agreeable style that our regret is deepened as we read them, that their author should not have completed his work. Besides these he has contributed to the various historical periodicals of the country articles on his favorite subject.

Mr. Otis has also written much on agriculture, horticulture arboriculture, and kindred themes. To his industrious pen the people of Barnstable county are largely indebted for the interest first aroused there on the subject of railroad facilities. He compiled column upon column of statistics, and never wearied until the steam-whistle was heard on Cape Cod. Among his political writings, the "Letters from Skipper Jack to my old friend that prints the Yarmouth Register," were immensely popular some twenty years ago.

Mr. Otis was the oldest surviving member of the Fraternal Lodge of Free Masons, and was for twenty-one years in early life the Secretary of the Lodge. He was a firm believer in the sublime principles of the order, and exemplified by his life the truths of Masonry. During the fierce anti-masonic excitement in this country, he never faltered nor disguised his sentiments, and held his position as an officer of the Lodge until the storm blew over. He never failed, when it was possible to attend the festivals of the order, and always appeared to greatly enjoy these social occasions. He was admitted to this Society July 21, 1847.

Mr. Otis was a man of deep religious feelings. He was for a large portion of his life a member of the East Parish (Unitarian) in Barnstable, but of late years became deeply interested in the doctrines of the New Jerusalem church, with which he formally connected himself within a few weeks. But he was no mere sectarian or bigot, and attached no undue importance to forms and creeds.

His liberality and public spirit were marked features of his character, and his private charities were numerous and discriminating. He never failed to aid, to the best of his abilities, a good cause, nor to help a fellow-man in trouble or distress.

Mr. Otis married, Aug. 15, 1830, Mary, daughter of Mr. Adino Hinckley, of Barnstable, whom he survived about four and one-half years. He leaves two sons, Henry and George.

Mr. Otis's memory will be kept alive in the hearts of his townsmen, so long as the noble elms which border their streets, many of which were planted by his own hands, remain to bear witness to his taste, foresight, and public spirit; and he will take his place in that long list of Cape Cod worthies, to the memory of whom he has been so tender and just, and whose character he has done so much to rescue from oblivion and neglect.

CHRONOLOGICAL RECORD

OF PROMINENT EVENTS IN THE TOWN OF BARNSTABLE
TO THE 200th YEAR OF ITS SETTLEMENT.

———

1614. The celebrated Capt. John Smith explored the coast from Plymouth to Provincetown. In his "Description of New England," published ten years later, he speaks of the Cape as "in the form of a sickle. On it doth inhabit the people of Pawmet, [Truro, Wellfleet, etc.], and on the bottom of the bay those of Chawm," [Barnstable and Yarmouth.]

1620. Dec. 8. O.S. The shallop with the company from the Mayflower passed Barnstable harbor in a thick snow-storm, while on their exploring trip which resulted in landing at Plymouth. [Mourt's Relation.]

1621. June. Gov. Bradford and a party in a shallop, from Plymouth, visited the harbor in search of a lost boy. They were hospitably entertained by Iyanough, the sachem of Commaquid.

1623. Owing to the killing of Witawamet, Pecksuot and other Indians by Capt. Standish, a great panic was created among the Indians in this region, and Iyanough fled to a swamp in fear, contracted a fever and died. [What was supposed to be the skeleton of Iyanough, was exhumed in East Barnstable a few years ago and deposited in Pilgrim Hall, Plymouth.]

1639. September. A grant of land was made to Mr. Joseph Hull and Thomas Dimock who were already occupying land in this town. Others from Scituate followed, and by December, Rev. John Lothrop and some thirty-eight families, mostly from Scituate, were established here.

1641.   June 17.   At a court held in Yarmouth, before Mr. Edward Winslow, Capt. Miles Standish and Mr. Edmund Freeman, three assistants, by virtue of an order from the General Court, the boundrary between Yarmouth and Barnstable was established.   Nearly a mile of territory from east to west and from the salt water on one side of the Cape to the other, was taken from Yarmouth and given to Barnstable—substantially the same territory as is now and since that time, has been embraced in the town of Barnstable.

1646.   May.   The first meeting-house was occupied by Mr. Lothrop's society.   It was near, if not within, the enclosure occupied by the ancient cemetery.

1653.   Nov. 8.   Rev. John Lothrop died.

1662.   Rev. Thomas Walley was recognized as the minister of the town.   Mr. William Sargent and Rev. John Smith had officiated for some time after Mr. Lothrop's decease, but had not been regularly settled.

1675.   March 26.   Lieut. Fuller and four men of Barnstable were killed at Rehobeth by the Indians at the opening of Philip's war, in a battle in which 63 English and 20 friendly Indians, under Capt. Pierce, lost their lives.

1678.   March 24.   Rev. Thomas Walley died, and was succeeded by Rev. Jonathan Russell in 1683.

1680.   Thomas Hinckley of this town elected Governor of Plymouth Colony.   He died in 1706, being at the time one of of the Council of the Province of Massachusett Bay.

1685.   County of Barnstable formed and Barnstable made the shire town.

1696.   The "Great Marshes" divided by vote of the proprietors.

1703.   Division of "the upland commons and salt marsh that had not before been divided."

1717.   The town was divided into two parishes.   The next year the church edifice in West Barnstable was erected and Mr. Russell remained with the society in that part of the town. Another edifice was erected on Cobb's hill, on the site of the present Unitarian church.

1757.   "The small-pox raged in town and many inhabitants died."

1774. Sept. "The Body of the People" as they styled themselves, composed of eminent citizens of this and adjoining counties met here and prevented the holding of the courts under royal authority. Commitees were subsequently appointed under the authority of the town to resist the measures of the King and Parliment.

1776. June 25. The town refused to instruct their representative in favor of a declaration of the independence of the colonies. There has been much adverse comment on this vote, but we believe that *refusal to instruct* the representatives was all that was meant. Though there were some Tories here, the great preponderance of the town was in favor of resistance to the measures of the British Government.

1783. May 23. James Otis, the patriot, died in Andover—the most gifted and eminent citizen the town ever produced.

1788. Feb. 11. Hon. Nymphas Marston, delegate to the convention to act upon the U. S. constitution, died at the age of 60 years.

Dec. 4. A Baptist society was formed on the "south side of the town"—Hyannis—and Rev. Enoch Eldridge was ordained pastor.

1791. Hon. Shearjashub Bourne of this town was elected a member of Congress from this district, which position he held for two terms. [The first representative from this district under the constitution, elected in 1789, was George Partridge of Duxbury.]

1800. The first United States census showed the inhabitants of the town to number 2,964.

1807. Feb. 11. Rev. Oakes Shaw, for nearly 47 years pastor of the church in West Barnstable died. He was the father of the late eminent Chief Justice Lemuel Shaw.

1810. Gen. Joseph Otis, a distinguished revolutionary hero, died in West Barnstable, aged 82.

By the U. S. census of this year, the population of this town were found to number 3,546.

1814. The British made a threatening demonstration upon this town in the fall of this year. The militia was called out, and companies from the neighboring towns responded, but the enemy abandoned the enterprise if they really entertained the design.

1816. The Hersey property situated in this town was sold in compliance with the terms of a permissory act of the Legislature. This property was in 1786 left to the thirteen Congregational Churches in the county by Dr. Abner Hersey for the purchase of religious literature, under the management of the deacons of the churches. The property sold comprised some desirable farming land.

1820. Population of the town 3,824.

1821. An almshouse was erected in West Barnstable on a farm some time previously bequeathed to the town for the support of the poor.

1825. The Barnstable Gazette and Nautical Intelligencer established in this town, W. E. P. Rogers, publisher. Sandy Neck Light-House erected the same year.

1826. An appropriation was made by Congress of $10,600 for the construction of a breakwater in Hyannis harbor.

1824. Oct. 2. The Court house, comprising the offices of Register of Deeds, Register of Probate and Clerk of the Courts, was burned, together with 93 folios of deeds and also deeds left for record, 3 folios of Probate records and the court records. A new County building was erected in 1828.

1830. Population of the town 3,975.

1832. County Court House erected. Samuel P. Croswell of Falmouth, Matthew Cobb of Barnstable and Obed Brooks of Harwich, County Commissioners ; J. and A. Taylor of Plymouth, contractors.

1839. Sept. 3. Grand celebration of the 200th anniversary of the settlement of the town. Oration by Dr. John G. Palfrey, dinner speeches by Gov. Edward Everett, Hon. Robert C. Winthrop, Hon. Wm. Sturgis and others. Brilliant ball in the evening.

INDEX

To

Genealogical Notes
of Barnstable Families

Compiled by

Charles A. Holbrook, Jr.

INDEX

-A-

DAVIS (cont.)
Experience, I: 284, 296, 300, 469; II: 149, 158
Frederick, I: 288
George, I: 282, 288
Gersham, I: 280, 283, 289
Gershom, II: 36, 46
Gustavus F., I: 285
Hannah, I: 26n, 173, 177, 186, 278ff, 282f, 288f, 292, 296ff, 299ff, 302, 341, 437, 515; II: 111, 148f, 153
Hitty, I: 441
Hopestill, I: 301, 529, 535f
Isaac, I: 7, 168, 281f, 285, 287f, 300, 302, 332, 432
Jabez, I: 294, 296ff, 299f, 302, 469, 536; II: 149, 158
Jacob, I: 300
James, I: 240, 280f, 283, 287ff, 297, 303, 305; II: 46
James, Jr., I: 30
James W., I: 288, 303
Jane, I: 19, 30, 280, 283
Jean, I: 283, 289
Jedediah, I: 26n, 297
Jefferson, I: 303
Joanna, I: 130, 133, 292; II: 28
Job, I: 177, 186, 300, 302
Job C., I: 289, 428, 436
John, I: 22, 167, 278ff, 281, 284f, 289ff, 292ff, 296ff, 299ff, 302, 334, 369, 391, 394, 399, 428, 482; II: 6, 54, 121, 124, 126, 148, 153, 159
John (capt.), I: 284f, 287, 340
John (Dr.), I: 284, 436; II: 15
John, Jr., I: 10, 26n, 297, 398, 428, 432
John, Sr., I: 156; II: 98, 125
Jonathan, I: 297f, 282, 301f; II: 9, 145
Jonathan (Capt.), I: 281
Jonathan, Jr., (Capt.), I: 10
Joseph, I: 37, 173, 180f, 278ff, 282ff, 288f, 294, 296, 298f, 301f, 395, 428, 443; II: 8, 15, 45
Joseph, Jr., I: 30
Joshua H., I: 303
Josiah, I: 278ff, 281ff, 284, 287f, 428, 432
Lewis, I: 302
Lois, I: 286
Lothrop, I: 284
Louisa, I: 286
Lucretia, I: 288
Lucy, I: 281, 449
Lydia, I: 280f
Margaret, I: 176n
Margery, I: 289, 292
Martha, I: 281, 284f, 287f, 301f, 428; II: 135
Martha (Patty), I: 287

DAVIS (cont.)
Mary, I: 37, 180, 212/213, 240, 276, 278ff, 281, 283, 287ff, 292f, 296ff, 299, 301ff, 399, 429ff, 432, 443; II: 45f, 98, 119, 122, 145, 166, 232
Mehitabel, I: 302, 340
Mehitable, I: 280f, 284ff, 287, 441; II: 6, 8
Mehitebel, I: 177
Mercy, I: 278f, 294, 296, 299f; II: 160
Nathaniel, I: 297, 300, 302
Nicholas, Nicolas, I: 22f, 26n, 31ff, 197, 277n, 289f, 291f, 294ff, 297, 299, 301f, 333/334, 366; II: 59ff, 62
Noah, I: 26n, 297, 300, 302
Nymphas, I: 443
Patience, I: 31, 223, 283, 289, 297, 301
"Patty," I: 287
Peace, I: 301
Phebe, I: 288, 443
Prince, I: 282, 287, 288n, 289
Priscilla, I: 301, 529
Prudence, I: 287f; II: 101n
Rebecca, I: 185, 276n, 280, 282, 287f
Reliance, I: 283, 289
Remember Mercy, I: 300
Rest, I: 301
Reuben, I: 300
Robert, I: 19, 276-278, 280, 282ff, 288f, 292, 296, 299, 301, 482n; II: 17, 135, 160
Robert, 2d, I: 278f
Ruth, I: 279, 287, 293, 296f, 301f, 298; II: 149, 159
Samuel, I: 283, 289f, 292ff, 296ff, 299ff, 302, 432
Sarah, I: 276n, 278ff, 281f, 287, 292, 295ff, 301f
Seth, I: 279ff, 302
Shobal, I: 297
Shubael, I: 223, 298, 300ff, 529; II: 93, 140
Simeon, I: 299
Simeon (Capt.), I: 529
Simon, I: 289f, 292, 296ff, 299, 301
Simon (Capt.), I: 301
Solomon, I: 281, 285, 287f, 298, 300, 302f; II: 6
Stephen, I: 32, 185, 279f, 282, 288, 297, 300ff; II: 135
Stephen, Jr., I: 282, 287f
Stephen, Sr., II: 140
Stephen G., I: 288
Susan, I: 281
Susannah, I: 10, 280ff, 284, 288; II: 145
Susy, I: 284
Tabitha, I: 224
Temperance, I: 288, 405

DAVIS (cont.)
Thankful, I: 280, 282f, 287, 298, 300, 302, 431f; II: 46, 140
Thomas, I: 233, 281, 284f, 287f, 302
Timothy, I: 224, 294, 296, 299, 301ff
Tristram, I: 279
William, I: 281, 285, 287, 289
William (Capt.), I: 246, 286f, 441, 443
Wm. P., I: 303
DAWES
Margaret, I: 55
DAXTER
Thomas, I: 246
DAY
Joseph M. (Judge), I: 236; II: 207n
Dead neck, II: 83n
Dead swamp, I: 277
"A Dealer," (trade), I: 277
DEAN, DEANE
Abigail, I: 327
Ann, I: 327
Archelaus, I: 327
Elijah, I: 246
Ephraim, I: 327
Eunice, I: 327
Hannah, I: 327
Jerusha, I: 246
Jonas, I: 327
Lydia, I: 57, 327
Samuel (Rev.), I: ii, 12, 17, 65ff, 86, 126, 140, 166, 168, 201, 252n, 266, 273, 279, 327, 330, 365, 371, 420, 422, 449, 461, 474n, 479, 489; II: 83, 113f, 116n, 118ff, 121, 153, 171, 186, 192, 194f
"Taunton," I: 327
Thankful, I: 327
Thomas, I: 327
William, I: 327
Dedham, MA, I: 21, 329n, 368n; II: 36, 58n
Deerfield, MA, I: 240
Defence (vessel), I: 190; II: 90
DELANO
Amy, I: 469
Jonathan, I: 469
Mary, I: 171
Philip, I: 171
DELANOY
Philip, I: 407
DELAP
Abigail, I: 196, 312
Catherine, I: 311f
Hannah, I: 314
James, I: 29, 304-312, 314
James (Capt.), I: 196
Jane, I: 309, 314n
Jane (Jean), I: 313
Jean, I: 306, 313
Mary, I: 311ff
Rose, I: 306, 309, 311ff; II: 234
Sarah, I: 306, 309, 313f
Temperance, I: 314
Thomas, I: 311ff
Delap's hill, I: 311
DENES
Mary, II: 163